Indigenous

Australian

Voices

Indigenous Australian Voices:

A READER

EDITED BY
JENNIFER SABBIONI,
KAY SCHAFFER,
AND SIDONIE SMITH

RUTGERS UNIVERSITY PRESS • NEW BRUNSWICK, NEW JERSEY, AND LONDON

Library of Congress Cataloging-in-Publication Data

Indigenous Australian voices : a reader / edited by Jennifer Sabbioni,
   Kay Schaffer, and Sidonie Smith.
         p.   cm.
      Includes bibliographical references and index.
      ISBN 0–8135–2491–1 (alk. paper). — ISBN 0–8135–2496–2 (pbk. :
   alk. paper)
      1. Australian literature—Australian aboriginal authors.
   2. Australians aborigines—Literary collections.   3. Australian
   aborigines in art.   I. Sabbioni, Jennifer.   II. Schaffer, Kay,
   1945–   .   III. Smith, Sidonie.
   PR9614.5.A94153   1998
   820.8'089915—dc21   97–30812
                                                                CIP

British Cataloging-in-Publication information available

This collection copyright ©1998 by Rutgers, The State University
For copyrights to individual pieces please see Acknowledgments.
All rights reserved
No part of this book may be reproduced or utilized in any form or by any means, electronic or mechanical, or by any information storage and retrieval system, without written permission from the publisher. Please contact Rutgers University Press, 100 Joyce Kilmer Avenue, Piscataway, New Jersey 08854-8099. The only exception to this prohibition is "fair use" as defined by the U.S. copyright law.

Manufactured in the United States of America

FOR MARCO

Contents

ACKNOWLEDGMENTS XIII
PREFACE: JENNIFER SABBIONI XIX
MAP XXXII
ABORIGINAL AUSTRALIA: A TIME LINE XXXV
INTRODUCTION: KAY SCHAFFER AND SIDONIE SMITH XLIII

Prologue

Self-Portrait, "Purrikinni" (Owl Man)	BEDE TUNGATULUM	2
Untitled [oral narrative from *Above Capricorn*]	EILEEN BELIA	3

Part 1: Politics and Land Rights

Citizenship	SALLY MORGAN	20
Assimilation—No!	OODGEROO OF THE NOONUCCAL TRIBE [FORMERLY KNOWN AS KATH WALKER]	21
Integration—Yes!	OODGEROO OF THE NOONUCCAL TRIBE	21
The Flowering	KEVIN GILBERT	22
Me and Jackomari Talkin' About Land Rights	KEVIN GILBERT	23
I Believe	KEVIN GILBERT	24
"Please mista do'n take me chilen, please mista do'n"	ERROL WEST	25

One Hundred and Fifty Years	JACK DAVIS	26
Mr. Don't Scratch My Rolex	LISA BELLEAR	27
Mad Souls	LIONEL FOGARTY	29

Part 2: The Dreaming and Connection

Road to Redfern	LIN ONUS	32
Reed Flute Cave	OODGEROO OF THE NOONUCCAL TRIBE	33
Song of Dreamtime	KEVIN GILBERT	34
"Sitting, wondering, do I have a place here?"	ERROL WEST	35
"There is no one to teach me the songs . . ."	ERROL WEST	37
Forgotten	MARGARET BRUSNAHAN	38
K'gari	OLGA MILLER	39
Marlu-Kurlu	PANSY ROSE NAPALJARRI	41
The Kangaroo	PANSY ROSE NAPALJARRI	41
Like Leaves	KEVIN GILBERT	42
Tree	KEVIN GILBERT	43
Cicada	JACK DAVIS	44
Black Cockatoos	JACK DAVIS	44
The Blackside	KEVIN GILBERT	45

Part 3: Family Dialogues

Pornum Athoy	ARONE RAYMOND MEEKS	48
Yantalpa-Ku	JENNIE HARGRAVES NAMPIJINPA	49
"Child, leave the tape recorder"	JENNIE HARGRAVES NAMPIJINPA	49
Ngati-Nyana-Jarra-Kurlu	RHONDA SAMUEL NAPURRURLA	50
The Two Mothers	RHONDA SAMUEL NAPURRURLA	51
Excerpts from *Auntie Rita*	RITA HUGGINS AND JACKIE HUGGINS	52
Granny Koori	KEVIN GILBERT	74
Grandfather Koori	KEVIN GILBERT	75
Mother-in-Law	LISA BELLEAR	75
Break the Cycle	LISA BELLEAR	76
Birth Control for Blacks	KEVIN GILBERT	77
Mary	KEVIN GILBERT	77
Artist Son	OODGEROO OF THE NOONUCCAL TRIBE	78
King Gunnadoo: The Australian Housewife's Lament	MARGARET BRUSNAHAN	79

Part 4: Station Life

This Mob Going Hunting	FATIMA KANTILLA	82
Excerpt from *When the Pelican Laughed*	ALICE NANNUP WITH LAUREN MARSH AND STEPHEN KINNANE	83
Excerpt from *Unbranded*	HERB WHARTON	95

Part 5: Urban Life and Dislocation

From the exhibition "Same Story, Different Places: An Urban Dreaming"	DARRYL PFITZNER MILIKA	114
"White man's vision"	ERROL WEST	115
Bitten	JACK DAVIS	116
Suburban Heroine	KEVIN GILBERT	116
The Black Drunkard	KEVIN GILBERT	117
Drumsticks	MARGARET BRUSNAHAN	119
Excerpt from *Bridge of Triangles*	JOHN MUK MUK BURKE	119

Part 6: Hardships and Resilience

Aboriginal Change of Lifestyle	ROBERT CAMPBELL, JR.	142
Hypocritic Sponsorship	GRAEME DIXON	143
The Other Side of the Story	KEVIN GILBERT	145
Baal Belbora—The Dancing Has Ended	KEVIN GILBERT	146
We Are Going	OODGEROO OF THE NOONUCCAL TRIBE	147
"Misty mountains tell me the secrets you hold, of men"	ERROL WEST	148
"I feel the texture of her complexion with both hand and heart"	ERROL WEST	149
Capitalism—The Murderer in Disguise	LIONEL FOGARTY	150
Need	JACK DAVIS	152
Imarbara I Am—Generation of Existence	LIONEL FOGARTY	153
Excerpt from *Don't Take Your Love to Town*	RUBY LANGFORD	154

Part 7: Communities

Inspection Day	ELAINE RUSSELL	180
Maturna-Jarra-Kurlu Kujalpa-Pala Wangkaja	PANSY ROSE NAPALJARRI	181
"Two women sit in the shade away from the hot sun"	PANSY ROSE NAPALJARRI	182
Fashion Statement	LISA BELLEAR	183
Double Standards	MARGARET BRUSNAHAN	184
Civilised	MARGARET BRUSNAHAN	185
One Way Street	JACK DAVIS	186
Pissing in Parks	LISA BELLEAR	186
Fellow Being	LIONEL FOGARTY	187
Excerpt from *Unna You Fullas*	GLENYSE WARD	188
Excerpt from *True Country*	KIM SCOTT	208

Part 8: Encounters with the Law

Definitions of Difference (detail)	REA	224
John Pat	JACK DAVIS	225
Escape!	GRAEME DIXON	226
Excerpt from *When the Pelican Laughed*	ALICE NANNUP WITH LAUREN MARSH AND STEPHEN KINNANE	227
One Hot Night	ARCHIE WELLER	229
Excerpt from *True Country*	KIM SCOTT	247

Part 9: Hidden Histories

Michael Watson in Redfern on the Long March of Freedom, Justice and Hope, Invasion Day, 26 January 1988, Sydney, NSW	BRENDA CROFT	252
Untitled (5/13), from the series *Patterns of Connection*	LEAH KING-SMITH	253
Artist Unknown	LISA BELLEAR	254
"I was thinking . . ."	BILL NEIDJIE	255
The Past	OODGEROO OF THE NOONUCCAL TRIBE	256
Holocaust Island	GRAEME DIXON	257
Are There Abo Schools?	LIONEL FOGARTY	258

A Letter to the Shade of Charles Darwin	JACK DAVIS	259
Historical Journals	LISA BELLEAR	260
Sue and Du: The Spirit of One Tribe Is All	LIONEL FOGARTY	260
Excerpt from *My Place*	SALLY MORGAN	262

GLOSSARY 287
BIBLIOGRAPHY OF AUTHORS' WORKS 295
SELECT BIBLIOGRAPHY OF INDIGENOUS AUSTRALIAN HISTORY, ART, AND LITERATURE 299
ABOUT THE CONTRIBUTORS 303

Acknowledgments

THE EDITORS would like to thank the following people and presses for permission to reproduce pieces in this anthology.

AUTHORS

Eileen Belia: oral narrative from *Above Capricorn,* ed. by Steven Davis, courtesy of HarperCollins Publishers and the author.

Lisa Bellear: "Mr. Don't Scratch My Rolex," "Mother in Law," "Break the Cycle," "Fashion Statement," "Pissing in Parks," "Artist Unknown," "Historical Journals" from *Dreaming in Urban Areas,* courtesy of University of Queensland Press and the author.

Margaret Brusnahan: "King Gunnadoo," "Drumsticks," "Double Standards," "Civilised," and "Forgotten." From *Raukkan and Other Poems,* courtesy of Magabala Books and the author.

John Muk Muk Burke: Excerpt from *Bridge of Triangles,* courtesy of University of Queensland Press.

Jack Davis: "John Pat," "Cicada," "Black Cockatoos," and "One Hundred and Fifty Years" from *John Pat and Other Poems;* and "Need," "A Letter to Charles Darwin," "Bitten," and "One Way Street" from *Black Life Poems*, courtesy of the author.

Graeme Dixon: "Escape," "Holocaust Island," and "Hypocritic Sponsorship," from *Holocaust Island*, courtesy of University of Queensland Press and the author.

Lionel Fogarty: "Mad Souls," "Capitalism—The Murderer in Disguise," "Are There Abo Schools?," "Fellow Being," "Imabara I Am—Generation of Existence," and "Sue and Du: The Spirit of One's Tribe is All," *New and Selected Poems,* courtesy of Hyland House and the author.

Kevin Gilbert: "I Believe," "Granny Koori," "Grandfather Koori," "Birth Control for Blacks," "Like Leaves," and "Mary," from *Black from the Edge* and "The Flowering," "Me and Jackomari Talkin' about Land Rights," "Song of Dreamtime," "Tree," "The Blackside," "Suburban Heroine," "The Black Drunkard," "The Other Side of the Story," and "Baal Beldora," from *The Blackside,* courtesy of Hyland House and the author.

Ruby Langford: Excerpt from *Don't Take Your Love to Town,* courtesy of Penguin Australia and the author.

Rita Huggins and Jackie Huggins: Excerpt from *Auntie Rita,* courtesy of Aboriginal Studies Press and Jackie Huggins.

Olga Miller: "K'gari" from *Fraser Island Legends,* courtesy of Jacaranda Press and the author.

Sally Morgan: Excerpt from *My Place,* courtesy of Fremantle Arts Centre Press and the author.

Jennie Hargraves Nampijinpa: "Yantalpa-Ku"/"Child, leave the tape recorder" from *Inside Black Australia,* ed. Kevin Gilbert, courtesy of Penguin Australia and the author.

Alice Nannup with Lauren Marsh and Stephen Kinnane: Excerpt from *When the Pelican Laughed,* courtesy of Fremantle Arts Centre Press and the authors.

Pansy Rose Napaljarri: "Maturnagarra-Kurlu Kujalpa-Pala Wangkaja"/"Two women sit in the shade away from the hot sun," and "Karlu-Karlu-The Kangaroo," from *Inside Black Australia,* ed. Kevin Gilbert, courtesy of Penguin Australia and the author.

Rhonda Samuel Napurrurla: "Ngati-Nyana-Jarra-Kurlu"/"The Two

Mothers" from *Inside Black Australia*, ed. Kevin Gilbert, courtesy of Penguin Australia and the author.

Bill Neidjie: "I Give You This Story . . . " and "I was thinking . . . ," from *Kakadu Man*, courtesy of HarperCollins and the author.

Oodgeroo of the Noonuccal tribe (formerly known as Kath Walker): "Reed Flute Cave," "Assimilation—No!," "Integration—Yes!," "Artist Son," "We Are Going," "The Past," from *My People* (3rd edition), 1990, courtesy of Jacaranda Press.

Kim Scott: Excerpts from *True Country*, courtesy of Fremantle Arts Centre Press and the author.

Glenyse Ward: Excerpt from *Unna You Fullas*, courtesy of Magabala Books and the author.

Archie Weller: "One Hot Night" from *Going Home —Stories*, Sydney: Allen & Unwin, 1986 (1st edition), courtesy of Allen & Unwin and the author.

Errol West: "Please Mista do'n take me chilen," "Sitting wondering," "There is no one to teach me," "White man's vision," "Misty mountains," "I feel the texture of her complexion," from *Inside Black Australia*, ed. Kevin Gilbert, courtesy of Penguin Australia and the author.

Herb Wharton: Excerpts from *Unbranded*, courtesy of University of Queensland Press and the author.

Artists

Cover Illustration: Bronwyn Bancroft: *My Land Escape*

Robert Campbell, Jr.: Aboriginal Change of Lifestyle, courtesy of Roslyn Oxley 9 Gallery.

Brenda Croft: Michael Watson in Redfern on the Long March of Freedom, Justice and Hope, Invasion Day, 26 January 1988, Sydney, NSW, courtesy of the artist.

Fatima Kantilla: This Mob Going Hunting, courtesy of Munupi Arts and Crafts Association, Pularumpi, Melville Island, Northern Territory, and the artist.

Leah King-Smith: Untitled (5/13), courtesy of the artist.

Arone Raymond Meeks: Portnum Athoy, courtesy of the artist.

Sally Morgan: Citizenship 1944, courtesy of Golvin Arts management and the artist.

Lin Onus: Road to Redfern. Copyright Lin Onus 1988, reproduced by permission of VI$COPY Ltd, 1997.

Daryl Pfitzner (Milika), Same Story, Different Places, courtesy of Unley Museum, Unley, South Australia, and the artist.

Rea: detail from *Definitions of Difference,* courtesy of Boomalli Aboriginal Artists Co-operative, Sydney, Australia and the artist

Elaine Russell: Inspection Day, courtesy of Boomalli Aboriginal Artists Co-operative, Sydney, Australia and the artist.

Bede Tungatulum: Self Portrait, 'Purrikinni' [Owl Man], courtesy of the artist.

The editors would like to thank Mark Selden, professor of sociology at Binghamton University, for his enthusiastic support for this project from the beginning. Having read a brief article about Sidonie Smith receiving a Senior Fulbright Fellowship to Australia (1994), Mark encouraged her to think about putting together a collection of contemporary writing by indigenous Australians. He generously facilitated early discussions with publishers in the United States about the need for such an anthology for educators and scholars. Sidonie acknowledges the opportunity provided to her by the Fulbright Program to spend six months in Australia in 1994 as a senior scholar.

Kay Schaffer gratefully acknowledges the Australian Research Council and the University of Adelaide for funding support and for approving her professional leave, which enabled her to work with Jennifer Sabbioni at the Edith Cowan University in Perth, Western Australia. Particular thanks go to Glen Phillips, head of the department of English at Edith Cowan University, who offered Kay an office in the department; to her welcoming and helpful English department colleagues at Edith Cowan; and Prem Hollis, the departmental secretary, who facilitated her stay in innumerable ways. Kay and Sidonie are also grateful to Kurongkul Katajin, the School of Indigenous Australian Studies at Edith Cowan, for its support of the project. Jennifer Sabbioni acknowledges the work of her former colleague at the University of Tasmania, Heather McRae, for helping her to shape her introduction. She is grateful, as well, to Don Gollagher for his library searches and research assistance.

For research support in the United States, we thank Deborah Dunk, an undergraduate research assistant who contributed energetically to this project by doing library research and began the glossary of terms that would be unfamiliar to readers in the United States. The University of Michigan provided research funds that supported Sidonie's return trip to Western Australia, enabling the three editors to meet and make final decisions about the shape of this volume. In Australia progress on the book was aided greatly by the research assistance of Sonja Kurtzer, Taasha Coates, Dennis Schofield and Phil Pring. We are particularly grateful to Dennis for his diligent and dogged tracking of permissions and reproductions, right up to the last minute, and to Phil for making the map for this anthology.

A number of gallery curators were generous with their time and advice about the location of the various art works for the volume, and for contextualizing many of the paintings and lithographs. Particular thanks go to Wally Caruana (Australian National Gallery), Nigel Lendon and Lucina Ward (Canberra School of Art, Australian National University), and Ken Watson (Art Gallery of New South Wales).

The overall design of the book owes much of its germination to a constructive conversation begun one hot afternoon by Kay with Barbara Milich in Perth. Barbara also generously read and commented on various first drafts of the introduction. The editors also thank a number of colleagues who agreed to read the final draft of introductory material, among them Adele Pring, Kim Scott, Tess McLennan (past curator of Boomalli, Aboriginal Artists' Cooperative in Sydney), Miriel Lenore, and Barbara Baird. Finally, heartfelt thanks to our families and friends for their patience, humor, and love as they lived with us throughout the project.

Preface

JENNIFER SABBIONI

It is a common assumption that all the indigenous people of Australia constitute one group, the Aborigines. However, we do not think of ourselves as "Aboriginal" but rather identify ourselves within our own communities. The first thing you are asked when meeting a member of another indigenous community is, "Where do you come from?" This allows indigenous people to associate you with a particular place. To explain it better to nonindigenous people, I could compare it to Europe. To the question, "Who are the Europeans?," the response is, a number of different peoples who live in Europe. The same variety occurs within Aboriginal and Torres Strait Islander society. Contemporary Aboriginal and Torres Strait Islander people refer to themselves as Murri (in Queensland), Koori (in New South Wales and Victoria), Nyungar (in Western Australia), Nunga (in South Australia), or Palawa (in Tasmania). These are the names adopted in the last decade by Aboriginal people from differing regional identity groups to replace the white man's collective naming of us as Aborigines. Within each of these groups are many more specific names, and even outside of them, for instance, the Yamajdis and Wongis in Western Australia.

Nonetheless, all Aboriginal and Torres Strait Islander people across Australia share many features that give unity and a common sense of identity in broader terms. Some of these features derive from a shared history of oppression and dispossession dating from 1770, with the landing of Captain Cook in Australia; shared experiences of racism and discrimination since the advent of European colonization, and of poverty and disadvantage; and a sense of a shared, though not uniform, indigenous culture.

Aboriginal and Torres Strait Islander people are linked by a system of kinship that governs day-to-day existence and the principles of interactive behavior. Kinship systems determine roles and responsibilities within families and extended families. A granddaughter has the same responsibilities toward her grandmother as toward her grandmother's brothers and sisters, since they are all her "grannies." As Robert Tonkinson says, "kinship provides a kind of blueprint for almost all interpersonal behavior among the Aborigines" (Tonkinson 1978, 43). In Aboriginal and Torres Strait Islander society an individual is constantly interacting with people who are identified in terms of relationship; and those relationships involve a whole set of rights and responsibilities between the parties. Some of the more important features of responsibility have to do with reciprocity (or the exchange of privileges and responsibilities among people from interrelated kinship groupings) and death rites (where these responsibilities are of particular significance). Kinship systems, however, vary across the continent; no two are alike, making it difficult, despite commonalities, to generalize about kinship and social structure within Aboriginal society.

INDIGENOUS ORIGINS AND THE DREAMING

Archaeologists date the earliest habitation of the Australian continent at between 60,000 and 120,000 years ago. Recent studies have pushed the date back even farther and presented the claim that indigenous people may have inhabited the continent for 175,000 years. Josephine Flood, in *Archeology of the Dreamtime* (1989), states that Aboriginal culture has the longest continuous cultural history in the world.

However, Aboriginal peoples reject this scientific approach to their origins. They consider the Dreaming to be their originating story. The Dreaming, sometimes referred to as the Dreamtime, encompasses the period of creation. During this period mythical beings emerged from the earth, the water, and the sky and assumed a variety of forms and identities. They roamed the vastness of a barren landscape, stopping and engaging in various activities through which they created mountains, rivers, water holes, flora and fauna, and the indigenous people, who were appointed as caretakers of the world that surrounded them. Rules and regulations were set in place to ensure a balance between humanity and other forms of life and nonlife. It can be said that the indigenous people of Australia were really the first environmentalists in the world.

In traditional Aboriginal and Torres Strait Islander society every person is assigned his or her own Dreaming (or creation) story, which is associated with a totem and kinship relations. Each person is also given responsibility for that particular Dreaming, which is continually reactivated through ritual, song, story, dance, designs, and totemic objects. Thus, in traditional Aboriginal and Islander cultures every person is an artist whose participation in ceremonies renews the relationship between people, the land, and the spirit world. On ceremonial occasions and in performances, participants, as guardians of the story, bring the world into being through their bodies, songs, and actions. Of course, there are differences in practices and stories among the hundreds of Aboriginal and Torres Strait Islander groups.

The Dreaming determines the system of values, beliefs, behaviors, and relationships that draw human beings, the natural world, landscape, and the spirit world into one interconnected entity. Dreamtime informs song, visual representations, political claims (including land rights), social order, concepts of law, and environmental ethics. Given the history of oppression and resistance in the two hundred years since white settlement, the Dreaming also functions as the basis for indigenous identity.

The Experience of Invasion

Armed conflict between Aboriginal peoples and Europeans began almost immediately after 1788 with the landing of Governor Phillip and the First Fleet on the shores of Botany Bay (near Sydney) and continued for approximately 140 years. In the eastern states of New South Wales, Victoria, and Tasmania, the period of conflict lasted from first contact into the mid-1800s. In the western states of South Australia and Western Australia and in more remote areas of Australia, where colonists took longer to penetrate, it began later and lasted longer. Many indigenous people believe that the conflict has never ended, as we continue to struggle against the invaders. Massacres were reported as recently as 1928, when twenty-eight Aborigines were murdered at Coniston, near Alice Springs, after spearing cattle.

According to Henry Reynolds, during the early contact and settlement period, which he refers to as the "Killing Times," about 2,000 to 2,500 nonindigenous people died against 20,000 Aboriginal people (Reynolds

1982, 99). Not all deaths were related to armed conflict. Large numbers of Aboriginal and Torres Strait Islander people were decimated by newly introduced diseases, such as influenza or measles, to which they had no immunity. Of the approximately 5,000 Aboriginal people inhabiting the island of Tasmania in 1803, by 1830 only 50 were left. In Queensland the killing times occurred in the 1850s when white settlers pushed northwest from Brisbane. In that decade, despite forceful, violent, and often successful black resistance, the indigenous population was virtually wiped out through an "orgy of slaughter" (Evans, Saunders, and Cronin 1988, 51).

Resistance

Before the 1960s historians glorified the achievements of the Europeans on the continent and ignored or underestimated, and in many cases excused, the disastrous impact of colonization on Aboriginal and Torres Strait Islander people. Yet throughout the time of European settlement, indigenous people employed strategies to maintain control over their land. And in recent years historians have recovered these histories of resistance, courage, and heroic skill. There is the story of Pigeon (or Jandamarra), who battled for approximately three years to protect Bunaba country in the Kimberley (in the northwest Northern Territory) from settlement. Walyer (or Tarenorerer), a woman warrior from Emu Bay in the Northwest of Tasmania conducted an individual resistance campaign against the British in the early 1830s. Yagan of the Nyungar country in southwestern Australia led Nyungars against the invaders; and Pemulwuy, the Rainbow Warrior, of the Eora in the Parramatta and Nepean regions of New South Wales, led his people in the struggle against the British until his death in 1802.

Protection Period

As the Killing Times ended, the population dwindled and conflict diminished. It was believed by the white settlers that extinction of Aboriginal peoples was inevitable. Social Darwinism provided an explanatory framework for that extinction. In response, state governments across Australia legislated for the protection of Aboriginal peoples beginning in 1860 in Victoria, 1880 in South Australia, 1897 in Queensland, 1905 in Western Australia, 1909 in New South Wales, and 1911 in the Northern Territory. Reserves and settlements were established where Aboriginal people

Assimilation

By the 1930s it was obvious that the protective legislation required revision. State and territory governments, driven by racist assumptions and self-interest under the guise of humanitarian concerns, began to float assimilation as a desirable goal. Aboriginal and Torres Strait Islander people would be assimilated, absorbed, and integrated into mainstream Australian society. The policy was delayed by World War II, and it was not until the 1950s that most states began to act upon it. The Queensland government maintained until well into the 1950s that Aboriginal people were not ready to be assimilated. In Tasmania the government continued to deny the existence of Aboriginal people right up to 1995, when they were forced by the federal government to give back sections of indigenous land to Aboriginal people in the state. By facilitating intermarriage between indigenous and nonindigenous people, the policy makers believed that indigenous traits would be bred out. Aboriginal descendants would become indistinguishable in the wider community of the European Australian population.

The assimilation period saw some positive outcomes, such as the fight for equal wages. From early settlement times, the indigenous people had been the backbone of the pastoral industry and had been paid for their services in rations of flour, sugar, and a minimal amount of tobacco. Following World War II, the Northern Territory recommended that Aboriginal people should be paid in wages, but on a scale below Europeans. Agitation for equal pay began in the 1960s. In 1965 legislation for equal wages was drawn up by the Arbitration Commission, but a "slow workers clause" was inserted which justified lower wages by stating that Aboriginal people work at a slower pace than their non-Aboriginal counterparts. In 1968 equal pay for equal work was finally achieved.

CONSTRUCTIONS OF IDENTITY

During this long history of contact, the nature of "Aboriginality" and the identity of "Aborigines" were represented through scientific, political, religious, and ethnographic discussions. Laws, government policies and reports, mission practices, newspapers, art, literature, and other forms of cultural production all sought to delineate Aboriginal identity. Contemporary indigenous Australians are heirs to this complex history of representations. Thus, there are a number of ways to understand identity within an indigenous context. One derives from the Western concept of biological determinism, which grounds identity in genetics and bloodlines. A second way, accepted by most Aboriginal people, understands identity in terms of actual social practices—kinship relationships, community acceptance, and living out a particular way of life that is a result of the history of colonization. Another approach, put forward recently by Aboriginal anthropologist, actor, writer, and political activist Marcia Langton, is to insist that "Aboriginality" has no fixed meaning but is constructed through social, political, and textual practices in everyday life.

The concept of biological determinism, a product of social Darwinism, was used against Aboriginal people to divide them from one another throughout the history of colonial practices in the nineteenth and early twentieth centuries. In the wake of an inevitable mixing of Aboriginal peoples and settlers, half-caste children, referred to as mongrels, were taken from their mothers, removed from communities, placed in missions, and adopted out to "good white Christian families," with the intention of "breeding out" the blood through biological as well as cultural assimilation. To this end, so called half-caste Aboriginal people were not allowed to marry people with darker skin; they had to request permission to marry and were denied access to traditional communities. These practices were justified as a means of "civilizing" indigenous Australians under the bureaucratic rubric of protection.

Such "civilizing" practices were the consequence of Western understandings of race. The concept of race that emerged in the early nineteenth century in the West was used to establish boundaries between groups of people across the globe, boundaries that were understood to be "biological" and thus "scientific." These differentiations were organized in a hierarchy ranging from the lowest to the highest form of human life. Aboriginal peoples and African Hottentots were assigned the lowest place on the scale of civilization and white (Western) peoples were assigned the highest place. Such racial theories contributed to concepts of racial superiority and inferiority and were invoked to make distinctions between authentic and inauthentic Aboriginal people—that is, between full-blood and half-caste Aborigines.

Western concepts of race also influenced the ways in which indigenous peoples were represented—as primitive, uncivilized, childlike, and doomed to extinction. Throughout the nineteenth and early twentieth centuries, photographers and ethnographers in fact created something called "Aboriginality," which was taken up and aligned with the policies and practices of the Australian state. Aborigines were brought into being as "others" within Western culture through these representational practices. Although we view these past practices with contempt, contemporary Aborigines use this archive of images and stories to reclaim personal and communal histories. We also use them, ironically, to mirror back to the former colonizers and their descendants their Western colonialist assumptions. Our use of white history moves beyond the "othering" machinery of the state and the continuing remnants of colonialist thinking as we take up anticolonialist positions. Yet despite this history of othering through biological determinism, contemporary Aboriginal people are beginning to return to "blood" as a basis of identity because of its potential usefulness in land-rights claims.

Aboriginal people understand themselves as having an Aboriginal identity in a number of ways. Because we now must deal with government regulations concerning the lodging of land claims, we have come up with three criteria that can be invoked to determine whether someone is Aboriginal: a person must be able to trace his or her heritage back to Aboriginal ancestors; must identify as an Aboriginal person; and must be recognized by the community as Aboriginal. Kinship relationships, ties to the land, religious rites and practices, as well as our shared history since European invasion are the most significant ways in which people can identify themselves as Aboriginal. However, a number of writers in the Aboriginal community now argue that there is no fixed identity; rather, identity is generated within specific social and historical contexts.

Marcia Langton, in her book *Well I Heard it on the Radio and I Saw It on the Television. . . .* , asks: "Who is Aboriginal? What is Aboriginal?" (Langton 1993, 28). She refuses the "fixity" of identity. Instead she provides three broad categories for the cultural and textual constructions of "Aboriginality":

• the experience of Aborigines interacting with each other in social situations within traditional Aboriginal cultures;

• stereotypes and mythologies of Aborigines from whites who have had no substantial contact with Aborigines;

• constructions generated through dialogue between Aborigines and non-Aborigines in which both subjects participate in their constructions as they try to find forms of mutual comprehension (33–36).

Langton argues that, in the main, whites do not relate to Aboriginal people but rather to stories of them told by former colonists. "Aboriginality only has meaning when understood in terms of intersubjectivity, when both the Aboriginal and the non-Aboriginal are subjects, not objects" (32). She argues that there is no fixed meaning for the concept of "Aboriginality." It emerges through dialogic exchange between Aboriginal and non-Aboriginal people, their imaginations, forms of representation, and interpretations that affect the understanding of what it means to be both Aboriginal and non-Aboriginal in Australia. Langton breaks through the one-sidedness of Western histories; her anticolonial, intersubjective approach refuses white knowledge claims that silence Aboriginal subjectivity.

Contemporary Issues

Today there are a number of pressing issues for Aboriginal and Torres Strait Islander people in Australia. Among these are the alarmingly high number of Aboriginal deaths in custody; the attempt to recover the Aboriginal past for the lost generations of children taken away from their mothers and raised in missions; and land rights. Aboriginal people believe that these issues must be resolved if any reconciliation between indigenous and nonindigenous people is to occur.

Aboriginal Deaths in Custody

The Anglo-Australian judicial system has been an instrument of oppression for Aboriginal and Torres Strait Islander people. Rarely has the law protected their lives, property, land, or civil rights. The judicial system harasses Aboriginal people, subjects them to alien legal proceedings, and needlessly jails them. The Human Rights Commission, in its Report of the National Inquiry into Racial Violence in Australia 1991, gives ample evidence of the high level of harassment and violence against Aborigines at the hands of the police.

The Royal Commission into Aboriginal Deaths in Custody was set up in 1988. The commission produced a massive report and made comprehensive recommendations for reform. In all, 339 recommendations were put forward. The analysis showed that most of the people who died in custody had suffered a common history: they had been taken away from their parents, institutionalized, dislocated, and had received limited education. Aboriginal people are at least ten times more likely to be jailed than non-Aboriginals, according to a paper written for the commission. An almost simultaneous publication by the Australia Institute of Criminology suggests twenty times is nearer the mark. Yet despite attention to the problem and a sympathetic reception to the recommendations by the police, press, and public, the rates of deaths in custody have increased since the recommendations were made.

The Stolen Generation

Of all the negative policies brought to bear on the lives of Aboriginal people, the most traumatic to our society has been that resulting in "the stolen generation": to assimilate Aboriginal and Torres Strait Islander people, young children were taken from their parents and communities and raised in institutions by nonindigenous people. The majority were told that they were orphans or that their parents and families did not want them. The trauma is a continuing legacy, and Aboriginal people suffer daily from their experiences. Robert Riley, who fought for social justice for Aboriginal people in the 1990s, was one victim of this policy. Unable to cope with the pain, the dislocation, and the traumatic experiences of his childhood, he took his own life in 1996. This is only one of many stories that illustrate how government policies impinge on the health, both of body and mind, of Aboriginal peoples.

An on-going inquiry into the stolen generation began in 1995.

Land Rights

The British claimed Australian lands through the doctrine of *terra nullius* (empty land). This doctrine held that Australia was an unoccupied territory, despite the long-term inhabitation by indigenous peoples. The doctrine provided the legal justification for the nullification of Aboriginal rights and sovereignty over land they occupied by denying any previously existing Aboriginal system of ownership.

Aboriginal relationship to the land is captured in this statement by activist Gallarrwuy Yunupingu:

> The land is my backbone. I only stand straight, happy, proud and not ashamed about my black color because I still have land. The land is art. I can paint, dance, create and sing as my ancestors did before me. My people recorded these things about our land this way, so that I and all others like me may do the same. I think of the land as the history of my nation. It tells us how we came into being and what system we must live. My great ancestors who lived in the times of history planned everything that we practice now. The law of history says that we must not take land, fight over land, steal land, give land away, and so on. My land is mine only because I came in spirit from that land, and so did my ancestors of the same land. . . . My land is my foundation. I stand, live, and perform as long as I have something firm and hard to stand on. . . . We will be the lowest people in the world because you have broken down my backbone, took away my arts, history and foundation. You have left me with nothing. Without land I am nothing (Yunupingu 1976, 9).

Toward the latter part of the 1960s demands for land rights became a central plank of the self-determination movement that emerged in Australia. During the 1970s and 1980s the land-rights movement gathered momentum as the federal government and various state governments set up commissions of inquiry to make recommendations for land-rights legislation. Yet state and territory governments were not prepared to implement the recommendations of these commissions. Great opposition to land-rights legislation came from mining companies and pastoral industries that wanted to maintain control over and exploitation rights to all lands. After the Labour government, which had been instrumental in establishing the inquiry in the early 1970s, was voted out of power, legislation in a watered-down version was passed by Liberal and coalition governments. Less land was made available and weaker mining vetoes were introduced. Land-rights legislation was subsequently rejected altogether in the 1980s by state governments.

The 1992 Mabo case renewed interest in land rights. Eddie Mabo was a member of the Meriam people of Murray Island in the Torres Strait. In 1982 he and five other Islanders began action in the state court of Queensland seeking confirmation of their traditional land rights. The five claimants argued that Murray Island (Mer) and surrounding islands and reefs had been inhabited and exclusively possessed by the Meriam people. The government view was that the British Crown, in the form of the colony of Queensland, became sovereign of the islands when they were annexed in 1879. Nonetheless, the Mer Islanders claimed continuous occupation of their land and argued that these rights had not been validly extinguished by British sovereignty. They sought recognition of continuing rights from the Australian legal system.

The case was heard over a period of ten years by both the Queensland Supreme Court and the High Court of Australia. During this time, three of the five plaintiffs, including Eddie Mabo, died, as did several witnesses. In 1985 the then Queensland government attempted to preempt the case when it legislated to extinguish retrospectively the islanders' claimed rights. The Queensland Coastal Islands Declaratory Act of 1985 declared that, upon the islands being annexed, rights were "vested in the Crown in right of Queensland freed from all other rights, interests and claims of any kind whatsoever." However, in 1988 the High Court ruled that this act was invalid as it was contrary to the Commonwealth Racial Discrimination Act of 1975.

After an unfavorable decision at the state level, those acting for Eddie Mabo appealed to the High Court of Australia. On 3 June 1992, the High Court, by a majority of six to one, delivered a favorable decision in the case entitled *Mabo and Others vs. The State of Queensland,* which overturned the doctrine that Australia was *terra nullius* at the time of the European invasion in 1788. Until then Aboriginal people had no rights to land based on prior occupation of the continent. The High Court followed the general approach of courts in Canada, the United States, and New Zealand in relation to issues of prior ownership of land by indigenous peoples. The court ruled that, though the Crown had gained title to the land of Australia on settlement, this title did not wipe out existing native title to the land. Therefore, Aboriginal and Torres Strait Island people could bring their claims to the court under the Native Title Act introduced in 1993. The Mabo case, however, did not involve a ruling on sovereignty, that is, on the legality of the British government's original acquisition of the territory of Australia. Such a ruling on sovereignty would have made even the court itself an illegitimate institution. Therefore, to avoid this implication, any claims to land must be framed in political rather than legal terms. At present, numerous claims by indigenous people are before various state and territory courts.

Prior to the Mabo decision, Australia lagged behind other countries in terms of land-rights adjudication. However, since the High Court's decision, it has become a world leader in legislating for indigenous land claims. Despite the legislation, few land claims have been successfully won to date. The present Liberal government, with pressure from the pastoral and mining interests in the country, is now threatening to weaken the High Court decision through new legislation to amend the Racial Discrimination Act. The battle for land rights has not been won.

Toward 2000

Aboriginal and Torres Strait Islander people in Australia have announced their intention to boycott the Olympic Games in Sydney in the year 2000 if their demands for land rights are not adjudicated within a reasonable time frame and the country's commitment to reconciliation is not honored. Actively preparing for Sydney 2000, we hope to bring world attention to the rifts and contradictions in contemporary Australian political and cultural life.

Despite the white view at the beginning of the twentieth century that Aboriginal culture was a dying one and that it was the responsibility of whites to "plump the pillows" of the dying race (by putting them in missions and Christianizing them), at the end of the twentieth century indigenous cultures remain dynamic and politically energized—a vital presence in Australian life.

All of this history shapes and regulates my behavior as a Nyungar woman living in the southwest of Western Australia.

REFERENCES

Evans, Raymond, Kay Saunders, and Kathryn Cronin. 1988. *Race Relations in Colonial Queensland: A History of Exploitation and Exclusion.* St. Lucia, Qld: University of Queensland Press.

Flood, Josephine. 1989. *Archeology of the Dreamtime.* Rev. ed. Sydney: Collins.

Langton, Marcia. 1993. *"Well I Heard it on the Radio, and I Saw it on the Television . . . "* North Sydney: Australian Film Commission.

McRae, Heather. 1992. *Aboriginal Studies* (Study Booklet). Launceston, Tas.: University of Tasmania.

Reynolds, Henry. 1981. *The Other Side of the Frontier.* Ringwood, Vic.: Penguin.

Tonkinson, Robert. 1978. *The Mardudjara Aborigines: Living the Dream in Australia's Desert.* New York: Holt, Rinehart and Winston.

Willmot, Eric. 1987. *Pemulwuy: The Rainbow Warrior.* Sydney: Bantam Books.

Yunupingu, Gallarrwuy. 1976. "Letter from Black to White," *Land Rights News* 2, no. 6, p. 9.

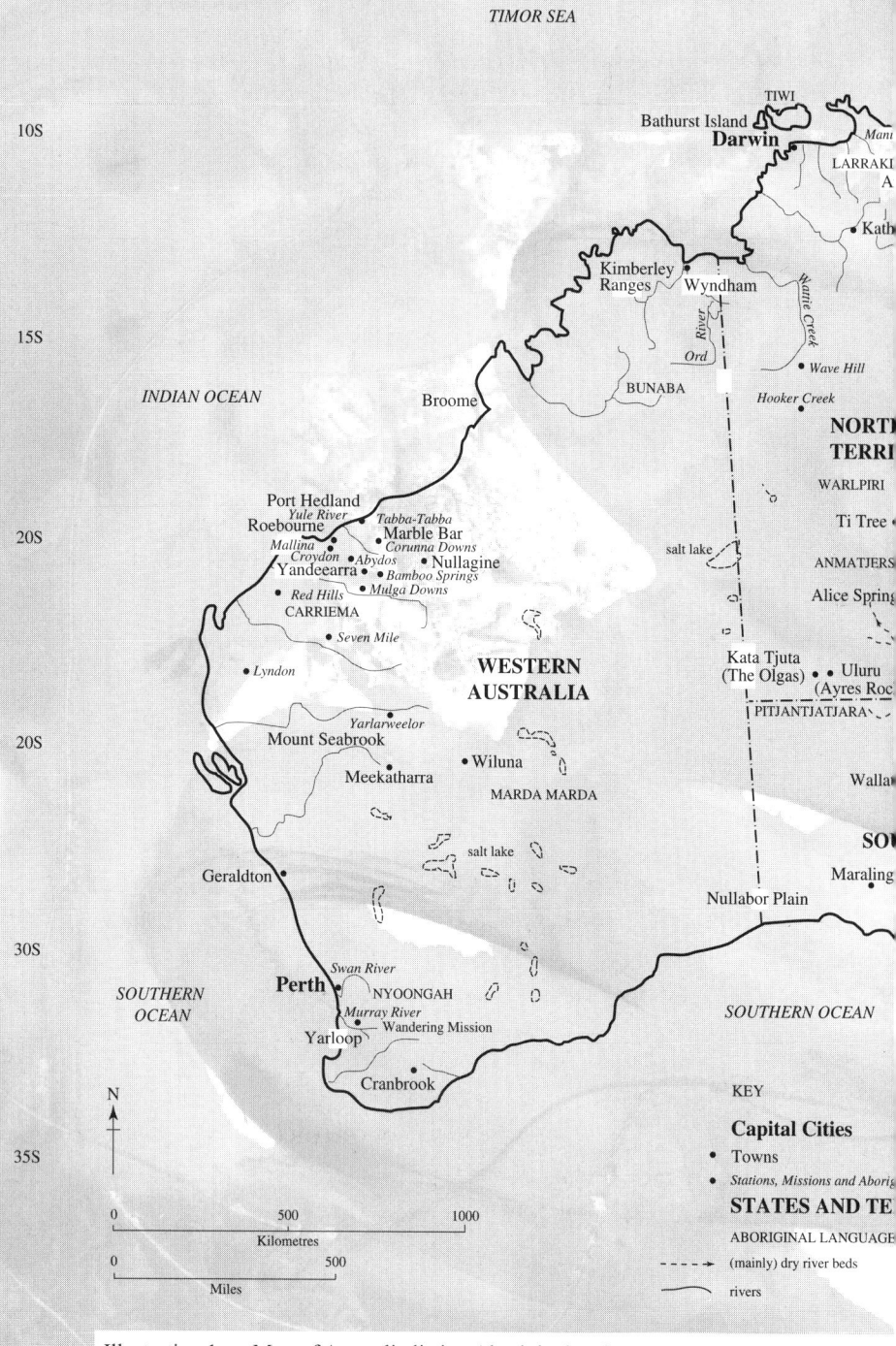

Illustration 1: Map of Australia listing Aboriginal and Torres Strait Islander Languages, States and Territories, geographic place names, towns, capital cities, stations and Aboriginal communities referred to in excerpts and poems in the anthology

Map prepared by Phil Pring

Aboriginal Australia: A Time Line

Some archaeological evidence suggests that Aboriginal inhabitation of Australia may go back 120,000 years. This time line, prepared by the Aboriginal Australian publication *Land Rights News* in 1988, was intended to provide some perspective on Australian history on the occasion of the bicentenary of the British presence. It first uses the archaeological abbreviation "BP" for before the present (in this case 1988), and then conventional dates. It has been slightly modified for this volume.

120,000 BP: Analysis of pollen and charcoal from Lake George, in the Southern Tablelands of New South Wales, suggests Aborigines were living in the area at this time.

35,000 BP: At Willandra Lakes district in Western NSW, evidence suggests an Aboriginal family's dinner camp—mussel shells, charcoal, and ash.

34,000 BP: Artifacts show Aboriginal presence on the Hunter River.

30,780 BP: An Aboriginal underground oven from this period at Lake Mungo, NSW, shows continuity with recent historical times.

30,000 BP: A man from the Lake Mungo area is buried in a shallow grave. His forearm bones are stained pink from ochre. This is one of the earliest known burials of distinctly modern man.

29,500 BP: Devil's Lair in Tasmania is home to Aborigines who leave bone tool artifacts, including unique bone-beads of split-pointed macropod shin bones. The cave is occupied from this time to 6,000 BP.

26,500 BP: The body of a woman from Lake Mungo provides the earliest evidence of ritual cremation in the world. The body is prepared with ochre before cremation.

23,000 BP: Aborigines are living at Malangangarr in Arnhem land and using ground-edge grooved axes. Australian technology leads the world.

22,000 BP: Deep in caves under the Nullabor Plains at Koonalda, Aborigines are mining flint and leaving grooved designs on the cave walls—early evidence of the close relationship in Aboriginal society of art and working life.

20,000 BP: At Devil's Lair engravings are being made. At Miriwan in Western Australia ground-edge axes are in use and in the Pilbara, hearths, steep-edged and notched scrapers go into the archaeological record.

19,000 BP: Meanwhile, in Arnhem, Northern Territory, grindstones are being used for hard fruits, seeds, and vegetables. But these grindstones are also used in ochre preparation—the aesthetic imperative is evident.

18,000 BP: Art at Ubirr (Obiri Rock) in West Arnhem land depicts now-extinct animals: the Thylacine (Tasmanian tiger), Zaglossus (the long-beaked echidna), and Palorchestes (the marsupial tapir).

17,500 BP: A rock shelter at Colless Creek on the Barkly Tablelands is occupied. This is the first inland Pleistocene site found that was not on a major river.

15,000–12,000 BP: At Kow Swamp in Northern Victoria, Aborigines are wearing kangaroo teeth headbands similar to those worn by men and women in the Central Desert in the nineteenth century.

12,000 BP: At the end of the glacial period, the seas rise, separating Tasmania from the mainland.

10,000 BP: Aborigines at Wyrie Swamp are using boomerangs of the returning type to catch waterfowl.

9,000–7,000 BP: Earliest visible evidence of Aboriginal belief connected with the Rainbow Serpent This becomes the longest continuing religious belief in the world.

7,500–6,500 BP: A burial at Lake Nitchie includes a beautiful necklace of thylacine teeth. It consists of 178 teeth from approximately forty-seven animals.

5,000 BP: At about this time a new, small tool is seen. Technology is developing in South East Australia. By 3,000 BP the technology has spread as far as Cape York.

1,000 BP: Archaeological evidence indicates that dugout canoes are being used along Australia's northern coast.

1588: Maccassan praus are sailing to the northeast coast of the Northern Territory. Trade between Aborigines and the Maccassans continues until it is stopped by the South Australian government in 1906.

1752: Dutch documents record the journeys of Maccassan trepangers to Australia, or Marege, as the Maccassans, call it.

1770: Captain James Cook claims possession of the whole east coast of Australia by raising the British flag at Possession Island off the northern tip of Cape York Peninsula.

1788: Captain Phillip raises the Union Jack at Sydney Cove and the invasion begins. The Aboriginal population is more than 750,000. Resistance is immediate. Within a few months of the arrival of the tall ships, Aborigines kill two convicts at Rushcutter's Bay.

1799: Aboriginal resistance flares with incidents in the Parramatta and Hawkesbury areas.

1804: Two years after the British flag is raised in Van Dieman's Land (Tasmania) settlers are authorized to shoot Aborigines.

1824: Conflict with Aborigines in the Bathurst district of New South Wales becomes so serious a threat to white settlement that martial law is proclaimed.

1830: Governor Arthur gets five thousand men to line up across Van Diemans Land to walk the length of the country in an attempt to force Aborigines into the Tasman Peninsula. The plan fails, and only an old man and a boy are captured.

1834: Western Australia's Governor Stirling leads twenty-five mounted police against Aborigines following attacks on the white invaders. Official reports say at least 14 Aborigines were shot dead in the "Battle on Pinjarra". Aboriginal accounts suggest a tribe is decimated in the attack.

1835: John Batman attempts to make a treaty with Aboriginal people. Blankets and goods are exchanged for 250,000 hectares of land. This treaty is the only one made with the original occupants of the land but is not recognized by colonial authorities.

1837: In London, a parliamentary select committee reports that genocide is occurring in the Antipodes.

1838: Three hundred Aboriginal resistance fighters attack a party of seventeen non-Aborigines, killing about ten. Some twenty-eight Aborigines are killed in retribution. At Myall Creek near Inverell in NSW, twelve non-Aborigines shoot and burn twenty-eight Aborigines. Seven of the murderers are hanged in December, but there is a cry of outrage from some sectors of the public who cannot understand why anyone should hang for murdering Aborigines.

1848: NSW police troopers are brought to Queensland to kill natives and open up the land for settlement.

1851: The colony of Victoria is established. A board for the protection of Aborigines is established and continues operating until 1957.

1868: One hundred fifty Aboriginal people are killed resisting arrest in the Kimberleys.

1869: Act for "Protection and Management of Aboriginal Natives" is passed in Victoria.

1870: The Overland Telegraph line connects Adelaide to Darwin and cuts Aboriginal land down the middle.

1876: Tasmania's Truganini, reputedly the last full-blood Tasmanian Aborigine, dies.

1890: Jandamarra, or Pigeon, an Aboriginal resistance fighter, declares war on white invaders in the West Kimberley. He holds the West Kimberley at bay for six years.

1908: The Invalid and Old Age Pensioner Act provides security for some but not for Aborigines.

1910: An inquiry is held after the Forrest River massacre in the Kimberleys.

1912: Maternity allowance is introduced but no allowance is payable to Aboriginal people.

1918: In the Northern Territory the Aboriginal Ordinance Act forbids mining on Aboriginal Reserve Land.

1928: Conniston massacre: whites admit to shooting seventeen Aborigines after a white dingo trapper is killed. Aboriginal records show scores more died.

1930: At Caledon Bay, a Japanese and three whites are killed by the local landowners.

1934: The Arnhem Land Aboriginal Reserve is declared.

1938: On 26 January an Australian Aborigines Conference is held in Sydney. It is the first of many Aboriginal protest demonstrations against inequality and injustice. In the white celebration of New South Wales's sesquicentenary, Aborigines from western New South Wales are trucked into Sydney and threatened with starvation unless they play their appointed role in the reenactment of the events of 26 January 1788.

1941: The Child Endowment Act is passed but no endowment is to be paid to nomadic or dependent natives.

1942: Darwin is bombed by the Japanese and many Aboriginal people are relocated in "control camps." Restrictions are placed on Aboriginal movement, especially of women. In Arnhem Land Aboriginal people make up a special reconnaissance unit in defense against the Japanese.

1949: The Commonwealth Electoral Act extends the franchise to Aboriginal ex-servicemen.

1953: Atomic tests, cynically code-named Operation Totem, are conducted at Emu, South Australia, on Maralinga lands. A black cloud, called the Black Mist, passes, leaving many Aborigines suffering radiation sickness.

1956: Operation Buffalo: another atomic blast at Maralinga, South Australia.

1957: Operation Antler: atomic testing yet again at Maralinga, South Australia. The presence of people on the nuclear test site is documented. The Federal Council for the Advancement of Aboriginals and Torres Strait Islanders is established.

1962: The Commonwealth Electoral Act is amended to give franchise to all Aboriginal people.

1963: In July a bark petition against mining on the Gove Peninsula is drawn up by senior men of the affected clans. On 28 August the petition is presented to parliament but is not recognized as valid because of "insufficient signatures." Although it is signed by most senior clan members, the parliament fails to recognize Aboriginal political structure. Also in August, a select committee on the grievances of Yirrkala Aborigines is appointed. From 1–3 October the select committee visits Yirrkala.

1965: The federal government adopts a policy of integration of Aborigines. Aboriginal people in Queensland finally get the right to vote in state elections.

1966: Stockmen and -women at Wave Hill, a cattle property in the Northern Territory, walk off in protest against intolerable working conditions and inadequate wages. They establish a camp at Wattie Creek and demand the return of some of their traditional lands. An Aboriginal Lands Trust is established in South Australia. Titles are held by a body consisting of all Aboriginal representatives for the first time.

1967: A referendum is held in May to change clauses in the federal constitution discriminating against Aboriginal people. People of full Aboriginal descent can no longer be excluded from being counted in the census. The federal government is prohibited from passing laws relating to Aboriginal people living in Australian states. With the changes to the constitution, Aboriginal people are recognized as Australian citizens with equal rights to vote. Aboriginal station hands are awarded the right to the same wages as white station hands The cattle industry reacts by phasing out Aboriginal labor and driving Aboriginal communities progressively off the properties that are their traditional lands.

1967–68: Desecration of the Weebo Site in Western Australia leads eventually to the Western Australia Aboriginal Heritage Act of 1972.

1970: The Gibb Inquiry looks into the situation of Aboriginal people on agricultural properties. The government moves tardily to create living areas, or excisions, on such properties.

1971: Noonkenbah station workers walk off. Gumatj elders Milirrpum and others take on Nabalco Propriety Ltd. and the Commonwealth of Australia in the Gove Land case, following up on the bark petition. Larrakia people hold a sit-in on Bagot Road, Darwin, as a protest at theft of their land.

1972: The Whitlam government brings in a policy of self-determination. The outstation/homeland movement gains momentum as thousands of Aboriginal people move out of missions and settlements and back onto traditional lands. Aborigines pitch their tent embassy outside Parliament House in Canberra. On National Aboriginal Day, 14 July, there is an Australia-wide strike and march by Aboriginal people. The Tent Embassy is forcibly removed from Parliament House by police on 20 July. The Aboriginal Heritage Act is proclaimed in Western Australia. In December the Whitlam government freezes all applications for mining and exploration on Commonwealth Aboriginal reserves.

1973: Justice Woodward of the Aboriginal Land Commission delivers his first report, pointing the way toward a new approach to Aboriginal land rights.

1974: In his second report Justice Woodward says "to deny Aborigines the right to prevent mining on their land is to deny the reality of their Land Rights."

1975: The World Council of Indigenous People is founded. An Aboriginal land fund is established to buy land for Aboriginal corporate bodies anywhere in Australia with funds from the commonwealth government (replaced by the Aboriginal Development Commission in 1979).

1976: The Aboriginal Land Rights (Northern Territory) Act is passed by the federal parliament. It represents a watered-down version of the 1975 Whitlam government bill but provides recognition of Aboriginal land ownership to about eleven thousand Aboriginal people. The Pitjantjatjara Council is formed.

1977: The first land claim hearing to Crown land at Borroloola commences. The National Trachoma and Eye Health program finds that of sixty thousand Aboriginal people studied, more than half have trachoma. The infection rate is as high as 80 percent in some areas.

Aboriginal Australia: A Time Line

1978: The Northern Territory Aboriginal Sacred Sites Ordinance, instituting prosecution for trespass and desecration of Aboriginal sites, is passed. The Kimberley Land Council is formed. The Northern Territory is given self-government by the Fraser government. On 3 November the Ranger Agreement is signed by the Northern Land Council and the Commonwealth of Australia.

1979: The Aboriginal Development Commission is established.

1980: The Pitjantjatjara Council advises the Aboriginal Affairs Minister of the possible radioactive contamination of Aboriginal people from Wallatinna Station, South Australia, by the atomic Operation Totem. The Black Mist of 1953 is brought to public attention with sight loss and skin rashes being reported. A number of Aboriginal people died as a result of the British Atomic tests and up to one thousand people are directly affected. Aboriginal people from all over Australia travel to Noonkenbah to help the Yungnogora people in the fight to stop the Amax mining company from drilling on their land. The Western Australia government, under Premier Court, gives police protection to an Amax convoy escorting the oil drilling rig. Yungnogora people and their Aboriginal and non-Aboriginal supporters form a human chain to defy the convoy. The confrontation draws national and international attention to Aboriginal rights. The drilling goes ahead but the moral victory goes to the Yungnogora people. The National Federation of Land Councils is formed (September), giving a national voice to the Land Rights movement through its membership of Land Councils from throughout Australia.

1981: The Pitjantjatjara Land Rights Act (South Australia) is passed, and a large area of the state is returned to the Anangu Pitjantjatjara—the corporate body of Pitjantjatjara people.

1982: A royal commission into the Maralinga atomic tests begins.

1983: A delegation of five Aboriginal people goes to Geneva to attend the United Nations Commission on Human Rights Working Group on Indigenous Populations.

1984: In September an Aboriginal land inquiry under P. Seaman is established. The prime minister announces the Aboriginal limited right to say "yes" or "no" to mining on Aboriginal land in the Northern Territory is to be removed. This is to happen in the context of Uniform National Land Rights.

1985: In the "Come to Canberra Campaign," joint land councils from the Northern Territory and the states go to Parliament House, Canberra, to protest the proposed amendments to the Aboriginal Land Rights Act of the Northern Territory and the inadequate provisions in Hawke's vision of Uniform National Land Rights. The Western Australian Government introduces a land rights bill but it is defeated in the Upper House.

1987: Northern Territory elections are held and voting becomes compulsory for Aboriginal people.

Addendum to the Time Line by the Editors

Since 1987 a number of significant events have occurred, some of which are noted here.

1988: A Royal Commission into Aboriginal deaths in custody is established. Also, white Australia celebrates its bicentennial year, which the white population designates as two hundred years of settlement as opposed to the Aboriginal understanding of two hundred years of invasion. On Australia Day in 1988, Aboriginal Australians and their supporters hold a major march and rally to call attention to two hundred years of white invasion and oppression of Aboriginal peoples. Many Aboriginal writers are published using bicentennial government funding. Publishing levels have continued since.

1990: ATSIC, the Aboriginal and Torres Strait Islander Commission, comprising an elected body of indigenous representatives from all states and territories that advises the government and administers funding for many Aboriginal programs, is established under the policy of self-determination by the federal government.

1992: The Australian High Court, in making its finding in the case lodged by Eddie Mabo and others, overturns the doctrine of *terra nullius* (unoccupied land) and paves the way for the lodgment of many "native title" claims, though few have been successful because of strict conditions.

1993: The United Nations sponsors the International Year of Indigenous Peoples. Paul Keating, the then prime minister gives his historic Redfern speech that acknowledges the injustices of the past—the first such by someone in that position.

1995: National inquiry on the "stolen generations" begins. Thousands of Aboriginal children were legally taken from their mothers under the policy of assimilation. The "Protector of Aborigines" was the legal custodian of all Aboriginal children until the 1960s. Many Aboriginal people are still trying to trace their families.

1996: National elections bring John Howard of the Liberal Party to power as prime minister. Liberal government challenges advances in land rights and proposes amendments to the Racial Discrimination Act to limit further claims.

Introduction

KAY SCHAFFER AND SIDONIE SMITH

MUCH of the history that shapes and regulates Jennifer's life as a Nyungar woman is reflected and reshaped in diffuse ways in the art and writings that follow. Some of these works were produced by people living in indigenous communities who have little contact with the outside world (except, of course, that which comes from bureaucrats, teachers, health professionals, visitors, and from adaptation to modern dwellings and the modern accessories of everyday life, such as television, satellite dishes, and Toyotas); some emanate from urban-based, Western-educated, and globally mobile artists and writers who are rethinking the relationships between traditional cultures, contemporary life, and their connection to the Dreaming. In all, twenty-four writers and twelve artists are represented here. They come from offshore islands and all six states of Australia. With the exception of the poetry of Oodgeroo of the tribe of Noonuccal (formerly known as Kath Walker), Jack Davis, and Kevin Gilbert, whose writing emerged in the 1960s and drew on their earlier political activism, the artworks, poems, and prose excerpts we selected have been published within the last twenty years. Several prose excerpts derive from oral narratives told by elders of the Aboriginal community whose families had been displaced through the processes of colonization. Some have remained within traditional communities; others now live in semirural and urban areas. Many contemporary urban artists and writers, trained in Western schools and traditions, find a sense of connection by returning to traditional cultures and shaping their art in the light of that experience. These contemporary, mainly urban-based, artists and writers acknowledge traditional values, ideas, beliefs, and behaviors as they explore a new sense of multiple identities.

We have divided this anthology into nine parts, each of which contains a blend of artworks, prose, and poetry: Politics and Land Rights, The Dreaming and Connection, Family Dialogues, Station Life, Urban Life and Dislocation, Hardships and Resilience, Communities, Encounters with the Law, and Hidden Histories. The sections encompass a range of issues arising from complex pre- and postcontact histories that inform contemporary Aboriginal and Torres Strait Islander life. The pieces could have been arranged around different topics, yet we framed the book in this way because we had several concerns in mind: Primarily, we wanted to convey the sense of the interconnectedness of indigenous life and the ways in which the Dreaming continues as a lived everyday reality even in the midst of radical social and political change. We hoped as well to dispel any notion of panaboriginality, of one homogeneous, indigenous culture. The artwork and writing capture some of the cultural diversity arising from different regional histories, from peoples living in traditional outback communities as well as those in the settled rural and urban spaces across the vast expanses of the continent. In addition, we wanted to demonstrate the innovation, change, and vitality of contemporary indigenous arts in Australia.

The thematic organization of artworks, prose, and poetry mixes genres—among them lithographs, photography, paintings, posters, fiction, memoirs, oral tales, and poetry—in such a way as to lend the book a visual, textual, and aural rhythm. In our selections for each of the nine parts, we have attempted to stage conversations, to set voices in dialogue with one another so as to emphasize the diversity of lifestyles and perspectives among the artists and also of regional identification, gender, class, and sexual preference. The anthology might be read as a series of interactive dialogues in which the authors talk to each other and also to "us," an audience of indigenous and nonindigenous, Western and non-Western readers.

On the cover of this anthology is Bronwyn Bancroft's *My land escape* (1993). The painting illustrates how indigenous artists negotiate Western and traditional genres and art practices as they cross cultural boundaries in innovative ways. Bancroft's title, for instance, ironically plays upon the influence of European landscape painting—but from an Aboriginal perspective. Here the conventional Western landscape is overwritten by floating male and female figures whose bodies bear traditional Aboriginal design features depicting native flora and fauna, thus blending Western and indigenous artistic traditions. Bancroft, an artist trained at the Canberra School of Art, is best known as a fabric designer. *My land escape* demonstrates her dramatic use of color and design. Here she emphasizes that landscape is not merely an "object" for representation but a space in which art, spirituality, nature, and land ultimately interconnect. Through this superimposition of design features on bodies and Aboriginal traditions on Western art forms, the artist achieves a number of notable effects: she comments on the transformative capacities of Aboriginal values, rituals, and artistic practices; overwrites the history of colonization of Aboriginal lands with the fluid signifiers of a vital, indigenous culture; and critiques Western artistic practices even as she invokes them. Her art, like the work of other artists and writers represented in this book, offers a fresh, contemporary understanding of Aboriginal life and culture.

The illustration that opens the Prologue to this volume, a linocut entitled *Self-Portrait, "Purrikinni"* (Owl Man) (1988) by Tiwi Islander artist Bede Tungatulum, shows a masked figure staring boldly at the viewer. (Tiwi Islanders live in communities off the Australian coast northwest of Darwin in the Northern Territory.) An anecdote about the genesis of this work points to the creative mixing of Western forms and indigenous cultural beliefs. Bede Tungatulum was asked to produce a self-portrait in a printmaking workshop at the Canberra School of Art—the self-portrait, of course, being a common generic form in the history of Western art from the Renaissance and a common assignment in art classes. For some days he struggled unsuccessfully to complete the project, without understanding why it seemed so difficult. It was not until he came up with the solution of painting a mask that contained the image of his totem, the Owl, surrounded by geometric areas of patterns, that he was satisfied he had produced a self-portrait. It is, however, one in which all signs of personal individuality are excised, both literally and symbolically. The designs Tungatulum uses in the background are typical of traditional Tiwi art and relate to Tiwi creation stories. It is critical to note that only members of Tungatulum's kinship group would be entitled to use these particular patterns and designs. The artist thereby retains his guardianship over the creation stories, affiliates himself with his totem, the Owl, and embeds himself in a kinship system that renders impossible Western notions of self and self-portraiture. The artist's extension of the idea of the self-portrait—using traditional patterns and designs relating to totem/kinship for a "self-portrait" that satisfies the demands of an art workshop—is an example of how

Aboriginal and Torres Strait Islander artists and writers maintain continuity with past cultural traditions while at the same time engaging in modes of cultural change and adaptation.

The life narrative of Eileen Belia follows, its orality captured in the rhythms of a poem. Hers is an all-too-typical story of one who was taken from her traditional tribal country in Queensland and brought up on a white homestead. Still, as she notes in her narrative, she escaped the worst experience of dislocation—being exiled to the mission on Palm Island off the Queensland coast. Like Bede Tungatulum in his self-portrait, Belia opens her narrative by locating herself within the kinship structures of her community. In the midst of cultural dislocation, she maintains ties to kinfolk, land, and heritage. Both artists adapt traditional images and oral forms in innovative ways by employing new techniques, materials, and forms of media to address diverse, contemporary audiences.

Aboriginal and Islander cultures have been largely oral cultures. The Dreaming ceremonies are communal performances. Creation stories, folktales, communal rituals are sung, danced, drawn, enacted. Thus, there arise inevitable problems in transforming oral forms into written texts. Oral forms are characterized by features that are untranslatable to the written page: the sound of the voice is elusive, intonation erased with transcription. Nor can a written text capture the crucial significance of the way in which ceremony is organized and performances at sacred sites are controlled. Readers will detect the influence of a continuing oral culture in the repetitions, the rhythms, and the speech patterns of Eileen Belia's narrative as well as of the other excerpts included in this volume—by Bill Neidjie, Sally Morgan, John Muk Muk Burke, and Kim Scott. Even those prose pieces and poems that seem to be totally within Western conventions generate something beyond, something more that cannot be contained or understood within those conventions. This element is often apparent to Aboriginal people when they hear or read texts; but it can be totally missed by non-Aboriginal readers.

The first thematic section, Politics and Land Rights, begins with Sally Morgan's 1987 poster *Citizenship*. Accompanying the poster is a statement by Morgan about the historical context framing this stark figure of a dog with a chain around its neck, the tag reading "Australian Citizen." "In 1944," she writes, "Aborigines were allowed to become 'Australian citizens.' [They] called their ... papers 'dog tags.' We had to be licensed to be ... Australian." Morgan refers to the years 1944–1967, which some indigenous people compare to the period of South African apartheid. During this time the Aborigine's Act (1944) permitted an Aboriginal person, deemed to be of good standing in the white community, to apply for exemption from the act to become an "honorary white person." Only in 1967, with the change in this practice through referendum, were Aboriginal and Islander people legally granted rights of citizenship. Even if permitted an exemption, Aboriginal and Torres Strait Islander people were subject to state laws and government policies designed to break down their culture in the name of assimilation.

The concerns of poets in this section span the period from the 1950s to the present. The writing careers of Oodgeroo, Kevin Gilbert, and Jack Davis began in the late 1960s and early '70s. Their poetry engages the politics of assimilation and integration, the hypocrisy of the assimilationist "civilizing mission," and the necessity for continued activism around land rights. The final poems come from the current generation of writers, Errol West, Lisa Bellear, and Lionel Fogarty. This poetry, characterized by uncompromising militancy, addresses today's political issues, such as environmental degradation, the lost generations of children forcibly removed from their mothers, and the destruction wrought on Aboriginal culture by contemporary global capitalism.

Lin Onus's evocative painting *Road to Redfern* (1988) introduces the second section, The Dreaming and Connection. A Melbourne-based painter, Onus traveled to Maningrida in Arnhem Land in 1986 as a member of the Aboriginal Arts Board to spend time, as he would often do until his untimely death in 1996, with the Gamerdi community. It was a journey that changed his outlook, his art, and his life. *Road to Redfern* refers to a predominantly Aboriginal, inner-city Sydney neighborhood. Although greatly concerned with the politics of contemporary life, the painting expresses a deep connection to the land. Through color, pattern, and design, Onus registers the importance of symbolic visual language within Aboriginal cultures. In this painting what at first glance appears to be an inverted evocation of the Rainbow Serpent (an Aboriginal creation figure from the Dreaming) in the diagonal linear design of the Gamerdi is actually a reflection in the rearview mirror of a vehicle traveling through a photorealist landscape. A contemporary automobile replaces the serpent's head, while ribbons painted in the colors of the Aboriginal flag—black for skin, yellow for sun, and red for land and the blood spilled upon it— float across the landscape, in the border between earth and sky.

Onus's painting is followed by several pieces that highlight the significance of the Dreaming. Poems by Oodjeroo, Kevin Gilbert, Errol West, and Margaret Brusnahan invoke the Dreaming as they explore the loss of sacred connections that followed invasion and settlement. The poems are followed by a folktale, retold by Olga Miller, a direct descendant of an elder of the Butchulla people of Fraser Island, off the central Queensland coast. Folktales like this were told by the elders to the children to prepare them for adulthood and, later on, to tell them the history of the people. This one tells of the creation of Fraser Island. The design that follows the tale contains features similar to those the Butchella women and men would draw in the colored sands of the area, or paint on their shields with juice from local berries or a stain made of crushed gum from the grass-tree, or weave into their dilly bags (carry bags made of string). As Miller explains, there is no separation between telling stories and other aspects of Aboriginal life. Nor are artists and storytellers singled out as special members of the community, although each clan had a "Keeper of the Records" to ensure that its private family history passed down. Nonetheless, all people in traditional communities partake in artistic production by telling stories, singing, dancing, painting their bodies, and other activities, while at the same time adaptations of traditional life continue as a remarkable feature of diverse contemporary urban-based communities.

Other poems by Pansy Rose Napaljarri, Jack Davis, and Kevin Gilbert express the connection between the natural, animal, and spirit worlds. Napaljarri's poem "Marlu-Kurlu," which translates into English as "The Kangaroo," was originally told in her traditional Warlpiri language. The version included here includes the original Warlpiri poem and its English translation. These poems and stories highlight the indivisible connections between the individual and his or her land, kin, rituals, and Dreaming affiliations.

A 1990 lithograph by Arone Raymond Meeks, entitled *Pornum Athoy,* opens the third section, Family Dialogues. It concerns many forms of family connection. Born in Sydney, but raised in Northern Queensland towns, Meeks traveled as an adult to the traditional communities of Northern Queensland where he was adopted by a traditional artist, Thanancoupie, and was given the name Arone (black crane) in a traditional "baptism" ceremony. *Pornum Athoy* (meaning "mother's love") is part of a series of lithographs he worked on upon his return. During this time Meeks discovered that he was HIV-positive. In this lithograph a female guardian spirit figure encompasses two androgynous spirit figures in an enclosure. Here Meeks adapts a Dreaming narrative and the guardian spirit form from rock art paintings to new artistic modes of family connection.

Different kinds of family dialogue emerge in the poems and prose pieces that follow. In the first few traditional-language (translated) poems, Jennie Hargraves Nampijinpa and Rhonda Samuel Napurrurla, both of whom are Warlpiri women living in a Western Australian desert community, playfully comment on the ways in which their children engage with white man's media and consumer products. In *Auntie Rita* (1994), excerpts of which appear here, Brisbane-based writer and activist Jackie Huggins and her mother Rita Huggins, who was taken from her "born country," the land of the Bidjara-Pitjara people (now the Carnarvon Gorge area of Queensland), are entwined in a double-voiced narrative in which they juxtapose Rita's life storytelling with Jackie's commentary. *Auntie Rita* presents a mother-daughter relationship in process, in which mother and daughter negotiate differences in their histories, experiences, cultural opportunities, and political perspectives. It also points to the intersections between historical and contemporary urban experiences and reveals the ways in which "Aboriginality" has been and continues to be constructed. To mark the different voices, the autobiographical sections by Rita appear in roman type; the sections by Jackie, which offer both a dialogue with her mother and a commentary that puts Rita's life in historical and politicized contexts, are in italics. Jackie acknowledges a debt to Alison Ravenscroft, a white editor, whose skills were a "crucial factor in a mutually satisfying outcome." As Jackie notes, not all collaborations work so well, an issue that is taken up in the next section of this volume.

The final poems in this section, by Kevin Gilbert, Lisa Bellear, Oodgeroo, and Margaret Brusnahan, capture in ironic, militant, playful, and poignant tones family quarrels around issues of gender, sexuality, politics, racism, and parental love. The poems and prose pieces gathered here emphasize the close family ties that exist within Aboriginal communities. As Jackie Huggins explains:

> Amongst Aboriginals is a very strong sense of kin, of family and belonging.... [W]hen others might turn from their parents, children and siblings, Aboriginal families, especially the mothers, daughters, sisters and nieces, do not. Other Australians might find the emotional expression of kinship bonds somewhat disconcerting, especially those which involve an extensive kinship system in the cities.... [But a]n extensive kin system works for a disadvantaged group as a strong resource in times of hardship (*Auntie Rita*, 99–100).

Fatima Kantilla's *This Mob Going Hunting* (1971) introduces the fourth section, Station Life. Kantilla, who comes from Bathurst Island off the northern coast of Australia, offers a humorous evocation of contemporary life on the station (ranch) where families pile into the back of a ute (pickup truck) with their hunting implements and head bush. According to Nigel Lendon, deputy director of the Canberra School of Art, this print was one of the most immediately popular prints produced and displayed at the school. Audiences responded to the humor and vibrancy of the illustration and also registered the significance of the automobile in indigenous societies, which allows the movement of outback peoples from stations to traditional homelands.

The two personal narratives included here in excerpt recall growing up in the 1950s and 1960s on white cattle stations, where the women worked mainly, but not exclusively, as domestics (maids, cooks, childminders, cleaners, gardeners, and sometimes musterers), and the men worked primarily as station hands (trackers, sheep drovers, stockmen, cattle musterers, horse breakers)—and where all of them earned little or no pay. One of these texts, *When the Pelican Laughed,* is the result of a collaboration between Alice Nannup and students Stephen Kinnane, who has Aboriginal ancestry, and Lauren Marsh, who does not. It began as an oral history project that Marsh and Kinnane initiated, focusing on oral histories of Western Australian Aboriginal women in domestic service. Nannup's narrative is the first of what they hope will be a series of research publications.

For many decades personal narratives have been the product of a collaborative process that brings Aboriginal and Torres Strait elders and activists together with white activists, students, ethnographers, and editors, with the goal of collecting the oral histories of traditional Aboriginal people and transcribing them. Often, as with Nannup, Marsh, and Kinnane, and Rita and Jackie Huggins in section 3, these projects—a sensitive process of cultural negotiation and dialogue—have been successful. But this has not always been the case. Collaborative projects are implicated in a history of colonialism, and indigenous peoples have often rejected them as appropriations of their culture. Too often in the past, scientists claiming objectivity and representatives from the dominant culture claiming to be sympathetic have attempted to study and portray the colonized. This unequal power relationship has resulted in editorial intervention and reformation of the narrative. Thus, the effects of such projects are complex: On the one hand they offer Aboriginal people a way to pass on their precious heritage and introduce their stories to the public sphere. On the other, when the story is "taken" by an editor, he or she may, even with the best of intentions, reshape the life to conform to certain Western expectations of life story and narrative. Moreover, collaborators sometimes bring to the project their own cultural expectations and projections of authentic Aboriginality.

Alice Nannup's *When the Pelican Laughed* (1992), warmly received by Aboriginal writers, tells of family ties and disruptions, nomadic life, mission experiences, and married life on the station, including giving birth in the hostile environment of a white hospital. Although divorced from traditional communities, the Aboriginal women in Nannup's narrative maintain vital links to their heritage. In the section "The Three Pebbles," for instance, Nannup remembers warnings emanating from the spirit world of the Dreaming, foretelling of family tragedies to come.

In *Unbranded* (1992), Herb Wharton describes the daily life of three male companions, one white and two black, who worked together on a large cattle station in Northern Queensland. He incorporates into the narrative the history of invasion, settlement, forced removal of children from their mothers, forced removal of elders to mission stations, and forced indentured servitude—even as he chronicles the stockman's belief in a better future when Aboriginal peoples would take their places as citizens in a modern Australia. Wharton's narrative attests to the fact that station life would have been impossible without the skilled labor of indigenous people, although only whites such as Sandy, who worked alongside blacks such as Mulga and Bindi, could expect to purchase land and become station owners. At the end of his narrative, Wharton leaves open the possibility of indigenous land claims as he tells of Sandy's fear, now that he has become a mature and successful white station owner, that Bindi, an Aboriginal elder, will lodge a claim to his lease on Red Hills. Yet, even as Nannup and Wharton describe the hardships of station life, they maintain a generosity of spirit and humor in their recollections of the whites for whom they worked, often in conditions that contemporary activists such as Jackie Huggins and Leah King-Smith have renamed slavery.

The idea of Urban Life and Dislocation, the title of the fifth section, is introduced by a set of images taken from Darryl Pfitzner's (Milika) exhibition "Same Story, Different Places: An Urban Dreaming," displayed at the Unley Museum in Adelaide. The exhibition resonates with the artist's family narrative, blending autobiography and history with a commentary on contemporary urban life. Pfitzner's great-grandmother, whose Aboriginal name was Milika, was a member of the Kokotha people from the west coast of South Australia. His grandmother was born of a liaison between

Milika and a prominent white pastoralist, who then moved the woman and her child to his property where they worked as domestic servants in the family home. The same fate befell the daughter (Darryl's grandmother) who, when pregnant with Darryl's mother, was transported from the west coast of South Australia to Unley, a suburb of Adelaide, to work as a servant in another household of the same white family. She thus experienced extreme dislocation. Although the paternity of the children was never acknowledged, they were baptized and given Christian names. The white family rose to prominence and erected an obelisk in the park to commemorate the pioneering spirit and heroic deeds of the early (white) settlers.

Pfitzner has placed a replica of that monument in the center of his exhibition. It is adorned not by commemorative plaques of white Australian history but by mementos of Aboriginal dispossession. Two groups of "blackfellas" and "whitefellas" flank the monument, thus reenacting the space as a camping (meeting) place for the two cultures. Pfitzner uses indigenous and introduced materials, images, shapes, symbols, and patterns to highlight the differences between the two groups. The blacks, who stand at uniform height to emphasize the communal nature of their society, are made from indigenous materials: red ochre, dirt, sand, and grass applied to stringy bark poles decorated with stones from the rivers and creeks of Adelaide. The whites, who stand in varied heights to emphasize the stratified and hierarchical nature of their society, are made from pine poles, an introduced species, on which red, white and blue stripes have been painted, and dressed in a parodic panoply of white costumes. Though the exhibition makes reference to the violence, rape, and dislocation that Aboriginal people suffered as a result of being divorced from their traditional place and transported into urban spaces, it deploys wit, humor, and irony in an ultimately optimistic vision. The wall piece, "Vision," mounted behind the blackfellas, carries this message by way of the rainbow serpent emerging out of the sun of a new dawn.

Poems in this section by Errol West, Jack Davis, Kevin Gilbert, and Margaret Brusnahan explore how urban Aboriginal people have been "bitten by the man," to use Jack Davis's phrase—bitten by alcoholism, drug addiction, broken relationships, poverty, and hunger. In the prose section from *Bridge of Triangles* (1994), John Muk Muk Burke tells of second- and third-generation ex-mission families adrift in an unyielding urban landscape. Drifting from town to town, the characters work to reconcile the harsh realities of contemporary life with their aspirations for happiness and family connection. Burke's evocative prose captures the nomadic lifestyle and unsettled relationships (often with errant white men) of women like Sissy and Rose, whose dislocation from traditional culture and family history of mission life form the background of the struggle to raise young families on the fringe of major cities like Sydney. Burke's narrative ends with a young boy's disillusionment with his place within Australian urban culture.

The sixth section, Hardships and Resilience, is introduced by Koori artist Robert Campbell Jr.'s acrylic painting *Aboriginal Change of Lifestyle* (1987). Campbell was born in the coastal town of Kempsey, New South Wales, and worked as a manual laborer before returning to the artistic customs of his childhood. His dense, brightly colored paintings humorously portray the suffocation and conformity caused by commercialized suburban living. The most striking feature of the painting presented here is the border that separates traditional Aboriginal life in the Outback in the top half of the canvas from the conformist suburban lifestyle in the bottom. Campbell superimposes an outline of Australia across that borderline. As is typical of Campbell's work, the artist includes the esophagus (painted in red to resemble a man's necktie) on each human figure. Symbolizing the spirit of all living beings, the esophagus provides a passage from the inside to the outside, a marking of a permeable boundary analogous to the boundaries between indigenous and nonindigenous cultures in Australia; it allows for a recovery of lost lifestyles.

Poems by Graeme Dixon, Kevin Gilbert, and Oodgeroo express a sense of despair and loss at the dispossession and degradation of Aboriginal culture as a result of white occupation and the loss of connection with traditional cultures, ceremonies, and lands. Other poems, like those by Errol West, although lamenting the forces of dispossession, speak of an ongoing connection to Aboriginal heritage and identity and affirm faith in the possibilities for continual renewal. The final three poems by Lionel Fogarty and Jack Davis, more militant in voice, celebrate a regenerated sense of Aboriginal identity located inside traditional systems of belief and a connection to all people trapped within what the poets see as the oppressive conditions of global capitalism.

Certainly themes of hardship and resilience permeate the excerpts from Ruby Langford's *Don't Take Your Love to Town* (1988), a personal narrative of a nomadic life spent struggling with poverty, harsh living conditions, and the heartaches of parenting, including the imprisonment of a son and the deaths of another son and daughter. Langford (who is now known as Ruby Langford Ginibi) tells of raising children by herself, of young people lost to drugs and alcohol, of people unable to find work and hope in the poor suburbs of Sydney. Yet Langford's narrative energy, her emergence as a writer, and her purposeful reconnection with Aboriginal culture—for political and spiritual sustenance and attentiveness to visitations from the spirit world—speak to an undeniable resilience.

Communities, the seventh section, opens with Elaine Russell's *Inspection Day* (1994). This painting harks back to the 1950s and '60s when government welfare workers or mission managers' wives would visit Aboriginal homes to inspect domestic conditions. This was a day all Aboriginal mothers dreaded, fearing that, if any fault was found with their domestic routines, the order and cleanliness of their homes, children would be taken from them and relocated in mission schools or adopted by white families "for their own good." The poignancy of Russell's canvas derives from its deceptively naïve style, which emphasizes the order and decorum of a stereotypical white suburban neighborhood. For Aboriginal spectators this canvas would evoke bitter memories of government surveillance and control.

Poems and prose pieces in this section evoke a sense of many kinds of communities and community relations. Poems by Pansy Rose Napaljarri, Lisa Bellear, Margaret Brusnahan, Jack Davis, and Lionel Fogarty partake of a number of dialogues, primarily among Aboriginal people, about generational differences, mixed heritages, neighborhoods, the politics of fashion, and the meanings of an Aboriginal community. Excerpts from Glenyse Ward's *Unna You Fullas* (1991) and Kim Scott's *True Country* (1993) explore two different educational communities and their cultures: one a 1950s mission school, the other a contemporary school in an outback community. Ward recalls moving into a new neighborhood in Perth and adjusting to a German Catholic mission school and its teachers. Here children are subjected to various shaming techniques, including physical abuse, sexual harassment, skin color differentiation, and racial discrimination. They are chastised as well for not speaking "proper" English as they are made to understand the inescapable mark of Aboriginality while being enjoined to assimilate into white Australian culture.

Scott's narrator is an urban-based, light-skinned Aboriginal teacher who spends a year teaching in a remote community school in the Kimberley region of Western Australia. The section "High Diving" offers a portrait, in contrast to Ward's, of students in exuberant play outside of school while Aboriginal mothers discuss their desire for the children to have opportunities in a larger world. In the section "Visitors in Great White Boats," the narrator assesses the effects of tourism in the outback and its contribution to the decimation of Aboriginal culture. These passages reveal the fragile nature of outback community life in the 1990s.

The eighth section, "Encounters with the Law," opens with a detail from photo-media artist Rea's series, "Definitions of Difference." The series was displayed in the 1991 exhibition in Sydney by Boomalli, a Koori artists' collective. Destiny Deacon coined the term "Blakness" and gave the show its distinctive title: "Blakness: Blak City Culture." The exhibition featured six photo-media artists exploring new, multiple selves emerging within urban communities yet simultaneously maintaining continuity with traditional cultures, beliefs, and identities. In her series Rea, who grew up in Gamiloroi country in the central west of New South Wales but now works in Sydney and Melbourne, studies the fragmentation and reinvention of the Blak body. The detail here shows the bare back of an androgynous Aboriginal body. A knotted necklace dangles between the shoulder blades; the words superimposed on the body suggest multiple readings of the image—the necklace, for instance, as the knot and loop of a noose—and draw attention to the political stakes of difference, in particular the issue of Aboriginal deaths in custody. The image is followed by two poems by Jack Davis and Graeme Dixon that relate directly to Aboriginal prison experiences.

Encounters with legal authorities can happen anytime, anywhere, and resistance takes many forms. Alice Nannup's piece "Radio Theatre: Geraldton, 1950," recalls a time when Aboriginal people were casually harassed in public spaces such as movie theaters. When, like Rosa Parks, Nannup resists by confronting the bad manners of the white racist audience, the police look on impassively. Two stories of violent encounters follow. Archie Weller's short story "One Hot Night" (1986) tells of suburban boys out for a night on the town that ends tragically. Kim Scott's excerpt from *True Country* tells of an interracial barroom brawl on the edge of a traditional Aboriginal community that results in the death of Franny, an Aboriginal youth. The piece evokes the working of Aboriginal justice or retribution as alternatives to the official legal system.

Readers may notice changes in the narrative style within this passage from *True Country*. Kim Scott has spoken of his discomfort with the style that came most readily to him when he began writing the book. It was only when he began to use an Aboriginal vernacular, with its characteristic vocabulary, rhythms, and syncopations, that he felt able to explore and tell the story in a voice appropriate to the subject matter. Only when he allowed the tensions (and collusions) between his narrator's own version of English, the silenced voice of his ancestors, and the various voices of the community to mix could he express Aboriginality in what was for him a more comfortable narrative voice. The potency of this blend of voices is exemplified in the passage where Billy, the narrator, confronts the raw issue of justice after the death of Franny. The language shifts in this section, finally resolving into a single unified voice of Aboriginal culture as Billy takes on the power of his heritage, growing strong through his identification with "us mob."

The ninth and final section, Hidden Histories, opens with a photograph by Sydney-based but Gurindji-identified artist Brenda Croft, entitled *Michael Watson in Redfern on the Long March of Freedom, Justice and Hope, Invasion Day, 26 January 1988, Sydney, NSW* (1988). The photograph was taken on Australia Day 1988, a national holiday that celebrates the white occupation of Australia, which began with the "voyages of discovery" of Captain James Cook and officially commenced with the arrival of the First Fleet in January 1788. Aboriginal people refer to this public holiday as Invasion Day. For the bicentennial celebrations, Aboriginal and Torres Strait Islander people and their supporters took to the streets in a massive protest that both disrupted and commented on official national celebrations. The protester depicted here, an urban Aboriginal youth who raises his fist in a gesture of defiance, wears an adaptation of a traditional red headband with the insignia "We have survived" and a tee shirt emblazoned with the Aboriginal flag. The writing on the tee shirt, "Cook Who / Cook-oo," plays on official Australian history by turning the explorer Captain Cook into a figure of derision.

The second illustration in this section, Leah King-Smith's untitled photograph from her 1991 "Patterns of Connection" exhibition, reveals another dimension of the nation's hidden history. Here King-Smith overlays two images—one a nineteenth-century photograph of an Aboriginal elder called "King Billy" by the whites, the other a twentieth-century landscape. King-Smith was employed by the State Library of Victoria to compile an index of all the nineteenth century photographs of Aboriginal people in the Victorian archives. Profoundly disturbed by the lack of documentation about the images and the anonymity of the figures photographed, she decided to mount an exhibition in which the photographs would be recontextualized. In overlaying the Aboriginal figure on a cleared landscape, she reminds viewers of a history of colonization that cleared the land of its inhabitants and separated people from their traditional lands. The highly reflective surface of the larger-than-life image not only restores the integrity of the figures in the old photographs but eerily reflects back to the viewer his or her own image, thereby implicating the viewer (as either formerly the colonizer or colonized) in the unwritten histories of colonization.

There are many hidden histories. In the poem "Artist Unknown," Lisa Bellear uses the occasion of an art exhibition to address the hidden history of unknown artists. The poems by Bill Neidjie and Oodgeroo lament the loss of a continuous indigenous culture. Those by Graeme Dixon, Lionel Fogarty, Jack Davis, and another by Bellear critique the legacies of colonization through a variety of voices and narrative techniques, including exhortation, irony, and verbal repetition; these works challenge colonial ideologies and reactivate the spirit of lost tribes.

Sally Morgan's *My Place* (1987), from which the final prose excerpt is taken, has become internationally known, with more than 400,000 copies sold around the world. The narrative tells of a young girl whose Aboriginal heritage was hidden from her by her mother and grandmother, both of whom suffered family dislocation through forced removal. In searching for her family history, Morgan recognizes the importance of writing the story down and of seeking out and interviewing family members, principally her grandmother, Daisy, and her great uncle, Arthur Corunna. In the last third of the narrative the text shifts from Morgan's voice to the voices of grandmother, uncle, and mother. Yet in the end Morgan cannot piece together the whole story because her grandmother Daisy chooses to maintain certain silences about her past.

Indigenous writers will continue to explore the silences of the past in Australia while at the same time moving beyond them to experiment with new ways of living with present realities. The dialogues constructed in this anthology illustrate the diversity of voices, positions, and histories of urban, rural, and traditional outback communities in contemporary Australia. The images, prose pieces, and poems presented in this anthology, although representative of contemporary Aboriginal and Torres Strait Islander culture, are the product of a long, continuous history. Auntie Rita's comments to her daughter Jackie Huggins about the importance of story provide a fitting background for the reading of this book:

> People tell stories about their lives and what's happened to them, the things they've seen. Everybody likes listening to stories. Some stories are very strong

and exciting; there are sad and happy stories. I like the sad stories coming out because it helps people. It gives Aboriginal people confidence to speak about our lives and to be listened to. I think it's good that Aboriginal people are writing down these stories. We've got a lot of things to say to the migaloos (whites). They don't understand it all, of course. (Huggins, *Auntie Rita*, 149)

"I like the sad stories coming out because it helps people"

Indigenous
Australian
Voices

'I give you this Story'

I give you this story.
This proper, true story.
People can listen.
I'm telling this while you've got time....
time for you to make something,
you know....
history....
book

I was thinking....
no history written for us when white European start here
only few words written.
Should be more than that.

Should be written way Aborigine was live.
That floodplain....
my father, my mother, my grandfather
all used to hunt there,
use ironwood spear.
No clothes then.

When I was growing up
good mob of people all around then.
Now people bit wicked.
My time never do little bit wrong....
otherwise get spear straight away.
Now.... little bit cheeky mob.
Old time they would all be dead now.
Old people were hard....
I frightened when young.
Only few people now,
but it easy for this mob.

Anyway, got to be made that book.
There's still time.
No man can growl at me for telling this story,
because it will be too late....
I'll be dead.

BILL NEIDJIE

Bede Tungatulum, *Self-Portrait, 'Purrikinni' (Owl Man)*, 1988, black and white lithograph, 50 x 40 cm. Courtesy of the artist.

Untitled (oral narrative from *Above Capricorn*)

EILEEN BELIA

First I got to tell you about my grandfather.
Kaitjindu,
That's his name,
My mother's father.
He was Belangu tribe.

My father . . .
He was Waluwarra tribe
His father was a Waluwarra,
And also his grandfather.

I'm come from two groups . . .
Waluwarra and Belangu.

I was born on the Barkly,
In a little creek,
Near Barkly Homestead
During a big ceremony.

Everyone was there for the ceremony,
Waluwarra, Belangu, Yirringa, Wakaya tribes . . .
All the tribes were there,
All mixed together.

But us mob,
When we finished there
We come back down to Headingly Station,
To our camp . . .
Belangu camp.
Big camp there.

We lived there for years and years,
My father,

My grandfather,
My great grandfather,
Belangu and Waluwarra tribes . . .
We lived together there.

I was born there,
Must have been in the 1920s.
Probably late 1920s I reckon.
I'm not sure but something around then.

My father and mother travelled.
They used to go all over to ceremonies
Over to Barkly,
Down the Georgina River to Roxborough Station,
That's where the main camp was.
We were really Georgina River people.

When my father took his wife,
That's the time he worked on the station,
He used to work from Headingly [Station]
He was drover.
Later when I come along,
We used to travel with him.

When we was travelling,
We all had horses.
We kids had our own horses.
They were all station horses.

At Christmas time we had holidays.
That's when we had ceremonies.
We travelled all around to ceremonies.
Travelled in our own buggy.
We had our own buggy and horses then.

While we were travelling,
We used to put our swags in the buggy.
Then walk on to visit the camps,
See all our relatives and friends.

PROLOGUE

The main camp was near Lake Nash.
Eighteen miles this side of Lake Nash.
We travel from Headingly to the eighteen mile camp.
That was the main camp.
Lots of Aboriginal people there.
All tribes.

From Lake Nash we travelled on . . .
We went to Beantree,
That's another big camp.
Then on to Barkly.

We used to have our own corroborees,
Just our ones.
No other tribe would dance there . . .
At Urandangi there
Only for Waluwarra that one.

When I was growing up,
I worked on the stations too.
I worked on Headingly, Rocklands,
Avon, Hoven, Carandotta.
I had a housemaid's job.

I didn't miss out on anything.
I still went to ceremonies and everything.
Whenever there was a ceremony,
Well they used to take me down there.

The policeman took us away to work.
We were about twelve years old then.
That policeman was really strict.
If we didn't go to work,
We got sent to Palm Island.
'Send you away from your parents', he'd tell us.
If our parents tried to stop him,
Then they got sent to Wurabinda Mission.
Grown-ups got sent to Wurabinda,
And children got sent to Palm Island.

One time old Fred and Dora Age got sent away.
They tried to stick up for their rights . . .
But they got sent away.
Dora was real fair skin,
And policeman said it wasn't right . . .
Can't have light woman living in blackfella's camp.
Fred and Dora stuck up for their rights,
So they got sent away.

We never had no schooling.
We weren't allowed to go to school.
They just took us away to work . . .
When we was twelve years old.

Headingly Station was my first job.
I stayed there a good while.
When the manager went away,
I went back to camp.

But that policeman used to check us up.
He'd come round the camp.
'Eileen Age . . .
Where's that girl?'

Well I got so as I'd look for work myself.
I'd go out after Christmas,
Leave my family,
And look for work.

I was lucky
Nearly every station I work for
They was good people.
They would feed me, clothe me,
And take me to town . . .
Mount Isa, Cloncurry, Townsville.
I used to get around with them.
But sometimes I said 'No,
I got to get back for ceremony'.
So they used to take me back,
Then pick me up when it was over.

Prologue

There was old Morton, Shaler, Smith.
Mrs Smith was on Carandotta
She was a good lady.
Old Morton was a German . . .
He was on Headingly Station.

Crowly was on Obon Station.
Alan Jack and Sue Jack from Rocklea Station.
They was nice people them two.
They never slinging off at dark people.

The Mortons used to take us down the corroboree.
They used to stay right through.
Then they go home late.
I had my own room in the main house.
They say,
'The door will be open when you get home'.
Then I'd stay for the rest of the corroboree . . .
We had to stay till morning.

When I was on Carandotta I was working for Smiths.
I was the baby-sitter for the two small kids.
I used to wash them, feed them,
Clean them, put them to bed.

Mortons used to have a buggy.
He used to come into Urandangi . . .
Come from Headingly for groceries.

Smiths got a car.
We travelled all the way to Townsville.
And they took me with them.
They took me everywhere with them.

All the way along we just camp out each night.
We each had a big swag
He was a real bushman Mr Smith.
He'd just chop a tree down and make a windbreak,
Make tea in a billy can.

It took us four nights along the road.
We had a flat tyre on that plain,
Down near Hughenden somewhere there . . .
Lot of timber there.
Mr Smith would say,
'We coming to that big plain now'.
So the kids would gather up the wood,

Chuck it on the back,
On the trailer.
There'd be plenty of firewood for later then.

I found a goanna . . .
Caught him and cooked him.
The Smiths ate him alright.
We stopped at that river,
Everyone went off to the toilet.
One of the kids yelled out
'Big goanna'.
Well they all off and into it.
We got him and cooked him.
They got into that tail.

Smiths saw me get that goanna fat . . .
I greased my foot with it you know.
It's like rubbing yourself with Vaseline ..
Stops your feet from cracking.

You use emu fat like that too.
That good for colds too that emu fat.
You can use that fat on your saddle too.
Mr Smith asked me what I was doing.
I told him.

Goanna fat and eucalyptus
That's the best medicine.
Rub your chest with that.
It's a bit hard to get emu fat now.

PROLOGUE

You can't keep emu fat in a jar . . .
I tried it in a honey jar once.
Not in jar, not a tin.
That emu fat just goes straight through.
If you put it in at night,
Next morning it'll be empty.

Well one time they took me to the pictures.
There was a big heap of sand,
And we all sat on that.
They had a cowboy picture . . .
That was my first time.

Those cowboys were shootin'.
And we was ducking behind each other.
Well we said,
'We got to get out of here or we'll get shot'.
So we grabbed the blanket we was sittin' on
And ran off.

I was living in the same house with the Smiths,
Down there in Townsville.
They bought me new clothes.
Shoes and socks.
I was dressed up like a white kid.
All flashed up.

I looked at the sea,
That big stretch of blue water.
'How far does that go?' I kept asking.

The Smiths was going over to Palm Island,
But I wouldn't get in the boat.
I stayed home.
I was frightened for that blue water,
But I was more frightened of Palm Island.
All that blue water round it,
No way of gettin' back to your family.
We always been cold about Palm Island.

If we didn't go to work,
Then we gunna be sent to Palm Island . . .
In the middle of the blue water . . .
In the middle of the sea,
And no way of coming back.

Well they already had some of our people.
They took them away to there.
So I was too frightened to go there.

The Smiths went to Palm Island,
Just for one day.
Then they came back.
But I wouldn't go,
No way.

Just after that they was bombing Darwin.
That German manager, Old Morton from Headingly,
He had to leave
But I don't know why.

Old Cowboy and Woodcutter,
They used to work for Old Morton.
That Slippery, Frank and Banjo at Amaroo Station . . .
They're called Morton cause they worked there.
They had no 'nother name before,
And he was good to them.

Same as my grandfather,
My father's father,
He worked for old Mr Age on Walgara.
So he took that name.
Before that he just had his straight out name,
And we kept that name on.

In those days young people was different . . .
The boys was in the single men's camp,
And the girls stayed with the old women.

Prologue

That way they didn't mix together.
Only married people were together.
Young people weren't allowed to drink.
Old people used to give them a belting.

Them days young people were different . . .
They had respect for old people.
Bur maybe if we started up the ceremonies . . .
Maybe they might change.
Maybe they might learn the corroboree.

My grandfather had the last corroboree.
That was at Urandangi

I used to talk to my grandfather,
Talk about our country,
Our background . . .
Whole lot of things.

Well one time
There was me and my two aunty,
Tibby and Rosie.
They were young then,
They didn't have no one [not married].
Rosie went to work at Hoven then
Tibby stayed on at Headingly.

Well, these two blackfellas come down drovin'.
They used to come down every year
They came down for race meeting this time
They was Pitjantjara men them two.
Anyway they come to Hoven this time.

Then while they there one night,
Rosie goes walking around down the dump.
Well she must 'ave been expecting them people eh?
And they took off with her.
From there they dressed in Kadaitja clothes.

Well everyone was looking for her.
She'd been missin' all night . . .
All the next day.
So they tracked her,
Followed her track.

Well that track came towards Carandotta,
There's another little place there,
Beanla . . .
A little camp there with a lot of people.

Well old Left Hand and Shorty
They got on to them two,
They was working some stations
So they got them two to track her.

They had old Joe Patterson
He was an old blackfella . . .
A tracker from Mount Isa
He was a Kalkadoon [tribe] that old fella
That was Henry Kitchener's mother's father see?

Alright,
They track them.
They seen that track
Seen where it went to this tree.
And they seen the clothes there . . .
Hanging up in this tree.

Well they must have put her in the other clothes . . .
Kadaitja clothes.
From there that footprint left that tree . . .
You think they could see it!

Well she must have been know something.
She know her two son been looking for her,
Because her toe mark there.
She just move her foot in that Kadaitja shoe
And she left toe mark for her two son.

<u>Well that policeman from Urandangi,</u>
He couldn't see no track.
'<u>They must have killed her</u>', he said.

But they could hear this bird sing.
Well, old people used to tell us that devil bird.

They follow that bird and climb a tree.
They could see something moving.
Well she just show herself to her two son.
She said, 'Sons, don't follow me.
I'm with the two travelling blackfellas'.
They couldn't really see her.
But they could hear her.

Well their hair started to stand up.
So they said to the policeman,
'We'll never find her no more,
She's gone.
She could end up in Alice Springs or anywhere'.

Couple of years later I was staying with Tibby . . .
Over on Carandotta.
Well that woman showed up that night.
All that came in was a ball of string.
Aunty Tibby said,
'Don't touch it'.
So we never touched it.
I just jumped straight up on the bed.
Then they come to this old cook.
They said,
'You know where my daughter and grand-daughter is?'
He said, 'Yeah, they over there in the hut'.
So we shifted up into the main house then.

We told the manager what happened
And he understand.
They was Gibsons, the managers,
And they come round Alice Springs
So they know about these Kadaitja men.

Alright,
Two years after
We find out she's at Alice Springs . . .
With those two blokes.

She was Jessie Kitchener.
Maybe she got family by them blokes now.
Jessie Katjundi, Jessie Kitchener,
She was my grandmother.

Cecil Moonlight,
He's Wangkungurru tribe,
He saw her there.

My grandmother . . .
My mother's mother
She not really belong to this country
She met my grandfather down Cluny Station.
He picked her up while he was droving.

When we had ceremony
Each tribe camp by themselves
We all have big corroboree at Urandangi
But each tribe got to be coaxed
If they don't come in for their dance . . .
Then big trouble.

Belangu and Waluwarra tribes,
They were close together.
My grandfather and great grandfather,
They were the big men for those tribes.

My father lived in the big camp.
That big camp at Headingly.
Well they had the same thing at Urandangi,
And they brought us into town.
But we only come in for race meetings or Christmas.
We do our twelve months on the station.
Not allowed to go away during that time,

PROLOGUE

Then come into town at Christmas . . .
Only once a year.

We used to get tucker and clothes,
And a few bob too.
The postman used to give us our money,
But the police used to take that . . .
We just blackfellas.

That time white fellas not allowed near blackfellas,
And blackfella not allowed to drink in the pub.
We was under the Act then.
But some station managers were good.
We used to eat in the kitchen with them.
Hoven and Carandotta Stations were good.
But Glenormiston . . .
Oh . . . that manager was no good.
The dark boys ate out at the wood heap.
They used to put their tucker in a big dish,
And have a big billy can of tea.
No cups, no spoon,
Just all dip their bread in.

Them days you not even allowed to get your money.
The policeman keep your money.
But when you go to get it,
You only allowed to have a little.
No matter you been saving it,
You only allowed to get maybe ten pounds.

Then when the Act finished,
Well it all change then.
One white man come along,
He said, 'How you get your money?'
We told him.
Then he gave us a little pocket book each.
After chat we always take our pocket book.
Then we can check up how much we got.

Then we see that some of us got a lot of money.
Well that's good then.
One fella even got enough to buy a car.

We weren't allowed into town.
Police used to chase us back down the river.
We weren't allowed to go to Mount Isa,
Same for all the working men.
Straight back to Urandangi.
'Get back down the river',
That's what they used to tell us.
We only allowed to leave for holidays,
Just one week before Christmas.
Then got to be back,
One week after New Year.

I got married when I was on Carandotta.
I was working for Crowleys then.
Crowleys took it over after Smith went.
Johnny Belia was working there then
When I married Johnny we stay together then.

Later, when we had kids we moved to Dajarra . . .
We wanted the kids to have some schooling.
Johnny used to travel back and forth to the stations,
But I stayed on in Dajarra.

That lasted about ten years,
Then we split up.
Now he lives next door . . .
He's pensioned off now.

But when I was a kid,
We had a good time before we start work.
It different now.

We free now.
But ceremonies all finished . . .
No one following up now.

PROLOGUE

Only old Dubbo Rose and Percy Age.
Percy, that Fred Age's son,
They the only two that can sing now.

Quartpot,
George Quartpot . . .
He's singing corroboree all the time.
He's always at it.
He talk Yirringa lingo.

Young people don't know it.
They haven't got the time to learn.
The old ways are just about gone.
Soon the Waluwarra will be finished.
Only my brother Johnny Age and me now,
That's all.

All Belangu gone now.
Soon Waluwarra will be gone too.
We only got one more chance.
We have to get the young people together.
Then we got to tell them . . .
Tell them how important this is.
Teach them the stories and songs.

I'm moving back to Urandangi soon.
Then my brother Johnny and me,
We can start with them young people
Percy can speak Belangu language,
So he can help too.

When you gettin' old, well . . .
You gotta leave a good story.
We just a few left now.
Me, Johnny Age and Jessie . . .
We gotta get that story together.
We should just slip out into the bush . . .
Take some young people and teach 'em.

I reckon I'm gonna try.

PART ONE

Politics and Land Rights

Sally Morgan, *Citizenship*, 1987, black and white limited edition screen print, 57 x 76 cm. Courtesy of Golvan Arts Management and the artist.

Assimilation—No!

OODGEROO OF THE NOONUCCAL TRIBE
[FORMERLY KNOWN AS KATH WALKER]

Pour your pitcher of wine into the wide river
And where is your wine? There is only the river.
Must the genius of an old race die
That the race might live?
We who would be one with you, one people,
We must surrender now much that we love,
The old freedoms for new musts,
Your world for ours,
But a core is left that we must keep always.
Change and compel, slash us into shape,
But not our roots deep in the soil of old.
We are different hearts and minds
In a different body. Do not ask of us
To be deserters, to disown our mother,
To change the unchangeable.
The gum cannot be trained into an oak.
Something is gone, something surrendered, still
We will go forward and learn.
Not swamped and lost, watered away, but keeping
Our own identity, our pride of race.
Pour your pitcher of wine into the wide river
And where is your wine? There is only the river.

Integration—Yes!

OODGEROO OF THE NOONUCCAL TRIBE

Gratefully we learn from you,
The advanced race,
You with long centuries of lore behind you.
We who were Australians long before
You who came yesterday,

Eagerly we must learn to change,
Learn new needs we never wanted,
New compulsions never needed,
The price of survival.
Much that we loved is gone and had to go,
But not the deep indigenous things.
The past is still so much a part of us,
Still about us, still within us.
We are happiest
Among our own people. We would like to see
Our own customs kept, our old
Dances and songs, crafts and corroborees.
Why change our sacred myths for your sacred myths?
No, not assimilation but integration,
Not submergence but our uplifting,
So black and white may go forward together
In harmony and brotherhood.

The Flowering

KEVIN GILBERT

When the white man took his bloodied boot
From the neck of the buggered Black
Did you expect some gratitude
His smile 'Good on you Jack'?
When your psalmist sang
Of a suffering Christ
While you practiced genocide
Did you expect his hate would fade
Out of sight with the ebbing tide?
In another time, another age
If fate had reversed the play
And a hard black boot pressed on your white throat
When released—what would *you* say
Friends and pals forever together in a new fair dawn?

Or meet like you and I shall meet
With flames and daggers drawn.

Me and Jackomari Talkin' About Land Rights

KEVIN GILBERT

He said
Don't be like the rest of 'em bud
a big loose mouth or a pen
Who's gonna lead us . . . and lead ya must
to git us our right place again
we're sick of the pain and the sneerin'
tired of bein' treated like dirt
we ain't fifth-raters—we're human
'cept they keep up the cripplin' an' hurt . . .
say what is the *word* for us Blacks now
where are we goin' to turn
if you're like the rest Christ help us—

I replied
Men have died in less hope brother
LAND justice is our cause
don't tremble at the sound of drums
or cringe at thought of wars
stand yourself up fiercely
gather strength from all your grief
and terrorise injustice if you must
to cure the thief . . .
and we'll stand there beside you
our land will glow applause
the big mouths too will join and lead
and pens turn into swords
our women with their eyes aglow
their suckling babes at breast
will MARCH AND BURN AND BLEED AND WEEP
AND WIN before we rest.

I Believe

KEVIN GILBERT

I believe
when the rain falls down
birds never fly up
The steel blue eyes of the cockatoo
jar wide in comprehension
of death descending
in white eddies
Today the pilot is grounded
yesterday the sun enabled him
to see the whites of our eyes
ranged in fear as he dropped
his helicopter blade
and cotton vermin poison on us
The cockatoos shrieked and choked
losing their feathers to the powder talons
death has many forms, they walk
to find polluted seed
waiting sometime, sore of foot
to catch a tourist bus
a few crumbs, a kind hand
mercifully wringing a neck to oblivion.
In the misting wet the big family
in the huge house keep wet inside
and praise God hallelujah
rain means more crop or insurance.
To me there is no longer a rejoicing
in possum skin or kangaroo rug
the rain means flu pain diarrhoea
baby sick bronchitis and no pay
at Wee Waa cotton, the miseries
get more miserable and someone
educated said: It's due to America
and American incorporation
with Australian enterprise.

~~Their country is a mess too
I believe.~~

"Please mista do'n take me chilen, please mista do'n"

ERROL WEST

"Please mista do'n take me chilen, please mista do'n"
These words echo through the channels of my heart and
   mind,
A black mother as rich as Croeses in love and loyalty doesn't
   meet the welfare's gait—why, I believe she has become
   too sad to hate what has been and too sick of heart to
   face the future.

The devastation visited on the Aborigine is the holocaust of
   the explosion of the nuclear family—in our people, the
   family goes on and on—it is as endless as we are.

A white man's view is finite, all things here have a beginning,
   and *they* produce the end
Above all things their major intention is to 'assimilate' our
   people—if the plaintive cry "please mista do'n take me
   chilen, please, mista do'n" is but the beginning
What horrors are at the end.

White man why are you threatened by the Aborigine?
Do you still hear that cry?

"Bring im along nar missus, bring im along"
I hear these words as if spoken to me—NO
I will not be parted from my chilen—my body born them
My love make them grow
My spirit need them
And they need me
Aboriginal man maybe don't have nothing
or so you say

but I as rich as Rockefella
While I got these little ones
"I tink ya know ut too"

You say we cannot mind our children—
you have better things—
I say "my fadda 'e
look afta me an 'e got nuthin"—
I can too.

One Hundred and Fifty Years

JACK DAVIS

Written in protest at the non-inclusion of Aborigines in the celebrations of 150 years of European settlement in Western Australia, 1829–1979.

I walked slowly along the river.
Old iron, broken concrete, rusted cans
scattered stark along the shore,
plastic strewn by man and tide
littered loudly mute on sparse growth
struggling to survive.
A flock of gulls quarrelled over debris,
a lone shag looked hopefully down at turgid water
and juggernauts of steel and stone made jigsaw
patterns against the city sky.

So now that the banners have fluttered,
the eulogies ended and the tattoos have rendered
the rattle of spears,
look back and remember the end of December
and one hundred and fifty years.

Three boys crackled past on trailbikes
long blond hair waving in the wind,

speedboats erupted power
while lesser craft surged along behind.
The breeze rustled a patch of bull-oak
reminding me of swan, bittern, wild duck winging—
now all alien to the river.
Sir John Forrest stood tall in stone
in St George's Terrace,
gun across shoulder,
symbolic of what had removed
the river's first children.

And that other river, the Murray,
where Western Australia's
first mass murderer Captain Stirling,
trappings flashing, rode gaily
at the head of twenty-four men.
For an hour they fired
and bodies black, mutilated,
floated down the blood-stained stream.

So now that the banners have fluttered,
the eulogies ended and the tattoos have rendered
the rattle of spears,
look back and remember the end of December
and one hundred and fifty years.

LISA BELLEAR

Him, that fulla over there,
        from the Lands Council
          he doesn't care
how us women feel,
    about mining,
        we milk our children

                    our tomorrow
on breasts filled with poisons
comes from that sludge
            in the river
'member how we could walk into
                mmm the clearest sweet
                                water
and the
        barramundi,
            all
                gone,
true, him that fulla up there!
I seen his
    mobile phone,
        toyota dreaming,
            nothin' but first class
                            travel,
where to now,
Canberra?
New York City?
I'd love to see them mob
                    at Geneva,
                    the ILO,
                    I'd tell 'em
                    our story,
                    women's business,
and show 'em, this is not our
                        way,
Aboriginal country
                is seeping
                in misery,
                death.

I weep for our dreaming
            hold
                me
                    sister
                        I
                            need

Your strength,
got to keep believing
　　that,
　　　　somewhere
　　　　　　someone
　　　　　　　　cares.

Mad Souls
LIONEL FOGARTY

I am a moody Murri
my temper as black as me.
I am a moody Murri
drink and smoke,
sail me away to Africa.
Yes, I'm a moody Murri
I live to swear
and shit anywhere.
I am the moody Murri
don't like Aussies
don't like Asians.
You'd love to meet me.
I'll tell you
go live where you come from.
I am the Murri black
here forever.
Sometimes can't stand my own people
some sell out
some sell off.
I am the blackfella you need
in governments.
If I am asked about, pay the rent
I'll give it a go mate.
I am the moody blue Murri.
Please don't take offence

your own negative reply.
I am not mad
but glad.
Roots grown out
Mingling with shining desire
Free our dreams
Yet you people miss what I am
and
I am the moody Murri
My temper as black as me.

PART TWO

The Dreaming and Connection

Lin Onus, *Road to Redfern*, 1988, acrylic on canvas, 60 x 120 cm, Copyright Lin Onus 1988, reproduced by permission of VI$COPY Ltd, 1997

Reed Flute Cave

OODGEROO OF THE NOONUCCAL TRIBE

I didn't expect to meet you in Guilin
My Rainbow Serpent,
My Earth Mother,
But you were there
In Reed Flute Cave,
With animals and reptiles
And all those things
You stored in the Dreamtime.
Pools of cool water, like mirrors,
Reflecting your underbelly.

The underground storage place,
Where frogs store water in their stomachs
And mushrooms and every type of fruit,
Vegetable, animal and fish,
Are on display.

Perhaps I have strayed too long
In this beautiful country;
The reed flutes are playing a mournful tune.
The cool air rushing through
The rock cathedral
Reminds me of the sea breezes
Of Stradbroke
And the reed flute seems
To be capturing the scene.
The slippery earth stone floor
Takes me back to mud sea flats,
Where seaweeds communicate with oysters
Fish and crabs.
Have you travelled all this way
To remind me to return home?
Uluru, your resting place in Australia,
Will not be the same without you.

I shall return home,
But I'm glad I came.
Tell me, my Rainbow Spirit,
Was there just one of you?
Perhaps, now I have time to think,
Perhaps, you are but one of many guardians
Of earth's peoples,
Just one,
My Rainbow Serpent,
Spirit of my Mother Earth.

Song of Dreamtime

KEVIN GILBERT

With our didgeridoos
in the heart of night
we piped to our God our song
our sacred chants filled the ever—Now
The Beginning covenant
The Essence of the presence
Our Dreaming Spirits Flow
and we held His hands
in the heart of night
and walked by His side at day
we rejoiced with His sacred angels
as they danced in the trees and clay
and leapt with love in the quivering stars
shimmered the trembling leaves
became a part of pirouetting waves
and the roar of the sea's great heaves.
Our sacred chants filled the ever-Now
we sang and danced with God
and loved with Him creation's gift
Our Dreaming Spirits Flow.
Hand in hand to the hunt were we

knee to knee in love
heart to heart in our sacred chant
all sacred our sacred mud
eye to eye in our testament
hand in hand the Son
we children of the one Great God
who fell to the vandals' gun.
Their poisoned flour sapped our lives
their greed stole our sacred land
but they couldn't change our chants to hate
our love to a less than grand
they could not steal our sacred song
nor make our God depart
nor raise His hand in vengeance
to those who kill our heart
while ever our pipes speak to His Being
while ever our camp-fires glow
He'll dance and laugh and cry with us
while His lost white children grow
and seek and learn to know His face
where the fire's red embers leap
He'll bring them yet to His covenant
and a Dreaming that they'll keep.

"Sitting, wondering, do I have a place here?"

Errol West

Sitting, wondering, do I have a place here?
The breast of Mother Earth bore me, yet long I host a shell of
emptiness, a human husk winnowed in the draught of history,
 my
essence ground on the mill of white determination.

I fight though mortally wounded, life blood and spirit ebbing
 away

<u>in the backwater of despair</u>, caused by long-winded politicians'
promises and administration's cumbersome gait;
another realisation of my hopelessness produces; another promise,
implementation of a band-aid gimmick, you had better hurry it's
getting late, red tape, budgets, strategies.
Rape!

Return me to my beloved land, let me be me, don't you understand?
All I want is a private dying in the arms of my Mother earth, she
too is suffering; as a mother must when her children are ripped
away from her love, and the safety of her arms, no more to be cradled,
tenderly caressed by her heavenly smoldering essence.
The Gubba-ment don't try its best, it really does reflect the spirit of the majority
While my body is complying, my spirit has unrest and decays, it does not matter what you say
all you do is 'smooth the dying pillow' an act which is constituted
of ignorance, hatred, or worse disinterest.

I long for my Mother Earth, though her craggy face has been altered by
concrete paths, her beautiful complexion pockmarked, scarred, ruined
by white man's highways, her enchanting brown eyes are glazed by
monolithic cataracts which reach to the sky. Yet for all her arid
beauty I ache for her embrace.

"There is no one to teach me the songs . . ."

ERROL WEST

There is no one to teach me the songs that bring the Moon
   Bird, the fish or any other thing that makes me what
   I am.

No old women to mend my spirit by preaching my culture to
   me—
No old man with the knowledge to paint my being.
The spectre of the past is what dwells within—
I search my memory of early days to try to make my presence
   real, significant, whole.

I use my childhood memories of places, people and words to
   re-create my identity.
Uncle Leedham, a fine black man is my fondest memory—
He could sing, he could dance and play the mouth organ or
   gum leaf.

His broad shoulders carried me and, as I remember, I found it
   a great pleasure.
I owe him and his contemporaries a debt—and I'll pay—
But there is no one to teach me the songs that bring the
   Moon Bird, the fish or any other thing that makes me
   what I am.

Like dust blown across the plain are the people of the Moon
   Bird—
Whitey said, 'You'll be better over there, you will grow
   again!'
Oh, how wrong he was—why the graves of children run four
   deep—all victims of a foreign disease.
They had no resistance to the legacy of the white invasion—
   or so they must have thought
I am their legacy and I'll not disgrace them,

But there is no one to teach me the songs that bring the
   Moon Bird, the fish or any other thing that makes me
   what I am.

Inside, a warrior of ages rises up—my soul he possesses, his
   righteous indignation is the cup from which I drink—
I do not want blood—just opportunity—to be.

But even with him within there is no one to teach me the
   songs that bring the Moon Bird, the fish or any other
   thing that makes me what I am.

Though wretched the invaders were—for me they created a
   greater wretchedness for they, at least, spoke their
   language, understood their role, yet it was nothing to be
   sought.

My great-grandparents knew their culture and it could not be
   taken from them,
Through the minutes since their life it was taken from me—
   though my warrior within says differently—

Even yet there is no one to teach me the songs that bring the
   Moon Bird, the fish or any other thing that makes me
   what I am.

Forgotten

MARGARET BRUSNAHAN

It's sad when my children want to know
Of Aboriginal legends of long ago,
Of dreamtime stories and corroborees,
Things that should have been taught to me.
How do I tell them that I missed out
Simply by being shuffled about

From one white home to another?
And that's how nobody came to bother
To tell me that I had a family tree
Or even that I was part Aborigine.

I had to wait until I was grown
To find my people on my own.
It's impossible to learn in a very short time
The language and culture of these people of mine.
I feel I am selling my own kids short
But how can I teach them what I wasn't taught?
So have patience my kids, I'm anxious too
To know these things as much as you.
Maybe in time we'll still this yearning
But remember my kids, I too am still learning.

K'gari

OLGA MILLER

1

This legend tells of the making of Fraser Island, a large sand island off the coast of Hervey Bay.

Way back in the First Time, Beeral, the God who lived in the sky, sent his messenger Yindingie down to make the land and other things.

Yindingie had a helper. Her name was K'gari (pronounced Gurri) and she was a beautiful white spirit from the sky. She loved helping Yindingie and worked very hard.

However, Yindingie did not want her to do too much, so he said, "You have been working very hard. I think you should have a rest now. Why don't you lie down on those rocks over there and have a sleep?"

He pointed to some rocks he had made in the sea, and K'gari went over and lay down on them. Soon she was asleep, for she had been working hard.

When she awoke. Yindingie had finished making a beautiful bay with lovely sandy beaches, little islands, a fine river and in the distance a lovely mountain.

"Oh," said K'gari, "what a beautiful place. I would like to stay here forever."

"You cannot do that," said Yindingie.

"Why not?" asked K'gari.

"Because you are a spirit and you live in the sky," he explained.

However, K'gari had really fallen in love with this beautiful place and she begged and pleaded until at last Yindingie relented and said, "Very well. But you cannot stay here as a spirit. I will have to change you into something else."

So he told K'gari to go and lie down on the rocks in the sea again, and when she had done this he changed her into a beautiful island.

He clothed her with trees and shrubs and ferns and lovely orchids. He made lakes to be her eyes and he put the sound of her voice into the swiftly flowing streams. He made some animals and birds and other creatures to live in her forests and lakes and sea. Then he made some people.

He taught all these creatures the Magic of Procreation, so that each kind could have "children." Then their children could have children and as time went by K'gari would never be lonely.

Olga Miller, *K'gari*, 1988, black and white lithograph, 15 x 11.5 cm. Courtesy of the artist.

Marlu-Kurlu

Pansy Rose Napaljarri

Ngapa, kanunju pamarrpa-wana,
karlimi ka pulya-nyayirni, karru-jangka
pamarrpa-kurra.
Jurlpu-patu kalu nyinami watiya witangka,
jinjirla kalu parntinyanyi kuja kalu pardimi yalyu-yalyu.

Marlu ka ngunami yamangka,
mata-nyayirni parnkanja-warnu.
Ngapa ka purdanyanyi,
kuja ka pulya karlimi.

Wardinyi ka nguna, yapa-wangurla luwarninja-kujaku.
jinjirla ka parntinyanyi,
matalku ka jardajarrimi.

The Kangaroo

Pansy Rose Napaljarri

Water beneath the hills,
running slowly from the creek,
towards the hills.

Birds sitting on the branch,
smelling the red flowers
that are growing.

Kangaroo is lying in the shade,
very tired from hopping around,
he listens to the water,
that is running very slowly.

He is happy, no people around,
to spear him.
He smells the red flowers,
so tired, he goes to sleep.

Like Leaves

KEVIN GILBERT

One by one
they all go down
like leaves
upon
layered leaves
the various stones
all strewn about
like crystal tears
are left to mark
the times
the loved ones grieved

One by one
we all go down
like leaves
upon
layered leaves
and I sometimes think
our love shines through
the various crystal
shining stones
placed near
where our loved ones grieve.

Tree

Kevin Gilbert

I am the tree
the lean hard hungry land
the crow and eagle
sun and moon and sea
I am the sacred clay
which forms the base
the grasses vines and man
I am all things created
I am you and
you are nothing
but through me the tree
you are
and nothing comes to me
except through that one living gateway
to be free
and you are nothing yet
for all creation
earth and God and man
is nothing
until they fuse
and become a total sum of something
together fuse to consciousness of all
and every sacred part aware
alive
in true affinity

Cicada

Jack Davis

Cicada, cicada,
you sing the whole day long,
and you have my memories
within your summer song.
You sing to me of willows
trailing tresses in the creek,
the cool caress of bluegum leaves
against a boyish cheek.

You sing a song of summer gold
fading in the west,
and a barefoot boy of twelve years old
knowing home is best.
None can ever equal
your tremulous warbling stress,
and though I often searched for you
I never had success.

Now some other boy will look
in high dry grass down by the brook
and you will leave with him, as these,
a host of childhood memories.

Black Cockatoos

Jack Davis

They come in the evening
in numberless flight
and settle in treetops
to herald the night.

The trees are alive
with their black and white sheen
the forest a backdrop
of dark vivid green.

The one on guard duty
is perched high alone
ready to warn
with a call of his own.

They will leave in the morning
with myriad sounds
to fly back to the ranges
their feeding grounds.

Their calling of *weerlark*
rings through the air—
How I long for such freedom
How I envy them there.

The Blackside

Kevin Gilbert

It's good to be
the Blackside
for we know that in this land
the fire-hardened tree survives
where others—yew and poplars
the fir and mighty oak
have never quiet adapted
to the heat and fire and smoke.

It's good to be the Blackside
fitting in with nature's plan
where she selected colour
for this masterpiece of land

and blended it superbly
with strokes of loving care
for each country has its colour
stark and strong and naked, bare.

It's good to be the Blackside
even though externals change
we tallow-wood and ironbark
are native, that's our point:
imported trees are alien
and the fairest English rose
even after generations
still remains an English rose.

It's good to be
the Blackside
when there's justice on our side
empowered by the spirit
and a firm and humble pride
in being on the Blackside
with nature and her might
the Blackside is the rightside
for this land: the colour's right.

PART THREE

Family Dialogues

Arone Raymond Meeks, *Pornum Athoy*, 1990, black and white litograph, 50 x 67 cm. Courtesy of the artist.

Yantalpa-Ku

JENNIE HARGRAVES NAMPIJINPA

Kurdu yampiya waya
manu pitiyawu kapanku
paniya ngawu-mani
nyanjarla-nyanjarla.

Waya-rlangu manyu-karriya
pulya-karri-karri
kapunpa langa rdulpardimi!

Yampiya kunjuru kaji kanpa papimi
manu jinta-kariji
pama-rlangu yampiya!
Kapunpa-nyanu jalpingki pirlirrpa-pinyi.
Ngurrju-nyinaya.

Yampiya kardiya-kurlangu
waya pama kunjuru pitiyawu
manu nyiya-kanti-kantiji!

Yantarni yawulyu-kurra manu purlapa kurra
yantarni wirlinyi-kirra manu wirntinja-ku
yantarni kajinpa nyuntu-nyangu warlalja kuruwarri
milya-pinyi.

"Child, leave the tape recorder"

JENNIE HARGRAVES NAMPIJINPA

Child, leave the tape recorder
and video alone. It will make
your eyes go very sore if you
look and look at it all the time.

Play the music a bit low,
or else, your ears will explode
from listening to it.

Leave cigarettes alone or they
might burn you and another thing
is, leave the grog alone too.
You might make yourself sick.
Be good!

Leave the White man's things
music, grog, cigarettes, video
and those other things as well!

Come to the ceremonies
come hunting and dancing,
come, so that you can know your
own culture.

Ngati-Nyana-Jarra-Kurlu

RHONDA SAMUEL NAPURRURLA

Nyinami kapala warlu-wana wuraji-wurajirla ngati-nyanu-jarra
wangkami-kapala yuntalpa-kurlu. Jinta-kariji Napangardi
manu jinta-kariji Nangala.

Rdijurnu Nangala-ju wangkanjaku wangkajalpa nyanungu-nyangu
yuntalpa-kurlu kujaka warrarda yanirni kutu-karirla pitiyawu-
jangka. Kuja-kulalpa Nangalaju wangkaja 'Ngaju-nyangu
Napaljarri-ji ka warrarda yani kutu-karirla
pitiyawu jangka?'

Nyarrpararla-mayi kalu nyanyi yartuwajiji mirni-marda
kalumpari yuwarli-patu-wana?'
'Paniya-jarraluju kalu murru-murru wangurlu mayi kalu
nyanyi manu pala-pala-wangurlu?'

Napangardilki-pa wangkaja 'Wara nyiya-wiyi ngaju-nyanguju yuntalpaju waya jukuka purda-nyanyi ngulaju mirntangali-jangka manu wuraji-wuraji-kurra. Walku-nyayirni junga-kalaka purdanyanyi, purdanyanyi, purdanyanyi tarnngangu-juku kapurnarla linpa-wangkami-wiyi Nangala-kuju?

'Kajinpa purdanyanyi ngula waya tarnngangu manu kilji-nyayirnirli kapurnpa warungkalku nyinami;' Kuja kularla wangkaja Napangardiji Nangala-kuju.

The Two Mothers

RHONDA SAMUEL NAPURRURLA

The two mothers both sit down near the fire at evening talking about their daughters.
The one is Napangardi and the other is Nangala.

The Nangala started to say a few words about her daughter.
She said, 'My daughter Napaljarri always comes after midnight from watching videos.
I don't even know where she watches videos, maybe somewhere in those houses.
Her two eyes don't even hurt and she doesn't even get cramp from watching the video.'

Then later the other woman Napangardi started to say a few words about her daughter too.
'Oh no wait till you hear about my daughter Nangala. She keeps listening to the radio, she listens to the radio from 8.30 in the morning until to 7.30 in the night!

'She keeps listening, listening, true. She never stops listening to the radio. I think I better put a stop to her. I said "when you listen to the radio so aloud, you will go deaf." That's what I said to my daughter Nangala.'

Excerpts from *Auntie Rita*

Rita Huggins and Jackie Huggins

Growing Up Cherbourg

My people were made to use English words at Cherbourg rather than our Pitjara language. If we used our own language in front of the authorities we would face punishment and be corrected in the Queen's English. The authorities tried to take away all our tribal ways and to replace them with English ones.

This is the way it was with our tribal names. My parents Albert and Rose were given English names by their white station owners. In turn my parents called their children: Barney, Clare, Margaret, Harry, Thelma, Rita, Violet, Jim, Ruby, Oliver, Lawrence, Isobel, Albert and Walter. It is known that at least the three eldest had tribal names as well as English ones, but we don't know anymore what they were. I don't remember whether I was ever given a tribal name. If I did, it was taken away from me when we were taken to Cherbourg.

My mother was such a fine woman. She was a big woman, although she dwindled away to a shadow before she died in 1972. She never had an argument with my father, at least not in our presence. Her work around the house was spotless. She would sweep the timber floors and then scald them with hot water and caustic soda once a week. Mama would even sweep the bare ground outside. It was as though she was in control of everything, her domain and her huge family. Our people went down to the store for rations and things for cleaning, like brooms, buckets, scrubbing brushes. They would get instructions and lessons how to use them at the store by the white officials. Mama would hide these new 'toys' up high in the trees where the kids couldn't get them. When Dadda came in from working, Mama would provide a dish, soap and towel for him before he sat down to have his meals. It was as if hygiene was a safeguard to this strange, new world we had just entered.

It must have been terrible for my mother and the others. Mama just had to do things. She had no choice. I think in her mind she must have said, 'My country, my culture, what I can do in the bush, have gone forever'. I believe she resisted a lot and never did all what the white people told her. She was never a believer of whiteman's medicine, saying it was barjun. She was a wonderful woman who evenly distributed her amazing love between all her fourteen children. The love we received from her was different from Dadda's. Although we loved and respected them both, there was a special warmth about Mama which was always there. She had a beautiful aura about her which went with her strength.

When my mother and the other women went to the hospital to have babies there was a lovely Matron Wren who always loved the Aboriginal people. But when my mother went there the first time to have Jimmy, her first baby born at Cherbourg, she felt funny about a white person touching her and a white person being the first person to touch her baby. She was so used to my grannie and my aunties and the other women in the bush delivering the babies. It really frightened her going into four walls and seeing all the instruments, a white matron and a nurse. I could imagine how she felt. It frightened her also when Matron Wren said, 'Let the baby come out', and when she did she'd look up to the heavens and think of her old mother and say, 'All finished . . . all gone . . . a new gunduburrie born now'.

We'd all rush her when she brought the new baby home. She had no napkins but we'd go to the rubbish dump looking for materials and clothes and take a knife to get the pretty buttons. Mama loved sewing, which the missionaries had taught her. The tip was in Murgon where the rich folk would throw out good things. We were too frightened to go to Murgon, frightened of the white men. Dadda would say, 'You go any further, they shoot you'. Mama would be holding the baby, looking around at where us kids would be while another held tightly onto her skirt. All the people in Cherbourg would say, 'There goes Rosie and her ducklings'. My younger brother, Wal, would come home after school and throw Mama's top up to suckle on her breast. He was about eight and it was as if she knew he was her last child. We still laugh about our baby brother today.

The government owned a store on the reserve where an official would ration out food, clothing and blankets every fortnight, but the food was only enough to last a few days. Mama usually went down with a sugarbag to collect what she could. She'd make whatever there was go around for the ever-hungry mouths. Among the rations was a lot of anything bad for health like sugar, salt, flour, tea, offal (including the inners of bullocks which we called running guts) and bibles and very little of any nutritional value. So Dadda and the boys would go hunting. They would hunt in the traditional way with spears, boomerangs and sharp sticks. In the early days, guns were not allowed to be owned by the Aboriginals on the reserves. Only the officials and the Black trackers carried them. A hunt would not pass unless several kangaroos, emus, goannas, possums, rabbits or our favourite—porcupines and carpet snakes (which still make my mouth water)—were found. Compared to the tasteless, stale meat we received in our rations, our bush tucker was always greatly appreciated. Although we had a wood stove, for many years Mama preferred to continue to cook outside.

Later, my sister Violet worked at a Murgon grocer and we would get scraps. The scraps were like Christmas to us, different sorts of things we'd never eaten before like fruit mince tarts and icing. Dinner was always on the table for Dadda when he came home. We boasted the best garden in Cherbourg at the time. There were lots of fruit trees in our yard. These were lemons, oranges, figs and mangoes.

Mama was very protective. She always kept an eye on us and knew where we were. She knew too well of the 'half-caste' kids who were taken away from their parents and her overprotectiveness as we saw it then was justified. The Aboriginal grapevine operated as much in those days as it does today. Except today it's faster with things like telephones. Word of mouth passed around the coming of the white people—how far away they were, the strange animals they owned and the terrible things they did to our people like shooting, poisoning and, the worst crime, taking our children from us.

She knew the value of money even though she hardly got any. She treasured it in a handkerchief which she would carry around with her. 'Spin it around' was her favourite saying and she would be careful with it to the last penny.

When letters were received from any of her children working away, she'd be overjoyed and get one of us to read it to her. Then we'd have to write back with all the news of home. How contented she'd feel that she could speak with her children when they were so far away. Her love was all consuming.

My father Albert was a proud man who lost a leg in a riding accident at work on one of the stations. He could still ride a yarraman as good as any able-bodied person. He had a particular fondness for his pipe, and for European swear words, particularly the f. word. While my father was a hard worker and good provider for all his family he never took on a whitefella's job. He never understood how migaloos work to a set time. The white way of working was so alien to our culture. Dadda was frustrated by the western way of doing things and in fact rebelled against employment forced onto other inmates. He never had and wasn't about to bow down to any whiteman. In a sense I suspect he was excused by the officials because of his disability.

Dadda would regularly play cards, which again were European inventions but which he liked. Cards had been introduced to the reserve lifestyle before we arrived in Cherbourg. Gambling schools were secretly set up throughout the settlement and the habit continues to thrive today. He would spend days at such events and then return home with family peace offerings of abundant bush tucker, including our favourite wild honey which was like lollies to us. In fact, every time the food supply was short he would disappear for days, and bring back more tasty food.

He set the highest standards for us and was intolerant if we did not meet them. Lessons like honesty, reliability, respect and loyalty. The value of his standards of life, humanity and pride, were realised by his children later in our lives. Immoral conduct like chasing another person's spouse was an unforgivable crime to Dadda but perhaps the wish he wanted most for all his children was for them to marry another Aboriginal person. Absolutely not a white. His dream came almost entirely true.

He was the toughest disciplinarian you could ever meet. Unlike my mother who was even-tempered, Dadda had a volatile temper which would erupt into full-scale fury and war when stirred. We were ingrained with a sense of honesty, good manners, morals and responsibilities and if we erred we would face the consequences from Dadda. His word was law and we dared not speak back or challenge him. It was unheard of and anyway not worth the punishment he would have dished out. He owned a stockwhip and some belts which hitched up his loosely fitting trousers. These would become almost lethal weapons when he singled out one or several of us for a hiding. There was nothing on earth like his floggings. I still shudder to this day when I think of them. I got one for stealing peaches one day from Nellie McIvor's trees.

Lucy, Patty McIvor and Nellie lived next door to us. I was about nine then, and was playing in our backyard with my good mate Barbara Evans. We suddenly felt hungry and both looked over the fence at the same time to the McIvor's fat, ripe peaches on the tree. Now we knew that this succulent fruit was heaven because Nellie often brought Mama over a huge basketful. Mm . . . I had indeed tasted their juicy flesh on a number of occasions before.

Without hesitation, I jumped the fence and began picking the heavily laden tree. In no time I managed to throw several peaches back over the fence to Barbara who immediately bit into them. Unfortunately in my haste and hunger I forgot about the McIvor's barking and ferocious dog Dodger who then chased me up the tree. Auntie Lucy came racing out to see what all the noise was about only to find me dangling from a branch with Dodger in hot pursuit. 'Gotcha!', she growled. 'And you can stay up there until Dadda comes home.'

By this time my best mate and loyal friend Barbara had disappeared from the face of the earth. I got gooly up with her at that and didn't speak to her for ages afterwards. I was left whimpering in the tree for about fifteen minutes before I heard a man's footsteps, followed by the distinct sound of my father's voice which grew louder and closer. Auntie Lucy must have told him. 'Knock off, Rita, you come down from that f'n tree, you thieving so-and-so!', he yelled. All the other curious kids who'd been hanging around scattered in a dozen directions.

I hung my head in shame. Dadda grabbed my arm tightly, and took me home where he shoved me in a room and reached for his stockwhip. The belting began. My tears poured over my cheeks as I closed my eyes. I had never experienced pain like that before. My mother never interfered when my father disciplined any of us. When the belting was over, Mum bathed my wounds with salt water after which she wrapped them in calico. This was only to prove band-aid treatment as the wounds were much more serious and I was later hospitalised overnight.

After that, I never took a hiding for granted—or stole Nellie's peaches again. Dadda felt a lot of remorse over that incident, bringing me fruit home daily for the next month. He spoilt me totally, gave me horserides and hugs. I could tell he was deeply sorry for what he had done by the look on his face every time he saw me. Of course, I still got scolded throughout my growing-up years like my other brothers and sisters, but never again would it be as severe as that belting. Dadda mostly didn't show much affection, being the serious and stern man that he was, but we loved him deeply just the same.

Dadda would listen to the radio for hours. He had a passion for the news and political stories. During the war he would leave it on one station only. We were never game to move the dial for fear of a belting. We never heard any music or other programmes. Dadda was a smart man, a bush lawyer by anyone's standards. He fought against the injustices of Aboriginal people on Cherbourg. He was called a stirrer by white officials because of his outspoken views and his arguments for better conditions. In fact, one Department of Native Affairs removals paper cites his occupation as 'black stirrer'. Many people in his community trusted his ability to deal with the authorities. Unfortunately, he was a lone voice, and had no strong support from other residents. Many Aboriginal people in those days were too afraid of white people and the system to stand up for themselves. Much of Dadda's anger he had to keep to himself. He was such an angry man and I realise now why this was so.

Aboriginal people at that time were so quashed in their attempts to speak out. My father was a great man who attempted to speak out but was ignored and put down for his efforts. He may have been as important to the struggle in his day as Charlie Perkins has been in his, but was never ever recognised for this. If it had been recognition he'd wanted, he lived in the wrong era. He had a regal presence about him. A 'man of high degree' although not in the clever man or medicine man mould but a man who stood out from others, a man of great intelligence and power. Those who knew my father recalled his strength and wisdom.

The degree of control that whites maintained over the reserves is made clear by the story my mother tells of her brother Harry's death in 1942, and the authorities' refusal to allow the family to attend his funeral. In order to leave the reserve or travel back there, Aboriginal people had to get a clearance from the reserve officials. This clearance was known as a permit. The permit system was standard procedure which operated from the Queensland reserves' inception in 1887 until the 1980s. Leave from the settlements was only granted in special circumstances for employment contracts, errands to other settlements and towns, medical treatment and, on occasions, funerals.

To Aboriginal people, the deep religious and spiritual significance of funerals places a huge onus on relatives and friends to attend these important events. A funeral is viewed as paying final respects to a worthy and cherished person. No matter whether the deceased was a close relative or community acquaintance, attendance is unashamedly commanded. Being one of the most honoured etiquettes of Aboriginal society, attendance may number in the hundreds. Absence at Aboriginal funerals does not go unnoticed, particularly if it is that of a close relative. Non-attendance therefore is largely scorned and considered an insult to the deceased and all surviving relatives.

My older brother Harry died when he was twenty-two years of age in Maryborough. He'd been working and was accidentally shot. We never knew what really happened. We were told it happened when Harry was cleaning his gun, then we heard it was when he was dingo shooting, but I think there must have been more to it than that. Mama cried every night at sundown when she heard. The houses had sticks to keep the windows up and when the sun went down Mama's wailing would be heard for hours through the open windows. We cried, too, at seeing her in such grief.

I remember my parents desperately wanting to go to Harry's funeral but the officialdom declined them a permit. I fretted to see them so hurt about it. Dadda made several attempts to go in his sulky but was refused by the superintendent. Thinking back on it, I wonder if it may have been punishment to him for his past behaviour. If denial was intended to hurt, it achieved just that.

While we had nothing materially in our childhoods on the mission, we were rich in other ways, rich in spirit. For us kids, there were always ways to be happy. I remember us making dolls out of bottles and cars out of rocks. We would go walking, fishing, hunting and camping inside the reserve. We were one of the few lucky families in Cherbourg to own a horse and sulky. That was like owning a Mercedes. But none of us was allowed to ride in the sulky without Dadda's permission and so none of us got to have a ride. It was used as transport mainly to and from Murgon which was about 5 kilometres away.

Murgon was the largest main rural town in the area. Other nearby towns like Wondai, Gavndah and Kingaroy were smaller places where the local pastoralists shopped. Murgon had all the modern-day things like a bank, post office, hotel, shops, railway station and when we would visit the town it was like exploring another world to us. Only non-Aboriginal people lived there then.

When we first arrived at Cherbourg all the children were sent to school. We'd never seen a school before. School was the place where we had the most contact with European ways. The lighter-skinned children would be separated from the darker children in classes with the idea of improving their learning. The teachers and missionaries were surprised when this did not happen. The dark-skinned children were just as bright as the lighter ones and some of the lighter ones were a few marbles shorter than the dark ones. I always thought how awful that system was.

I first went to school when I was eight. There were two teachers and the principal, Mr. Crawford, who'd give the boys almighty whacks with the cane. Auntie Janie Sunflower used to teach us at the school, too, and she'd take us for physical education, and play the piano-accordion and a mouth organ. It was nice to have one of our own people there.

Our room was a shed and in the front was the school office near the river. The school today is in the old 'top camp' area. At school there were about six European children in their starched clothes, the children of the white officials, and they mostly stuck close together. Sometimes we'd play with them but, I guess like them, we preferred our own mob. We never went outside the reserve on excursions to Brisbane like the white children and there was never any mixing with them outside school hours.

We used the old slates to write on. We were taught basic reading, writing, arithmetic, and a lot about European history, Captain Cook, and sewing. We were never allowed to draw or dance, which we were naturally good at. I don't remember the white teachers ever encouraging us to do things we wanted to do, or what we were good at. Instead, sewing!

As I've said, we were told not to speak our Aboriginal language, although we still spoke it out of hearing of the whites. We lost most of the Pitjara language, but we learnt Wakka Wakka words. That was the name of the local Cherbourg tribe. My brothers and sisters still know some words of that language. Although we can't speak it fluently anymore, the words we know are precious and carried on to our children and their children.

When I was twelve I was sent to the mission dormitory by the superintendent. I was very frightened. It was pretty rare to have escaped this experience for so long. I was put there as punishment for seeing boys. Just because we spoke to the boys, the officials thought we were doing niggi niggi. A Black tracker came to our house and took me to the dormitory. It was because of Fletcher Brown, my first boyfriend. I would tuck scones under my calico bloomers to give to him and he would hide gingerbreads in his shirt. We had a puppy love relationship until he died when he was sixteen from tuberculosis.

The dormitory became home then. We were discouraged from thinking of our real home with our families. It did damage here but it could never sever the ties we had with our families. We were allowed visitors but my parents kept my brothers and sisters away in case they were kept in there, too. We were allowed to go home at weekends.

The dormitory was a two-storey wooden building with huge verandahs around it. It was near the teachers' residences. You could have eaten off the floors they were kept that spotless. An Aboriginal staff acting under orders of the superintendent controlled the dormitory routine like clockwork. Nancy and Charlie Chambers who were distant relations of ours were in charge of at least a dozen cooks, cleaners and other minders. Strict control and discipline were part of dormitory life. There was a range of chores to do such as making beds, washing clothes and linen in huge boilers, and scrubbing out the dormitory. We would go to school after breakfast and played after school. Then there were prayers, and dinner—

mainly stew—which we ate in a huge dining room using enamel plates and cups. And then to bed.

It felt strange going to bed where there were three or four girls, not sisters. The boys were put into dormitories, too, but they were separated from us. The beds were lined up beside one another in long rows on either side of the room. My hair was completely shaved off because it was infested with lice. That was common on the mission.

I didn't like the dormitories but we deserved what we got because we didn't do what we were told. Sneaking around and talking to boys and all that business.

No, Mum, none of youse deserved it. They brainwashed you into believing you were responsible and it was your fault. It was about white paternalistic control and surveillance. Would you have sent us to a home? Even though you continually threatened us as small children, 'I'll put you all in a home if you play up'. I used to be terrified you would, so tried not to play up often—even though this never worked. No one deserves to be forcibly removed from their families.

When I was thirteen, me, Betty Hart and Iris Hegarty were imprisoned for a week in Cherbourg gaol for seeing boys. Again, they thought we were doing niggi niggi, but we weren't. It was the only time I've been in gaol. We only had one blanket and one pillow and it was cold and we huddled together to be warm. It was so dark and scary in that place. They'd shaved our heads bald and gave us only bread and water. We never even had any munyoos. When they took us out, we had to do the housework at the dormitory, scrubbing the floors with our bare hands.

Unlike a lot of reserves we sometimes had corroborees. We would always go down to watch. Auntie Janie Sunflower would sit down and by just pounding a pillow she'd make this mellow sound which would blend with the other music. Women would sing but not dance with the men. Fires were lit by the traditional way of rubbing two sticks together. Men continued the dances and songs late into the night. The men were good dancers and would go down to Brisbane to dance for white people.

After school we would wander off to the local swimming place known as the Bogey Hole at Barambah Creek. In summer this place would attract the kids in droves, seeking out the cool water. Most of us would strip off and dive straight in. The boys preferred to climb out on the thick limbs of the tree and show off their different styles of diving. They all made sure that the girls they liked would be watching. Sometimes we would drift down on logs, splashing, singing and skylarking away. The younger children often came with us and it was our duty to look after them. We might only have been ten years old but we were guardians to a bunch of babies. We would make sure that they had as much fun as we did. So much fun in fact that it became hard for us to get them out of the water. The older children would take them home whether or not they were their brothers or sisters. It was always like that when I was growing up. We had such a deep sense of loving for each other.

The Bogey Hole would also be used for baptism services by the Aboriginal Inland Mission. My brothers, sisters and I would sneak down on Sundays to see who was getting thrown back in the river. As we hid behind the bushes we used to wonder why everyone in the water was screaming and throwing their hands up in the air. We thought they must be drowning or something, but how could they be? Everyone knew how to swim on the mission.

Uncle Moses lived on the mission farm which grew many of the vegetables we saw but never had the opportunity to eat. Most of it went to the white officials. My friends and I would see him ploughing every day, going up and down the furrows with his faithful old horse and broken-down plough. Now, I had learnt my lesson well and good not to steal anymore but my friends had not. So while I stood guard and watched Uncle Moses doing his chores my mates stole the tempting vegetables. Sweet potatoes were the tastiest. My friends would take them home and give some to my mother who thought that Uncle Moses had given them to us.

One day I was not so quick. I was distracted and Uncle Moses caught my friends outright. He had a habit of waving a stick around and this time held it higher than normal and shouted to them to drop their loot. They hurriedly jumped through the barbed-wire fence where I was waiting on the other side. Uncle Moses was not fast enough to catch anyone and, as he ran towards us, someone called out something that our gang would remember for a long time and still rings in my ears today:

Moses, Moses,
when you die
your mundie closes!

Growing up in Cherbourg for my mother was a struggle and a privilege. There was an affinity and a cohesion between everyone. A Cherbourg experience has not yet been written which sheds light on the ever-growing success stories emanating from that community, in terms of Aboriginal activism throughout the country. Perhaps the younger generation has learnt many gracious and crucial lessons from their peers, for many Cherbourg descendants are now at the peak of their professions in Aboriginal community affairs such as Aboriginal education, legal and health organisations, and comprise large numbers in government and non-government positions.

THE GRAND EXPERIENCE

I came to Brisbane in 1959. It was closer to my own country and to my family. Ayr held too many memories for me, I saw Jack's face everywhere. With my four young children, I moved to Inala, a Housing Commission area in an outer suburb of Brisbane. We were one of the first Aboriginal families there. Inala is an Aboriginal word for good camping place by running water, and the place always did have a very Aboriginal sense about it. I could see them in the old days living there, sitting around the campfires telling the stories, singing and dancing. Now Inala has the highest population of Aboriginals and Torres Strait Islanders in Brisbane.

Being in a city was very hard for me at first. Looking back, I think that the changes I went through at that time were too big. Without Jack, and in a new place, I felt very lost. I was grieving beyond belief for my precious husband. My life felt like one big, empty hole with no way to climb out. I was very angry that Jack had died and wasn't with me and our children.

I had very little resources for raising a family all on my own. The only job I knew was domestic service. But it was impossible when three of my children were under three years of age. What money there was came from Jack. He had always been a good provider, and he was able to support us after his death as well. He had contributed to a superannuation fund from which I received a small fortnightly cheque, as well as a war widow's pension from Veterans' Affairs. This money was a godsend and enabled my family to have shelter, food and clothing.

However, I didn't always use the money in that way in the first years after Jack died. My grief swallowed me up and I looked to things that would take me away from my cares. I loved to go out at night and let my hair down. Actually, in those days I wore it up in a beehive. I spent money on good times and alcohol, and sought relief in the friendship of other men. I just wanted to have a good time—anything away from the grief.

I spent a lot of time at The Grand Hotel in Mary Street, down by the wharves It was a concrete pub with a small, shabby lounge and a public bar. Many Murries used to meet there. People from all parts would come together to catch up on news of friends and relations. Every Friday and Saturday night The Grand would come alive to the beat of the juke-box and the hum of voices filling the dimly lit, smokey rooms. Women would sit on the men's laps and, while chairs were scarce, the laughter and beer were not. It was a place where everyone felt like one big family, fights and all, and boy-oh-boy, were there some fights.

In those days there were plenty of 'captains' who were willing to share drinks, smokes and their company with us. But they didn't get it all their way because sometimes we'd beat them at their own game. The power for once was in our court until we tired of it all, then we'd leave. They'd get gooly up, but who cared? Lonely old guys, too, would wander in from the streets into the Murrie pub where they knew they'd be listened and spoken to and given some respect, if they deserved it. We'd even give them taxi fares home. A lot of younger Murrie women were also regulars at The Grand. When the ships came to town the sailors would be buzzing around and I don't think they could resist the temptation. Someone must have told them about us. As they told me later, The Grand was important to these young women in their growing up. They learnt to deal with a society that was very different from their own. Something of their identities as young women was formed at The Grand, as well as some streetwiseness and the ability to deal with hungry white guys.

It was here at The Grand that I met one of the loveliest people in my life, Harry Hapameni, a merchant seaman from Finland. Harry would stay at our place on his weekend leave. We'd all go for bush walks and picnics which Harry just loved. I could have easily fallen in love with him, but what was the use? He would soon be going home to Finland and I would never see him again. I was an Aboriginal woman and could never leave my land for anyone.

The way in which relations between women worked was very interesting. We'd always be loyal to each other and defend one another, but when it came to a man two women wanted, it would be every selfish thimbun for herself. One day a woman I used to call a friend pulled my hair down the toilet because she was jealous of her date's attention towards me. Betty Hart was my best friend and backstop at the time and came to my aid. Betty had been a school pal at Cherbourg and could outfist the boys any day—a real tomboy. She was well known as a good fighter and would put off any bully. I always felt safe around her. If anyone hit me, she'd take it up for me and bash him up. We had a lovely sisterly friendship all our lives. Betty never had any children but would spoil my children as if they were her own. My children loved her very much in return.

Although she was very protective towards me, I sometimes hated going to the pub with her because she would get jealous if her boyfriend so much as looked at or spoke to another woman. Her round, black, red-lipped face was scarred by fights and if a white person who she didn't know so much as glanced at her she'd say, 'What the f'n hell are you looking at? Haven't you seen a Blackfella before?' She got worse when she'd had a few drinks. She was such a wild woman. Everyone was scared of her.

Betty changed in the 1970s when she found the Lord. She became a committed Christian, involved in full-time Church work. I was so happy for her. I saw that gentle side of Betty that I knew so well begin to out-shine and take over. She began dressing better, really looking after herself and had a special glow about her. Betty remained a loyal friend until her death in 1986.

My mother had much loyalty and generosity towards her friends. It wouldn't be rare to bring them home to sleep. They'd always be women though and sometimes we'd get a fright to see another person sleeping in our room on a mattress on the floor or to have our brother or sister in bed with us while the friend slept in one of our beds.

Although we had only a little ourselves, we still shared whatever we could. Mum would usually feed her friend the next morning and then send her home in a cab. She felt sorry for them because sometimes it would be the only feed they had had in days. She collected all the strays and brought them home like the caring person that she was.

We never winced about this, though, because Mum seemed to get a lot of satisfaction from this. Besides, her friends were always nice to us and gave us a few bob if they had it, which wasn't often. We called them all Auntie and even today they acknowledge us fondly. One time, Auntie Caroline Doolan wanted to take me out to the Birdsville Races with her boyfriend because I was her favourite. Needless to say, I never saw Birdsville. Actually, a few of my aunties promised me many things which I never got. They were so loving to all of us which made up for lots.

Little did I realise how in those days I was neglecting my children who began to suffer. I usually left them in the care of my second-eldest daughter Gloria who was only in her early teens herself. I think now what a burden and huge responsibility it was for a young girl to take care of her younger sisters and brother when she should have been the one who was going out all the time. I don't know what Gloria had felt about all this because she never complained—not to me that is. She may have to her friends but she was such a beautiful and generous spirit who was kind and understanding to everyone.

My children told me much later in their lives how they were hurt by my not being there. How my priorities were solely about me and my life. I was so busy having a good time that I'd spend most of our money on drinking and socialising. My children paid the price, but I couldn't see it. As long as I was having fun, who cared?

Yes, Mum, I hurt a lot about the bad old days but they are gone now. Writing about them has proved an extraordinary healing process for me and I'm sure you won't mind me telling a few yarns.

I remember when I was eleven, and wore that scungy old green seersucker dress constantly to school until it was in tatters. One day, this freckly, skinny, smart alec schoolboy asked, 'Don't they stock those dresses in other sizes or colours?' Ngaire was into recycling at an early age and would mix and match two outfits to go around for as long as she could. And, well, Johnny just didn't care, did he? He had a persistently runny nose and needed hankies more than clothes. Neither did we have any shoes and would walk to school barefoot. However, in those days many of the other kids in Inala hadn't shoes either so it didn't seem to worry us. Can you imagine your grandsons doing that today? It would be a real shame job, ey?

Vegemite sandwiches were the norm for lunches and some days we were so broke that you'd wait until the bank opened on pension day before you could take our lunches up at recess. Our hungry little faces would faithfully greet you as you handed the lunches over the fence. 'Thanks, Mum', we'd appreciatively say and scurry off. As soon as that 'motherly' duty was performed you'd get done up perfectly and rush off into town. You were always immaculately decked out like a queen, with dress, jewellery, handbag and shoes all matching. We'd just sit and watch you. Everyone commented how great you looked and, being a real Leo, you just loved the flattery.

I can still see Johnny, who was about nine, over at the local Commonwealth Bank agency withdrawing twenty cents for some margarine. I think there was only about fifty cents in the account anyway. The shop assistant must have felt so sorry for him because she ignored the withdrawal and gave him the money out of her own purse. We can laugh about that now.

I realise now why my daughters give their children everything. It's because they missed out on such a lot of material things in their time. They can't bear their children to go without while they have the money. Sometimes I criticise them for spoiling their children as I think it's healthy for kids not to get everything they ask for. But I can't blame them because they know the real meaning of being poor when they were young and what it is like to go without.

My spending went on for years. We always seemed to be broke except on pay day and it would be gone again in the following few days. To tell the truth, I never knew how to budget. We had very little to spend anyhow and Jack had always handled the household money. I never learnt the value of money and how to make it last until the next pay. It was in one hand and out the other, all in a matter of days. I'd get so excited the day before pay day and never really plan how to spend it. All I knew was that soon I would be having a good time. My fortnightly thrill was coming up and I would look forward to the next one. I didn't understand hire-purchase either. It was a quick way of getting goods like fridges and washing machines without much cash. So I would sign up. Soon I found myself unable to keep up the repayments. I would hide in my room when the bill and rent collectors came around. They would get abusive to my children when they told them Mum wasn't home.

Spending on the wrong things meant I couldn't keep the roof over our heads. Rental arrears began to mount up. I had no one to blame except myself. One cold July day in 1969 a Housing Commission rent collector caught me at home when the children were at school and served an eviction notice. My kids were angry with me when they realised what was happening. We were going to get evicted from our house and not only would they lose their home but their school and friends as well. They never forgave me for that. It was a huge disruption to our lives. A long series of moves around Brisbane followed. If I'd known what would happen I would have paid the rent, arrears and all. For years we didn't have a real home anywhere, just temporary, seedy, accommodation to look forward to.

We moved to the inner-city area where times were tough. I got in boarders, one at a time. The kids didn't like having an extra person but it helped with the rent and food. One star boarder was old Frank who must have been eighty years old and still working. He was bald, toothless and had suffered a stroke years ago. He had worked as a carpenter all his life and would cause his employers some fright because he refused to give up work. He'd travel up to eighty miles a day to work. All he had was four weetbix for breakfast and I would pack him sandwiches for lunch. Poor old Frank was never any trouble to me.

I remember one slack week, we had nothing in the house to eat—no muntha or anything. Johnny the animal lover had a pet duck called Harvey that used to roam around the yard, just minding his own business. My brother Oliver was staying with us and was used to having his meat at night. As there was no meat I had no hard feelings in baking up Harvey for the evening meal. Oliver loved it but all the kids could do was to stare down at their plates. They had put two and two together. Suddenly Johnny jumped up and said, 'Where's Harvey?' The next morning with tears and bookah streaming down his face he went outside to pick up the scattered duck feathers.

It's been very hard for Rita to talk about these days. In fact, I know you don't like to be reminded of them, do you, thimbun? I believe these are the hard years that have added and made you the person that you are today. No one is perfect, as you've always told me. You need not feel ashamed anymore.

Despite the hard times we had, all of us would say that we had a beaut childhood somehow. Sure, we'd complain, off-load and fight because they were ways of relieving our anxieties. It was probably our closeness as children which gave us the security and love we felt so deprived of at times. But insecurity and loneliness weren't even issues because we had each other and, besides, you always came home to us in the end. You could have told us all to get nicked and put us in foster homes but you chose to keep your children and we love and respect you for that.

My mother blames herself for those years, but they are not problems that were peculiar to her, but ones common among Black urban communities. Aboriginals in Brisbane were not only faced with the difficulties of being newcomers, but they were dealing with a cultural shift from the reserves or rural areas and small country towns to an urban area. Aboriginal people had been moving to the capital cities, because of greater employment opportunities and greater freedoms that emerged after the war. With freedom from the reserves came the unlocking of rights that had previously been completely unattainable for them but that had been taken for granted by non-Aboriginals: freedom to move around the country without permission, to earn a wage and keep it, the prospects of jobs and education, a chance for a life over which we had some control and, most important of all, the freedom to express oneself. Not all Aboriginals who came to the cities liked the life or were able to find work, but a significant number stayed. By the mid 1960s, approximately one in every five Aboriginals lived in the capital cities, a dramatic increase on the pre-war period. It has been estimated that about five thousand Aboriginals lived in Brisbane by 1965.

Most white Australians would have had no knowledge of what my mother's generation of Aboriginals faced in the shift to the cities. White Australians knew virtually nothing about the places my mother's people came from except for some ill-conceived notions derived from the media. It was, after all, the days when the practice was strong of taking children away from their families in the name of protection. The myth abounded of Aboriginal degradation, hopelessness and inferiority, part of the collective unconscious of the white nation. While the most violent acts of persecution of Aboriginal people were usually confined to the more remote frontier regions, nevertheless racial prejudice and discrimination persisted in the cities.

It wasn't uncommon, for example, for Aboriginal families to be forced to lead a life of urban itinerance, moving house perhaps four or five times a year, because of the attitudes of white neighbours and landlords who had no tolerance for Black ways. So, for instance, offering a place in our homes for transient or homeless relations and friends was (and still often is) viewed with great intolerance by whites. It was expected of Aboriginal people living in cities that they undergo huge cultural change, conforming to white ways.

There weren't many Aboriginal people living in Inala in those days and poshy white people especially were very backward in their attitudes and understandings of us. And today not a lot has changed in that respect at all. I have heard many stories from my people of how they get discriminated against by real estate agents, by lawyers, by doctors, and the ways they get treated by bus drivers and taxi drivers, and by people in shops and hotels. It happens all the time.

I remember the time when my children were little in the '60s, Johnny got a rash on his arm. I took him to the local doctor who took one look at me with my three other children in the waiting room and, when it came my turn, said, 'You're Aboriginal'. I wasn't sure if it was a question or a statement. I thought how strange it was for him to say that. I told him my son had an itchy rash on his arm. He didn't even bother to examine my child but said right away, 'He's got scabies. I'll prescribe some lotion which everyone in the house must use and you'll have to wash all your clothes and bed linen'. It didn't feel right somehow but I went home and did exactly what he had told me, even though none of us other than Johnny had the rash. A week later Johnny still had it. A friend took one look at Johnny's arm and said it was an allergy of some sort and I should take him off dairy products for a while. Two days later the rash disappeared. He'd been cured and I'd been conned!

What could I do? I'd been taught to trust and respect doctors, people in authority. I wasn't confident enough to challenge him. Perhaps today it would be a different story because I have had heaps of experience with doctors and other health people who have tried to pull the wool over my eyes. I would now demand a proper examination, or get a second opinion if I didn't feel satisfied. Just because he had seen a lone Aboriginal woman with a mob of kids in his surgery he presumed that we were dirty.

In the years after the war, Inala was a dumping ground for migrants and thousands of people with nowhere else to go. It was no wonder that Aboriginal families would find their way there. I suppose it was like Elizabeth in Adelaide, or the western suburbs of Sydney. When we moved there in the late '50s, it seemed that mostly everyone was a battler, gunin gunin. The crime rate was not as bad as it is today. We were all so poor, Aboriginals and whites. It didn't matter what colour your skin was. Some of the whites were worse off than we were, and that was saying something! Public transport didn't exist, and without a car you felt pretty lonely. Some of my nephews had old cars they'd done up and they would take us for drives.

I didn't have a car then and used taxis when I had to. That's how I met my good friend George Hodges and his family. He'd taken me into town from Inala in his taxi one day in 1964. We struck up a good friendship and I liked him so much that he became my personal chauffeur (at a price) for the next ten years. Sometimes the kids and I would get bored and we would tear off to the Gold Coast or up to see my mother at Cherbourg in George's taxi! When Mama first saw George she said, 'Who that withew?' I said, 'He's our taxi driver, Mama'. It didn't take long for Mama to like him. George was a tall, well-mannered man who was reliable, honest and a damn good taxi driver. My children liked him a lot, too. He was a good friend to me. His children were about the same ages as mine and on weekends my children would stay with him and his wife at the time, Rae. They spoilt my children rotten. It was nice to know such lovely people.

One time, Johnny must have been feeling lonely without a father because he always had his mum and three big sisters nagging him. He proudly asked, 'George, will you be my daddy?' George's face went red and he nearly died on the spot but couldn't refuse those big brown eyes. 'Yes, mate, I will'. Johnny called him Dad from that day on.

When George's taxi pulled up, we would get so excited because we knew we'd be going on a long trip. Mother would usually prepare us well in advance for the destination and while we loved going to the beach we'd balk at Cherbourg because it was a long, hot ride for five hours. This trip was pretty monotonous and we'd anxiously wait to get there as fast as we could, and play 'I Spy' all the way. I'd usually win because I cheated by changing the object every time someone guessed it.

On arrival in Cherbourg our Gran would hug, kiss and greet us warmly. She never knew we were coming. We just turned up, which is always the way with Aboriginal families. No formal phone call or message needs to be given that you are coming. You just turn up. Everything gets accommodated. While Grannie would take us inside and give us cordial and biscuits, George and Mum would get a cup of tea. George would automatically lie down in a bedroom after the long and noisy drive. He was such a gentleman and I can never recall him telling us to shut up. Mum did that quite handsomely, come to think of it.

I often recall those days and how strange it must have been to see an Aboriginal woman and her back-seat load of children being driven around everywhere by a white taxi driver. George didn't seem to mind, though. He had enormous respect for my mother and perhaps, in his own way, felt a little sorry for us, too.

Journeying

... In 1988, after finishing her degree in history and anthropology at the University of Queensland, Jackie did a diploma in Aboriginal education at Flinders University in South Australia. As part of her course, she spent eight weeks teaching in Ti Tree, two hours' drive north of Alice Springs, and John Henry (who likes to be called John these days) and I went with her. John was three years old then and I was glad to look after him while Jackie was teaching. We were given a house across the road from the school. My grandson was so cute. Every morning, he would perch on the sink to wave his mum goodbye.

It was a good chance to meet the local Aboriginal people and learn their customs. They were Anmatjera people and I formed a wonderful friendship with the school's laundry lady, Nita Napparula. Nita was a tall, strong woman. Her hair was curly and reminded me more of the Torres Strait Islander people.

Being 'outsiders' and new in town some Adelaide friends called in on their way from Katherine. They asked about us at the service station. The local, white, school bus driver was having his tea in the diner. Our friends went over to him to find out where they could find us. He replied that he knew of an Islander family who were living in the town, and swore black and blue that we weren't Aboriginal (good-go). This was because we spoke a different language and my hair was frizzy. Usually my hair is thin and straight but I'd recently had a perm which had sent it crazy.

It was then that I realised how different we were, not only to the whites in town, but to the Aboriginal people. I am sure they saw Jackie as a white person because she was a teacher and couldn't speak her own language apart from the Aboriginal English we use between ourselves. For the first time in Jackie's life she suffered from an identity crisis—she was too black to be white and too white to be Black. And I am not sure they knew what to think of me. Here I was, this little old granny looking after a small boy but still very different from them. They were very wary of us but I was determined to be myself and break down the barriers. Acceptance took some time, but it did come. After school and in the early evening the children and their families would come around and it was not unusual to have twenty people in the house. Acceptance came more quickly for me, though, than it did for Jackie as she was seen as a boss figure. The kids called her 'Miss Jackie' at school and at home.

I have always been strong about my Blackness. From my earliest days my mother, family and friends helped me to feel pride in being Black, and I've been reminded of my difference by whites ever since. Without that early reinforcement I'd be a confused person now. Until Ti Tree I had never questioned where I stood in the world. I was a Black person within a white world. But in Ti Tree I was a Black person within a Black world that was different from my own and I experienced something of a culture shock.

But all the same, here the white world still wielded the power.

My uneasiness was apparent to the young Black children that I taught and their families. The children were my greatest critics. We all weren't sure what to make of each other. They were privileged in their own way but I felt as though I had a privilege that exceeded theirs but could never exceed the white privilege. But what is privilege anyhow and who really holds it? They probably pitied me the most.

Jackie would come home and tell us how her day was with the children. She did not approve of the white teaching but loved the children. They weren't cheeky and gave her a lot of satisfaction.

One day she asked a class of five white children and twenty Aboriginal children whose families had been living the longest in the area. A young white girl put her hand up and claimed that her grandparents had been living in the area for over fifty years. Jackie turned to a young Aboriginal boy and asked him how long his people had been there. 'I don't know, Miss, maybe thousands of years, ey?' 'Try 50,000, Sean', she said. With that, the Aboriginal pupils' pupils lit up like brown beacons across the room. She saw their proudness. They sat up quickly and had huge white smiles all over their mitha mitha faces. It seemed the white children were always in competition with the Aboriginal children. That is except when it came to sport. The Aboriginal kids always won. The white kids didn't like it either. For once in their lives the Aboriginal children had them beaten.

The days were beautiful and clear. I love the desert, so arid and majestic. At night we would sit outside in the glorious sunset. I would think about the old people who lived in the area long before I had ever seen this country. How contented they must have been.

During a long weekend we hired a car and went to Uluru, a place I had only dreamed about. I was overcome by its presence and beauty. A kindred spirit had opened up inside me. For one of the very few times in my life I was speechless as we drove around it. I noticed every little crevice and wondered how all the old people once survived in harmony around it. We drove into the Aboriginal township but it was deserted. We found out later all were at the Barunga Festival in Katherine.

When we were camping, I met a young English tourist, and I invited her to the Olgas with us the next day. Jackie was a bit cheesed off because I was always inviting strangers along. As we drove past Uluru, I pointed out the Aboriginal warrior's face on the rock. The English lass swore she could not see it. I've always wondered if it is only something Black people can see, as every Murrie I have spoken to who has been to Uluru has seen it.

To me there seems more of a spiritual presence at the Olgas than Uluru. Perhaps this is so because there appeared little European tampering here, and less goings-on by tourists. They'd climb the Rock out of an effort just to say they climbed it. I wonder if they thought about its sacredness, though. How typical, I think, of white people who are satisfied with the result rather than the purpose. My daughter refused to climb on her 'Mother's heart', as she described it. That trip was so brief but I'll never forget that beautiful place.

Sometimes white people don't think we have a right to be there. Or they have expectations that all Aboriginal people will be the same. Like the time Jackie and I went over to New Zealand for a holiday. It was an eye-opener for me. I saw another beautiful country and lots of sheep. This was a strange feeling to leave my country. I was a little frightened but had my big backstop with me. I'd never been out of Australia before.

When we arrived in Christchurch we went straight to our motel room and in the morning met up with people who were on our coach tour. We were a very mixed bunch of people—Americans, Australians, Canadians, Japanese and Europeans. I spotted a big, tall, Yankee tourist staring at us and said to Jackie, as I so often do, 'Thilly-wujaburri!' ('Big, white eyes watching us'.) He asked us 'what' we were and when I said we were Aboriginal he shook his head in disbelief and said he'd just been to Australia and, no, we weren't. Fancy saying that! I was very angry and told him that we knew who we were. I knew I had jarred him by the look on his face.

A Scottish lady, Ella, shyly came over and said, 'Excuse me, dear, are you . . . are you . . . the Aborigines?' Now we were the exotics. When I said, 'Yes', she took me over to meet her husband. They were nice people, and the four of us became good friends. We dined with each other every night. One night we were enjoying ourselves so much that I stayed up till the wee (pardon the pun) hours of the morning drinking. What I didn't know was that it was straight Scotch on the rocks I was drinking. Jackie retired to bed much earlier (as she couldn't handle the pace). I can still see her peering down the hall to see if I wouldn't fall over. It's strange that I never felt slightly tipsy although I must have drunk many, many glasses. I remember matching them drink for drink, but it had no effect on me. My sleep that night was rock solid. In fact, the next morning the bus driver said he had heard snores from our room. I'm not sure if that had been me or Jackie.

It was so interesting seeing a different land. My only regret is that we never met any Maori people.

Our experience in New Zealand showed the preconceived ideas people have about Aboriginals. Because we did not fit the stereotype of the 'savage' we were not considered 'real' Aboriginals. You meet this often. Like the time it was said to me that I didn't sound like an Aboriginal because I didn't have an accent. Styles of dress, speech, abode, where we shop or what car we drive do not lessen our relation to Aboriginal culture and identity. Nor do they heal the emotional scars from our experiences living in western society.

The ultimate insult is 'You're not a real Aboriginal'. Non-Aboriginal people are not expected to comply to one particular model and neither should we. We come in all shapes and sizes, and from different places. We have always had to conform to white Australian society, but imagine what a different country Australia would be now if non-Aboriginals had had to adopt Aboriginal ways. Non-Aboriginals have a lot to learn from Aboriginals, things like respect for one another, cooperation rather than competition, non-materialism, looking after the country, taking care of family and respect for elders.

Granny Koori

KEVIN GILBERT

Dear Director of Aboriginal Grants
My association needs $55,000 bucks
To purchase silky black ladies' pants
A quota to cover each area, the Territories—
State by state
To conceal from the prying eyes of the world
The Aborigines' poor buggered fate.
There's few men with ESSENTIALS among 'em
We think lots of bloomers will meet
Requirements of dress as befits them
While women fight for Black kids on the street!
Blackblokes think they're great 'lovers' and 'manly'
A MAN 'cause he drinks lots of grog
They leave it to women to battle
Far as 'love' goes—so does my dog!!
A *real* man stops children from dyin'
A *real* man don't belt up his gin
A *real* man don't grog away money
To let wolves of hunger come in
A REAL MAN in old tribal custom
Held to the law and its way
He didn't starve kids or his missus
Not like the weak Blacks of today!!
So expedite bloomers first mail please
We've hoped for too long they'll be *men*

Now we'll cover their doongles with panties—
And start out all over again!!

Grandfather Koori

KEVIN GILBERT

Now Granny, get yer fanny
Out of here, I'll have *my* say
'Course the Blacks are kinda useless
Since the whitess come here to stay
With 200 years of bribin', baccy flour grog an' tea
Each has made its mighty inroads on a people who were free
But they're *not* the free no longer, they're the chained and crippled now
And it takes a lot of courage for a man to face his hour.
Sure, the women march for justice while near all the men stay home
But there's a small few men there with you—little bricks are building Rome
Solid bricks and solid women with love's cement in their hand
Will block and build a nation—once they've won their bit of land.
Once we've won our bit of land back we'll put bludgers to the rout
And we'll fight and form our empire—further out, much further out.

Mother-in-Law

LISA BELLEAR

Took me thirty years before I left your father
Battered wife syndrome, well that's the term the
Social worker used at the neighbourhood centre
Oh I didn't realise I was being abused. On the bad days
I never left the house, told friends, not that I had many
I was visiting a relative who had taken poorly
Look at me sweetheart, you've made the right decision

Believe me, you have to think of Stacy, and don't forget
You have to take care of yourself. Mothers have rights
Mothers have needs too. I'll not make excuses for
Your behaviour, you have to work through that, nor
Can you say it was all Larry's fault. Honey don't cry
Together we'll be okay, you've got to stop hating yourself
Alright, the court order allows fortnightly access visits
On the proviso he's not been drinking—listen he's not
Doing right by you or Stacy, coming here drunk. He
Hasn't even bothered to shave. Darling, he may still care
He may even still love, but rules are there for the protection
Of the child, and for the sanity of the mother. Maybe the
Next time you will be able to welcome Larry inside but
For now, tonight, the situation, the reality is no, and if
He's still there in five minutes, Larry knows the score
There's a train, or there's a police van
It's up to him

Break the Cycle

Lisa Bellear

Hit
me
again
and
i
swear
i'll
call
the
cops/
brother
got
to
stop

fightin'
me
i'm
your
sister

Birth Control for Blacks

Kevin Gilbert

Don't you take that pill
He tells me
Don't you listen to them whites
They're all out to kill us,
Race-wise
Just to save 'emselves some fights.
'Member how they tried to kill us
Poisoned flour and with the gun?
Now they're out to git ol' Jacky
While he's at his bit of fun!

(How he bores me as he beds me—
Now if I could change *their luck*
I'd make every man among 'em
Have a baby—every fuck.
Soon we'd see 'em every morning
Like a boar-pig at its swill
Swallow trough-loads while they're singin'
HALLELUJAH!!! for the pill.)

Mary

KEVIN GILBERT

Don't be too hard on the males, Mary
when you cry out that they are not men
and too many children are dying
where in God's name will it end
why don't the men speak and stop it
and why don't they speak out or die
as men with some courage to face it
without the wine courage they buy
remember when you sit in the ashes
as tears fall for your kids lying dead
that you're also part of the problem
guilt equally falls on your head
your trust in the whiteman is legion
you trust in the flag you salute
stars with the ensign of England
the symbol of vandals and brute
you cling to the white Woman's Weekly
and yearn for the world of TV
while women of much stronger fibre
make molotov cocktails for tea.

Artist Son

OODGEROO OF THE NOONUCCAL TRIBE

To Kabul of the tribe Noonuccal (Vivian Walker)

My artist son,
Busy with brush, absorbed in more than play,
Untutored yet, striving alone to find
What colour and form can say,
Yours the deep human need,

The old compulsion, ever since man had mind
And learned to dream,
Adventuring, creative, unconfined.
Even in dim beginning days,
Long before written word was known,
Your fathers too fashioned their art
Who had but bark and wood and the cave stone.
Much you must learn from others, yes,
But copy none; follow no fashions, know
Art the adventurer his lone way
Lonely must go.
Paint joy, not pain,
Paint beauty and happiness for men,
Paint the rare insight glimpses that express
What tongue cannot or pen;
Not for reward, acclaim
That wins honour and opens doors,
Not as ambition toils for fame,
But as the lark sings and the eagle soars.
Make us songs in colour and line:
Painting is speech, painter and poet are one.
Paint what you feel more than the thing you see,
My artist son.

King Gunnadoo: The Australian Housewife's Lament

Margaret Brusnahan

The history books are full of men
Who have all done famous deeds.
These are men who have shown that when,
If needed, they can lead.

There's Alfred the Great and Captain Cook,
And Churchill, he led too.
But I have a man that could fill a book
With what he's Gunnadoo.

He was gunna cut the trees next week
But the wind beat him to that.
He was gunna fix the roof's slow leak
But he's been busy having a nap.

He's gunna mow the lawn one day
If only he gets time.
He'll be able to bale it up for hay,
It's way up past the line.

He's gunna fix the cupboard door
And unblock the bathroom sink.
He's gunna put tiles on the floor,
Pity his back got that kink.

He's gunna lift that gate a bit,
He's gunna build a cage;
But like he says, "Why overdo it?
Work only makes you age."

When I look at things in horror
He comes in right on cue,
"I'll fix all that tomorrow,"
Says my love, Gunnadoo.

Pleading falls on deaf ears,
So what else can I do?
But resign myself to many years
Of promises, with Gunnadoo.

PART FOUR

Station Life

Fatima Kantilla, *This Mob Going Hunting*, 1990, black and white lithograph, 37 x 48 cm. Courtesy of Munupi Arts & Crafts Association, Pularumpi, Melville Island, Northern Territory, Australia, and the artist.

Excerpt from *When the Pelican Laughed*

ALICE NANNUP WITH LAUREN MARSH AND STEPHEN KINNANE

KANGAN GIRL

. . . When I was born they gave me to an old man. My group is garimarra, and balyirri is my straight. They did it by the men picking who they wanted as their mother-in-law. Like when this old fella was around fifty, and mother was having me, he said, 'If that's a girl, that's my woman.' Well I was born a girl, worst luck.

It was never the old women that chose, it was only ever the men. They had it all their own way. A woman used to walk about four or five yards behind her man, carrying a baby on her hip, a bundle of wood or something on her head, another bundle on her back, and have children walking along with her. She'd do all that while the man was walking along carrying a couple of spears! I tell you what, the men had it made.

Anyway, when I was about nine going on ten, this fella I was promised to used to come over to the station to see me. He was waiting until I was old enough, however old that was, and he'd say, 'When you're ready to come with me, you're coming, whether you like it or not.' This was all in Aborigine of course, and he'd come over demanding a feed.

When he'd come, Mother would go off and hide herself because she was forbidden to mix with her son-in-law. She used to say to me, 'Make it, make him a cup of tea. Go on, give him what he wants.'

He'd be saying to me, 'You my woman, you feed me.'

I said to him, 'Mirda, nyinda buga,' That means, no! you buga, you stink.

'Never mind about the buga,' he said. 'You my manga (woman).'

Sometimes he'd come around and Mother would have made a loaf of bread, one long loaf, and he'd just break it into four bits and gobble it down.

'He's just greedy hungry,' I'd say. Mother would say, 'Never mind, never mind, you just feed him.' He'd eat everything, like if we had any cold meat or anything he'd eat it.

He always used to come when Tommy was away from the station. How he knew that I don't know but that's when he'd come. So when Tommy came home one day I told him this fella had been carrying on and bullying me around. 'He wants to take me away. He reckons I'm going to be his wife,' I said.

'Huh, over my dead body,' he said. 'If he comes around while I'm here I'll shoot him.'

My mother was a bit upset and she said, 'Oh, you can't do anything like that!'

Thinking about it now, I think this must have been one of the reasons why my mother decided to leave. Another reason was, after Old Ned died, the Aborigines reckoned my mother shouldn't be living on the station without another husband. I think they'd been on at her for awhile, threatening her about breaking the law, and she got that way she just wanted to leave.

She had the urge to take Ella and me back to Abydos to see our relations, the Lockyers. This was the station I was born on and she wanted me to see it. Tommy came with us on this trip and I remember it so well. We took the wrong track and it was just a spinifex blur. The poor horse went down a hole and broke the shaft on the dray. Tommy said to stay there while he went and found a tree to make a shaft. By joves, he used to carry everything with him; he had axes, chisels, and goodness knows what else in this cart. So, anyway, he fixed it and we were on the road again.

We couldn't reach Abydos that night so we camped out on the road. We had tea, then pulled all the gear off the dray and slept on top of it. The dingoes were really bad and there were a lot of snakes around too. It's an experience I've never forgotten. Those dingoes were howling around but Tommy wouldn't shoot them. He just kept them away. He and Mother took it in turns—Mother would sleep while he kept watch, and then she'd keep watch while he slept.

One time I peeped over the side of the dray, and in the moonlight I could see the white of this dingo's chest. He went, 'Wooooooooooooow,' and I jumped back under the rugs. Those dingoes were that game they'd sneak up and try to pull food away.

After we returned to Kangan my mother got really restless. One night her and Tommy were playing crib when I heard him break down and start crying. I was in bed and I didn't know what they were talking about, but I just buried my head because I didn't want to hear him cry.

The next morning when I got up he said, 'Come on, we're going into Wodgina today . . . did you know your mother is leaving?'

'Is she?' I said.

'Yes,' he said, and I could see he was upset.

'Well, I'm not going.'

'Look,' he said, 'you've got to go where your mother goes. You can't stay with me.'

So he took me into Wodgina because he knew he was going to lose me. We ended up staying the night and the next day we went back home.

A couple of days after our trip, Tommy packed us up with the sulky, two horses, some food and things, and Mother, me and Ella went off to Mallina Station. It took us about three days to get there, and on the way we stayed with Mr Ben Hewitt for the night. He was prospecting with another man, Mr Wilson, and they had a gold mine on the Yule River. The next morning we crossed the Yule and stayed at Mount Satirist for the night. Then it was on to Mallina.

Mallina Station was owned by Mr and Mrs Campbell and it was one of the bigger ones around. There was Croyden, Satirist, Mallina and Munda, all big stations up there. Aborigines would live down at the camps or in cottages, and the station owners lived up in their homesteads.

My mother, Aunty Minnie and Aunty Silvie Lockyer all worked up in the kitchen and the house. They had a chinaman cook there and Mother used to be like a kitchen maid. There was another woman too, and she worked in the house cleaning. There was always work on Mallina, you'd never ever come there and just sit around. Mrs Campbell would make sure of that. Always plenty to be done, like cleaning windows, cooking, gardening or watering fruit trees.

Women worked as musterers and stockworkers as well, not just charwomen and cooks. Aunty Minnie, Aunty Silvie, Miss Greenwood, myself and a couple of others used to ride out mustering sheep. My mother would stay back in the kitchen. We'd go way out to bring the sheep back and it would still be dark, just as the sun was breaking. The earlier you went the better, because if you left after sunrise it'd be a bit too hot for the sheep to travel in.

We used to take our breakfast with us and eat it out there on the way back. It used to be really beautiful, with all the colours changing going from browns to reds around us, and I just loved it.

It wasn't long after we got to Mallina that I went with Aunty Minnie and Uncle Bill to Balla-Balla Station. We were there for awhile—until Tommy got in touch with them because he was going droving. Aunty and Uncle always went droving with him, so they went off and I went back to my mother.

When I got back to Mallina Mother had got together with a man named

Captain. He was a marda marda like me, except his father was Ceylonese. Captain was working on Mallina when we first got there but I don't remember much about him; only that I didn't much like him because he took Mother away from us.

Captain decided he wanted to go over to Munda Station to work, so we all went with him. Mother worked up at the house and us kids used to stay in the camp all day, waiting for her to come home. This camp was by the river. We were with a lot of other Mulbas and we'd just swim nearly all day.

It was when we were back on Mallina that the scouts started to come around. They were sent up from the Aboriginal Affairs in Perth to come and look for the half-caste kids. My mother would say, 'The scouts are back so you'd better be careful,' and she'd tell us to stay in the bunkhouse all day. She was working in the kitchen so she'd bring down a sandwich and a bottle of water and say, 'If they come around, get under the bed and don't talk, just keep quiet.' So we'd get under the bed and stay there until we couldn't hear anything. Then Ella would jump up and have a look and say, 'No, he's gone now,' and we'd be able to come out. Really, because Ella wasn't fair like me she didn't have to worry, but Mother would hide her with me in case they got hold of her and asked questions.

Because we used to hide they could never catch us. Then, this one time, and I remember it as clear as daylight, the Aboriginal Affairs man ended up staying the night. He stayed up at the station house with Mr and Mrs Campbell. They had a conversation together and that must have been when they made all the arrangements.

After his visit the Campbells talked to my mother, my aunt, and my Uncle Paddy about me and Doris. Doris was another fair one like me, and they told them they were going to take us down South to educate us, then bring us back home to our family. I was really excited about going, it sounded like a real adventure. Besides, I thought, it was a good way for me to get out of marrying that old fella I was promised to. But I didn't know, I never even thought of it really, that there were other plans for me.

And it is my belief, too, that if my mother had known what was going to happen she would never have let me go. But she had no reason to think anything other than what they said, because, when she was a young girl, the owners of Abydos Station took her, Aunty Minnie, Aunty Silvie and Aunty Louise down to Bindoon. The station owners went on a holiday and took these four girls with them to help out, and while they were there they went to school. Then afterwards, they all came back to Abydos, and I suppose my mother just thought it would be the same for me.

So, as soon as it was agreed upon, they took me and Doris from the camps and put us up in the station house with the Campbells. We both had to work while we were there—washing dishes, sweeping the verandahs, scrubbing out the bathroom and toilet, things like that. They used to say to us, 'You're our children now,' but they didn't treat us like that. Doris and I shared a room in the house, but we ate on the verandah where we washed up and not with them.

Now we were up at the house we weren't allowed to go past the gate or leave the yard any more. I wasn't allowed to play with Ella either, but she used to come and sit on the other side of the gate. There was a big garden up at the station yard and we used to pull up radishes and things and push them through the wire to her and talk.

I was very lonely up there at the house and I was missing my mother and my life on Kangan. Now that I look back on it, I think if I'd stayed with Tommy on his station I would never have been taken.

When Aunty Minnie had finished droving, she came back to the station and was working with us up at the house. For a while my mother was working there too, and at night, after the washing up was done, she used to come and see me. My mother made sure she never went home without coming to see me first. I was at a bit of a loss to know why I had to be drafted away like this, but she used to say, 'Don't worry, don't worry Wari, you'll be all right.'

Aunty Minnie was younger than my mother, probably only about eight years older than me. One day she had to be rushed to Roebourne to have an operation because she was having a baby and something went wrong. She had to have a caesarean, which was a dangerous operation in those days, and she ended up losing that little baby.

Then one day Tommy came over Mallina way and Mother got to hear of it. I was up at the house with Mrs Campbell and she came over and spoke to her. Then she came to me and said, 'Tommy's down at the mill and we're going down to see him tonight. Then you can tell him you're going to school.' So I was all excited and we went down to the mill where he used to camp by the creek. It was sundown and he was cooking his tea, curry and rice, and he offered us something to eat.

We stayed and ate with him and then we sat around talking until Mother said, 'Well, we better get back now. But you must tell Tommy what you're doing.'

Of course Tommy pricked his ears up and said, 'What's going on?'

'Well,' I said, 'Tommy, I'm going South to school.'

'Who says!'

'Oh, Mr and Mrs Campbell are taking me down and Doris is coming too. We're going to go to school down there and when we're finished we'll be coming home.'

He was very upset. 'Well,' he said, 'that's the finish of it then. What's the good of me living out there, hanging on to the station, if you're not going to be around.'

'Well, Mrs Campbell's promised to bring them back,' my mother said.

But he wasn't happy about it, and he did go and see the Campbells himself, and they assured him everything would be all right and I'd be coming back.

We said goodbye to him after that, and on the way back to the house I was thinking about what Tommy said about wanting to toss it all in. I was really baffled so I said to Mother, 'Ngangka, that's funny. Tommy reckons he doesn't want the station because I'm going South. But when you said you were leaving I wanted to stay, and Tommy said I had to go where you went, and now he doesn't want the station any more!'

'Well,' she said, 'that's because you are a part of him. It's a big shock to him that you're going South, because he thought when you grew up a bit more that you'd go back and look after him.'

When she said this I didn't really understand what she was getting at, and I don't know why, but I just didn't take it any further.

When it was getting close to the time we'd all be leaving, Miss Greenwood, who was Mrs Campbell's niece, took me with her over to Portree Station. She had friends over there and she wanted to have a farewell party with them before she left.

While we were there she stayed up with the station owners, and I stayed down at the Aborigine camp. One night I was sitting with everyone around a big camp fire when I felt something crawl up my back. I put my hand up to grab it, and it grabbed me—twice!

This big bloke named Paddy said, 'What's the matter, what's the matter?'

'I don't know,' I yelled. 'Something is biting me.'

I thought it was a snake, see, but it was a big long centipede. Paddy looked and there were two big bites, so he got some safety matches and broke two of them on my back. He reckoned the sulphur would go in and do something about the poison.

Well, I ended up sick, and Miss Greenwood went back to Mallina and left me there at the camp. We'd ridden across by horse but they took her back in the car. They could've taken me back in the car too but they didn't. I had to stay there until my Uncle Sam rode across to get me.

When I got back to Mallina my mother had had a baby daughter to Captain, and she was only a couple of weeks old. They named her Myrtle, and not long after I got back they took Ella and went to work on Croyden Station.

I was very upset to see them go, but now I'm older I understand that it was getting close to the time when I'd be leaving, and I don't think my mother wanted to see me actually leave. I also wouldn't be surprised if the Campbells had told her to go so I wouldn't be so restless.

When it was very close to when we'd leave, Mr and Mrs Campbell's son, Noble, and Miss Greenwood, took me over to Croyden to say goodbye to my mother. My dear old Uncle Paddy had given me a tin of cling peaches and I said to Mother, 'Uncle said to take this and remember him.' It was a big tin of peaches so she said, 'Well, you can't take it with you, so we might as well eat it.'

So I spent time with them, and my baby step-sister was a bit older then and she was really beautiful. Then, when it was time for me to go back to the station, I said goodbye to everyone, not realising that this would be the last time I would ever see any of them again.

THE THREE PEBBLES

When we left the settlement we travelled to Yarlarweelor Station in Meekatharra. [My husband] Will worked out in the yards and I worked up at the station house cooking and doing housework. We were supposed to get thirty shillings a week pay between us; ten shillings for me, and twenty for Will. We were told by the department that we had to stay for twelve months, but when the station owner and Will had a falling out we had to move on and were never paid our wages.

From Yarlarweelor we moved on to Mount Seabrook Station, and again Will worked outside while I worked up at the house. But we weren't there for very long before we moved to an outcamp on the station. It was called White Well, and Will was looking after the flock out there.

I started up a lovely garden while we were at that place. I had flowers on one side of the mill, and vegetables on the other side. I grew everything; apple cucumbers, long cucumbers, radishes, tomatoes and iron-bark pumpkins. We used to have a water trough out the back that I used to clean everyday to make sure there'd be clean water for the animals. So to water my garden I made all these little lanes in the sand leading down from the trough. Then, when I pulled the plug, everything would get a good watering.

While we were living out there I had my first baby. In the middle of February the manager, Mr Campbell, came out and brought some food. He said, 'This is for Will. You're not having any of this food Alice, you're coming back with me. We don't want you to have the baby out here, we'll take you into Meekatharra a good fortnight before.'

So I packed up a few things and took off with Mr Campbell. Will wasn't too happy about me going—he thought there was still plenty of time—but Mr Campbell just said I was going.

On the following weekend Miss Arnott, who was Mrs Campbell's sister, and Marjie Campbell, who was the boss's daughter, and myself, all took off in a Chev ute. It had been raining and we travelled along with Marjie driving, Miss Arnott in the middle, and me near the door.

Anyway, we got to this slippery part of the road and, being wet, the ute got out of control. I remember that very clearly. Marjie couldn't hold it and we sort of spun straight around and were facing back to Mount Seabrook. We all got such a fright. Marjie got out and checked everything was okay with the ute, and Miss Arnott was saying, 'We better go back and get Mick to drive us in.' But Marjie was going, 'Oh no, we'll be all right Aunty.'

So she got back in the ute and started it up, and we slid around for a while getting back on to the road. When she hit the road she took off again, and every time she'd put her foot down Miss Arnott would say, 'Please Marjory . . . we'll go for another spin and we might roll over.' But Marjie reckoned we were all right, and that was how I got into Meekatharra.

I knew nobody in Meeka, so they took me to a boarding house in town. This was a boarding house for railway workers, and it was run by Mrs Williams and her daughter Annie. Miss Arnott and Miss Campbell went and saw Mrs Williams and she said she had a room, so they left me there to wait to have the baby.

Well I was a boarder there, the boss was paying for my board, but I wasn't treated like a paying boarder. I had a little room and I just sat in there all day with nothing to do, and no one to talk to. At meal times I ate in the kitchen while all the other boarders were served in the dining room. It wasn't that I wanted to eat with them, because they were all men, but I should have had the same treatment as the other boarders. I thought Annie and Mrs Williams would sit and eat with me, but as soon as the men were finished they'd go and have their meal in the dining room, and never invite me.

Then, when I was in my room, Mrs Williams started to call out to me and say, 'Could you come and peel some potatoes?' or, 'Could you wash these dishes?' and anything else that needed doing. She'd put a meal on and she'd say, 'Would you like to just keep an eye on this while Annie and I go down the street?' Well, that wasn't my job! But I'd say I would because I didn't have anywhere else to go.

I'd been there for about a week I suppose when I decided I'd go out for a walk down the street to Garrick's. I wanted to buy a couple of little pieces of material so I could sit down and make something for the baby. While I was in town I went into another shop and I met an Aboriginal lady named Mrs Ingram. She saw me there, walking around, and she came and introduced herself. She asked me where I was staying and I told her I was up at the boarding house. I asked her where she lived and she said, 'Behind the hotel, just near the creek.' Anyway, we talked for a bit longer and as we were parting she said, 'Come back tomorrow Alice, and we'll talk some more.'

I went back to the boarding house feeling very pleased I'd met her, because she was a lovely person. As soon as I got back Mrs Williams started up, wanting me to do this and wanting me to do that. I was getting cross about all this, because I wasn't getting paid for all this work and the boss was paying them to have me there. Aside from that, they wouldn't talk to me other than asking me to peel vegetables or do some other work. I mean, if they wanted to befriend me they could have come and got me and asked me down to the kitchen to have a cuppa with them or something.

The next day I went and met up with Mrs Ingram and she asked me if I was happy staying at the boarding house.

'No,' I said, 'they don't talk to me, unless they want me to do something for them.' I told her how my board was being paid but I had to do work for them.

'Well,' she said, 'if you're not happy there you can come and stay with us.'

I jumped at this invitation, and I went back and told Mrs Williams I was off.

'But you can't,' she said. 'You can't go without letting the Campbells know.'

'I don't have to let them know,' I said, 'and I'd rather go and stay with these people because it's a bit lonely here.' So I got my things together and moved down to stay with the Ingrams.

Mrs Ingram had two daughters, and I shared a room with them. Not long after I moved in there was a big electrical storm. I got so upset with all the thunder and lightning that I went into labour. One of the men from where I was staying went out to try and get a taxi. But what had happened with the storm was the creek had flooded and I couldn't get across.

It was a very frightening experience for me having that first baby, and I wouldn't wish it on anyone. Luckily Mrs Ingram was experienced at delivering babies and she helped me through it. I had a little boy who we named Ronald George; Ronald after a relative of Will's, and George after Uncle George Ring. Then, the next day, as soon as the water went down, the doctor came across to see me.

I had milk fever and was very sick, so I ended up in hospital. This was Meekatharra Hospital and it was very different for Aboriginal women in those days. We weren't allowed in the main ward where all the other women would be, we had to be kept separate in a little place that was just like a meat-house. It was very small and hot, and because my baby wouldn't drink, they used to express the milk from me and give it to him on a spoon. I had little Ron in the room with me but they'd take him away to feed him.

Will was out on the station and I didn't have any visitors or anything. The nurse came over a few times during the day, and that's the only person I ever saw. It was just me and my baby in this little meat-house, and I used to bawl all the time. After about six days it was time for me to leave, so Will came and got us and took us back to the outcamp at Mount Seabrook.

We stayed at the outcamp until shearing time, then we went back to the main station to work. Then, when Ron was about five months old, we moved in to Meekatharra. Will got a job working for the butcher, tailing cattle, and taking them to the slaughter yard, and I got a job in a cafe. One day I had been walking along the street when I saw on the door of a cafe that they needed some assistance. I applied for the job and got it. I worked out the back in the kitchen and laundry, and I'd go there everyday and take Ron with me. I really enjoyed this job, and Ron was such a good little baby, he'd just sit up in the laundry and watch while I worked.

One afternoon Will came home from work and said to me, 'Your Uncle Lou Bassett's up at the sale yard.' I was that surprised. 'Really?' I said. 'What's he doing here?'

'He's brought some cattle down to sell and he wants to see you.' Lou and Will had got talking and Will told him he was married to Alice Bassett from Roebourne.

'Does he want to see me in town or do I have to go up to the sale yard?'

'No, he said he'll meet you in town,' Will said.

I was that excited to see him. We met in town and he asked me to have lunch with him. I had little Ron with me and Uncle Lou thought he was just great.

During lunch we talked about home and I asked him for news about my family. He said he hadn't seen my father for a while, but as far as he knew they were all doing well. He told me a few stories about what had been happening around the place. I was so relieved to hear everyone was well, because I was always thinking about them and wondering how they all were.

When it was time for Uncle Lou to go he said he wanted to buy me something, so I asked him if he'd buy me some material. I didn't want him spending a lot of money on me, just some material to make Ron some new rompers and a few things suited me fine. So we went off to the store and I chose what I wanted, then we said our goodbyes and he went back to where he was staying.

It wouldn't have been long after I'd seen Uncle Lou that a strange thing happened. One night I was sitting up feeding Ron, when a pebble came in under the tent door. Will saw me staring at it and he said, 'What are you looking at?'

'I don't know for sure, it's a sign.'

'What sort of a sign?' he asked, because he didn't believe in signs.

'A little stone just rolled in,' I told him.

Only a few seconds later another little stone rolled in. 'Did you see that one?' I asked.

'Nuh, you're imagining things,' he said.

'Well, just keep your eyes open,' I told him. 'Might be another one coming.'

Then, sure enough, a third one rolled in. 'You saw that one didn't you?' I said.

'Yes, and I'm going out there to see who's hanging around.' Will ran outside, and he shouted and carried on for whoever was out there playing tricks to show themselves. But no one was out there, see.

I said to him when he came back inside, 'No, Will, it's a sign.' I didn't know what it meant, or who it was from, but I knew it was meant for me.

We left Meekatharra soon after this, because the butcher Will was working for wanted a couple up at Wiluna. We had a camp way out in the bush, about nine miles out, at a place called Cockyarra Creek. I didn't really like living there much, and at one time we moved even further out in the bush.

While we were out there, once a fortnight I used to come into town with Will and some friends. While they went off together, I'd take Ron and we'd go to the pictures. I was walking down the street one afternoon when I saw this lady across the road. I was really looking at her, because she looked like an old friend of my father's, a German lady, Mrs Buggenthia. Anyway she stared at me too, then came rushing across the street and threw her arms around me.

'I've been looking for you,' she said.

'Why?' I said. 'What's the matter?'

'I've got news for you. but I can't tell you here. Come with me.' Mrs Buggenthia took me into a cafe and we sat down. She took Ron off me and hugged him a bit, then she ordered two cups of tea. 'Not good message, not good news,' she said.

I looked at her and waited for her to go on. 'Your sister Ella, and the baby . . . finished. Your mother so broken hearted she throw herself around and kill herself. And then your father, foul-play. Somebody come there and find your father dead.'

After a bit more talking I found out what had happened. Mr Ben Hewitt had been in contact with Mrs Buggenthia and asked her to try and find me to give me this terrible news. Ella had been having her first baby and she had a very cruel husband. He kicked her in the tummy and burst her bladder killing both her and the little baby she was carrying. When my mother found out she was so heart broken with grief, she had thrown herself around and around, damaging herself until she died.

Then someone had been sent to tell my father about what had happened and found him laying dead in his little shack. From what I've been able to piece together, Tommy had gone back to Roebourne to live after he'd come down to Perth that time and been barred from seeing me.

When Mrs Buggenthia told me all of this it hit me like a ton of bricks. I didn't know how everyone was going, but I never dreamt of anything like this. It hadn't been long since I'd seen Uncle Lou and he'd told me everyone was doing fine back home, so I suppose he hadn't got the news yet himself. I just sat there, not knowing what to do. It was such a shock, I was in a complete daze.

After a while Mrs Buggenthia asked me what I was going to do. 'I'm going back home,' I said, and I picked up Ron and walked outside. This was the saddest day of my life, but I was too shocked to even cry.

A chap walked past me in the street and I heard myself ask him if he'd go and find my husband. He must have done that because Will came to me and said, 'What's wrong'

'I want to go home,' I said.

'But we've only just come in!' Will said.

'Yes I know, but I want to go home because I just got very bad news. My sister, my mother and my father, are all dead.'

I suppose it spoilt the evening for the other chaps who'd come in with us, but I didn't know what else I could do, where else I could go. Anyway, Will was agreeable, so we bought a few stores and headed back to our camp. All the way home my heart was heavy with grief, and all I could think about was the three pebbles that had been sent to warn me.

Excerpt from *Unbranded*

Herb Wharton

This is the story of three men. The dreams, the goals and the memories they shared. Their background beliefs and the colour of their skin were different, but never a bar to their friendship. They were the best of mates, each helping the other to achieve his ambition. They shared the past, planned the future, shaped their dreams, then made them happen.

As the sun set behind the red mulga hills, the clouds reflected colours of the rainbow: crimson, violet, gold, red. The hilltops and trees were silhouettes against the darkening sky. Two roos, their shapes outlined darkly, hopped along the ridge heading for the sweeter, greener grass that grew on the flats below, where surface water was everywhere, the gilgis full as the wet season came to an end.

At the foot of the hill a campfire glowed and horses fed close by. No sound of horse bells, only the rattle or click of hobble chains. Two men sat around eating cornbeef stew; a billy of tea stood close to the fire and the bedourie oven. Packsaddles and bags were stacked close by with the swags. Two bags near the fire held cooking and eating gear, a piece of calico spread out acted as a table. On it lay tea, sugar, salt and pepper, a bottle of hot sauce, a tin of golden syrup and a half eaten damper, besides a few tin plates and knives, forks and spoons.

The men ate in silence after a hard day of chasing wild cattle, throwing some by the tail, dehorning and castrating them where they fell, always hunting them into the herd. For the last few weeks they had been gathering their herd of unbranded cattle which was growing larger by the day: that was why there were no horse bells. Hearing them, cattle would move away. But another reason was that these men did not own the country or the cattle they mustered. The land was part of a pastoral empire owned by some rich absentee landlord who resided overseas. The men saw nothing wrong with helping themselves to the unbranded cattle that roamed in untold numbers on this vast, badly managed station known as Mulga Downs. They reasoned that they were doing the owners a favour if the owner could not manage and brand his herd; they were helping to control the herd and tame some of those unbranded cattle.

One of the men rose and walked to a tree where a night horse was tied. As the last bit of daylight faded he rode about fifty yards to where another man was riding around the outside of the yard, which was made from hessian about six feet high rolled out around the trees, used as posts. As the two met they talked for a while, then the short, stout white man rode back to the fire, leaving the tall Aboriginal man to watch the herd.

Sandy, the white man, washed in a shallow dish, then ate supper. Across the fire sat Bindi, another Aborigine. He was average height, slim, and wiry looking. He was silent as he stared into the flickering fire. This land was once Bindi's tribal land. For a moment he imagined he saw in the flames the image of a hundred tribal men as they danced long ago. Tomorrow, he thought, the coals and ash from the fire would cool, then like spirits of his tribal past the ash would scatter across the red brown land. He was one of the last of his tribe who practised tribal rites and knew the secrets handed down by word of mouth. He had no interest in who owned and branded the alien white man's meat. His only feeling was for the land itself. To get back some of his tribal land was his dream and to pass on to his sons a culture almost lost, the legends from the Dreamtime past.

Across the fire Sandy was also deep in thought, recalling his father's years of toil to save and buy the small block of land that was now called Red

Hills Station. For years he struggled, droving to help get the station started, then died of a heart attack, leaving Sandy—his only son—to carry on. Sandy's mother had died when he was a boy and he was raised by an aunt, until his father took him droving or mustering. Now he was the owner of Red Hills and he had his own dream. He thought of his father's years toiling for the big overseas owned stations. Sandy did not want to be neighbour to the big stations, he wanted to have his own cattle empire. He concentrated his thoughts on the herd of cattle held behind the hessian yard. Here on Mulga Downs country they were miles from home. It was unlikely they would see anyone as the roads were impassable and pack-horses were never used on Mulga Downs. The men had worked on Mulga Downs before as stockmen and knew the country. They had planned the muster well in advance, waited till the time was ripe. The task was almost over. If they were caught now Sandy would be finished. If they succeeded he would be on his way to his cattle empire. For weeks they had mustered in what they jokingly called their "back paddock." Working from dawn till dusk, taking turns at night watch. All day chasing and throwing cattle, galloping after fresh mobs, shouldering them into the herd, changing horses sometimes four times a day. Never relaxing, always on the alert, cattle always trying to break away from the herd. Sleeping in swags, living hard, they kept going. Now they were almost finished.

The three men had one thing in common. All had a strong dislike of the manager of Mulga Downs, a mean old red-faced bastard who seemed to know nothing of cattle or how to manage the millions of acres he ruled from the safety of the veranda, where he sat and sipped his whisky. Never leaving the comfort of the big old homestead, he skimped and shortchanged the stockmen he employed. Anyone could get a job here, men never stayed long because of the conditions and the tucker—or lack of it. That was why the manager was nicknamed "Sugar-Bag." Even when mustering was in full swing and men wanted more food out in the mustering camp, he would never send out more than could be put in a sugar-bag. One time when the men complained about having no vegetables, he said, "Okay, I'll send some out." Next day a jackaroo turned up with a sugar-bag. In the bottom of the bag were three potatoes, two onions and a packet of dewcrisp to last eight men two weeks.

Nowadays Mulga Downs was rundown because of the cheap labour Sugar-Bag employed, mostly jackaroos from the upper-crust mob. "Marsupials," they were referred to by the stockmen whose bosses they would become. Ability meant little on the big stations. If you didn't attend private school you would be a stockman until you died, especially if you were an Aborigine, no matter what knowledge you had of the land or stock. This was why Bindi and Mulga had decided to help Sandy duff the mob of unbranded cattle from the vast unfenced acres of Mulga Downs. Now they were almost ready to head back to Red Hills and stamp its brand on these cleanskins.

Sandy finished eating, then spoke to Bindi about the day's muster. They estimated they had four hundred head now. They spoke of the weather. Would it be best to head for home tomorrow? Rain seemed to be getting closer and if it did rain heavily then all traces of their tracks would be washed out. Not that jackaroos would be likely to notice anything amiss when they mustered here later in the year.

Soon they stoked up the night log on the fire and crawled into their swags. The night was warm. From the gilgis came the croak of frogs and the sound of crickets and a thousand other insects. Mosquitoes whined. A plover called; from far away came the lone, mournful howl of a dingo. Sometimes, riding around the herd, Mulga broke into a curse or a song to let the cattle know he was there. If he remained silent he might frighten the sleeping cattle; they might wake and see the mute figure riding by. That was one way to start a cattle rush or stampede, as the Yanks would say.

Mulga, unlike his fullblood cousin Bindi on his mother's side, or Sandy, who was related to him on his father's side, held no ambition of winning a cattle empire or regaining his tribal land. The world was his kingdom. He had been reared in one of the camps or yumbas that used to exist on the fringe of western towns, where the Murris lived in tents or shacks made from saplings, tin and bags. To Mulga, his independence was worth all the empires. In the yumbas, for years men and women had fought for equal rights and education. They had escaped the church-run missions, the tea and sugar handouts of government rations. They worked on the stations, laboured on the roads, in shearing sheds, along the railway lines. They still hunted the tribal meat sometimes, and some still listened to the stories of the old people—legends handed down by word of mouth. Meanwhile, the kids were sent to the white man's school to learn his legends.

Mulga's father had instilled in his son the importance of all sorts of learning. The first thing Mulga learned about in school was prejudice, which was also rife in the township. During those early days in school he soon learned to run fast or stand and fight. He also learned what interested him most and realised early on that ignorant people were the biggest racists and usually the dumbest folk around.

At school he could beat most of the others at their own games. He beat them in exams, even though he played the wag a lot. Yet he realised early in life he would have to fight for anything he sought. The only things Mulga sought were some answers and independence. He soon found that even the history books did not tell the true history of the land. At school he learned of the discovery of this great land by white sailors. A wide uncharted unmapped land. At night he listened to the tales around the smoky fires. How the birds and animals came to be. The stories told in stars, rivers, hills and sky. These stories not in the history book told how the land was charted, mapped and known to a race of people for thousands of years, their footprints stamped upon the ground for all to see, like roadways. Fifty thousand years of footprints were stamped upon the earth long before white explorers came or white settlers followed.

Quite early in life Mulga realised that not everything he read and heard was true. The history books told of massacres of a handful of settlers by the so-called ignorant savage black. But they did not tell why the black man fought back. They did not tell of the wholesale murder of thousands of men, women and children by the ignorant savage white tribes in their quest for land rights. This history Mulga learned at night around campfires. He learned, for instance, about the forced removals of the elders to the mission stations. Of the slave conditions on some stations, the pittance paid to some workers.

Mulga left home young to go droving. Since then he had roamed the outback working at all sorts of jobs, mostly stockwork. He fought for better wages and conditions on the stations for both black and white. Equal rights and education for his own people was his call. Although he had a deep feeling for the land, he believed no tribe, clan or religious creed owned any patent on the earth. The earth belonged to all. To Mulga, the soil itself was sacred. All life came from the earth and when people died they returned to it. All life depended on it.

As Mulga came to understand the white written history, then learned of the unwritten black history of Australia, it seemed that everything went wrong for the Murri about 150 years ago. Too many white criminals were imported to Paradise, where they built gaols. Later, their leg irons undone, those criminals shot, poisoned or gaoled the Murris, were granted land rights and became the white oppressors—they who had been the oppressed. Today, it was the blacks who were calling for land rights. Could the oppressed blacks become the black oppressors of tomorrow? No, it was not in their nature. Australia was too small a country for divisions of any kind. Education,

Mulga thought, was the key to everything. He dreamed of a standard legal and education system regardless of state borders or religious beliefs. Surely it was possible for everyone to enjoy a similar lifestyle and still have different beliefs . . .

Now, as Mulga rode round the herd, he saw no crime in mustering cattle neglected by the men on whose country they ran. For years station workers were not paid what they were worth. In the law courts station owners had argued that being a good stockman was not a trade, so that they could go on paying the same wage to every employee. The squatter always opposed wage rises, claiming that being a good stockman was unskilled work. Managers like Sugar-Bag and the men he represented Mulga held in contempt. He worked for them and did his job to the best of his ability. He owed no allegiances to such men, although he had met and worked for bosses he liked and respected. He took delight in helping Sandy take cattle from men like Sugar-Bag, who would never get their hands or clothes dirty. The owners raped the land, taking all the profits overseas. When the land was flogged bare and over-stocked they screamed for government handouts or else moved on, investing in something else.

Mulga also wanted to see some justice, the demise of an oppressive government ruled mainly by these who represented the graziers' empires. The graziers ruled like feudal lords and controlled the local shire councils. It took only fifty votes to elect one of these squatters, yet in the towns it took one thousand votes to elect someone to the council. These men were a law unto themselves.

Mulga realised that money was everything. Principles seemed to matter little if you were a member of the ruling squatter class, the oppressive government or the police force. Mulga wondered how some of these men could take oaths to uphold the law and the integrity of society. He also noted with disgust decisions made by judges and magistrates clearly biased against the Murri. He wondered that so much value could be placed upon the book upon which the white man swore his oath of truth and honesty: to him it made a mockery of justice. He thought that men should be made to swear on something more substantial than a book. Maybe they should stake their wealth, their integrity or life itself.

As Mulga rode around the hessian yard most of the cattle settled for the night. He looked up into the night sky, and now his thoughts went far beyond cattle empires and governments. Mulga was fascinated by space, the vastness of the universe. By comparison the Earth seemed insignificant, like a grain of sand in the desert. Already he had seen a man walk on the moon: now his ambition was to witness a flight to the stars. His ambition went beyond Sandy's cattle empire or Bindi's territorial boundaries.

At ten o'clock he woke Bindi and handed him his pocket watch. Bindi would wake Sandy at one o'clock. In the daylight hours they did not need a watch; they started work before the sun rose and finished after it had set. Lunch time was when they had time off and the cattle rested.

Next morning at four o'clock Sandy woke the other two sleeping men. Bindi reheated the stew, turned it into a curry and cooked some johnnycakes on the coals and ash, while Mulga unhobbled the horses and brought them back to camp. Catching his day horse and pack animals, he tied them to the trees. Bindi finished eating, rolled his swag, caught his horse and relieved Sandy, who turned the hungry night horse free to eat.

As Sandy and Mulga sat eating by the fire they talked of the day ahead. Should they head for home now they had plenty of cattle? In the north heavy clouds were building up: even as they ate a few spits of rain came down. They decided they would head for home. For the last few weeks they had mustered around in a huge circle and were now only about twelve miles from Red Hills station. The men finished eating, rolled their swags, filled the packbags. Then, saddling up, they rode to the herd, leaving the packhorses tied to trees.

The big bank of clouds grew darker in the northern sky as the men opened up the yard and let the cattle out. With whips and curses they steadied the lead, keeping the beasts from rushing off. After they were settled Mulga quickly undid the hessian yard and rolled it into bundles. He walked the packhorses to the rolls of hessian, and threw them on top of the packbags, securing them with a surcingle and cross-straps. Then, gathering the horses, he headed them in the direction of Red Hills.

The horses needed no steering: heads turned for home in the greyish light. Rain began to fall. With the horses leading the cattle followed, the three men chasing wayward beasts back into the mob. Some horses, impatient to be home, began to trot. Sandy rode in the lead to steady them while Bindi and Mulga worked and cursed the mob as the rain became a steady drizzle. As they headed home they picked up a few extra cleanskins but did not look too hard for more. The sun was now hidden behind the clouds and as the rain became heavier the cattle were easier to control. Heads down they followed the horses, seeking safety from men and rain amongst the herd. They reached the boundary fence. The ground was squashy underfoot as they opened the barbedwire fence in a stony creek that was now a few inches deep with red muddy water. As the cattle walked up the creek bed, all trace of their tracks was washed out where they went through the fence. The rain was now a steady downpour. Between two hills they stopped to change horses and rest the cattle. Nothing seemed to move in the whitish wet shroudlike landscape except a big old roo that stood up and gazed down but did not leave the safety of a cave just below the crumbling rocky hilltop. Horses and cattle, heads bowed, stood silent as the rain continued to fall.

From there on the trip home was easy going. The men reached their home yard in pouring rain and the cattle followed the horses straight inside. They led the packhorse to the garage-like shed that was their house, stowed the packs inside, placed some horses in a small paddock and turned the rest loose. Water now lay everywhere as the old packhorses were relieved of their burdens and turned loose, unhobbled for the first time in weeks. They sought relief from their itching backs by rolling in the soft wet mud. Then, shaking themselves, they trotted off down the paddock to a well earned rest.

Inside, the men busied themselves lighting a fire in the old wood stove in one corner of the huge shed, a recess cut out and enclosed with tin. A chimney poked up through the roof. Outside, Bindi was splitting pieces from the woodstack and carrying them inside. An enormous black cast iron kettle stood on the stove. Sandy lifted it from a tap that protruded from the wall. The water came from the big rainwater tank on the side of the shed. Close to the stove hung saucepans and frying pans, and along one wall ran planks of timber stacked with bottles of sauce, honey, pickles, tins of meat, fruit, treacle, milk, coffee and other things. Beneath were drums of flour, tea and sugar, dried fruits, rice, custard powder and foods in packets, well protected from the rats and mice and the weather.

Away from the wall stood an old table and around it were grouped half a dozen four gallon drums. From the rafters hung a tilley lamp. There was a big kerosene fridge. As Sandy heated a meal of tinned curry and Bindi split the wood, Mulga busied himself cleaning the fridge inside and out and filled it from a drum of kero. Tomorrow they would be able to store fresh meat. With a yard full of cattle and the fridge going, they would have fresh meat tonight.

They sat down at the table and realised that this was the first time in weeks they could relax. They felt relief and a sense of achievement. They had set out to do a hard and dangerous job. Day and night they had had to guard their herd. Now they could laugh and joke. The cattle were safe behind a six-foot wooden fence. They discussed what had to be done. They finally decided to draft the Mulga Down branded cattle from the mob and take them back through the fence. Holding them here was dangerous; they could not sell them and they would only eat Red Hills grass. Besides, if it kept raining there would be no tracks coming or going to Mulga Downs. By tomorrow they would have only their own cattle on Red Hills.

After a short rest the men walked to the cattle yards and forced the mob into smaller yards. As Bindi and Mulga worked the gates Sandy drafted the cattle through the yards. Occasionally a micky bull or some old cantankerous cow charged, but the rest of the cattle followed the leaders through the drafting yard.

In no time they had finished. About eighty branded cattle were drafted off. Bindi and Sandy caught horses from the paddock and as Mulga opened the gate to let them go they rushed from the yard, heading home. The men steadied the lead for a while as some old cows on the tail, their cleanskin calves still in the yard, wanted to stay, but a good flogging with a whip got them moving. Bindi went with Sandy for a couple of miles then returned to help Mulga kill their meat.

Gathering knives and bags, they drove the Land Rover to the yard, through wet slushy ground. The rain had now eased to a steady shower. They drafted off a branded Mulga Downs cow then shot her and swiftly began to skin and bone the carcass where it lay, cutting steaks, roasts and chunks of brisket to be salted. As blood sometimes upset the cattle, later they would return to move the skin and offal. On a sandy ridge at the back of the shed stood the meathouse, a small, single gauzed-in room with a high tin roof to catch the breeze. Inside, two pipes ran from wall to wall and from them hung steel and wire hoops. A bench ran along one wall with a round chopping block cut from a Gydgea tree. As the men hung up the fresh meal, Bindi began salting the meat to be corned, cutting long deep slashes in the flesh, rubbing in salt, then stacking it in a heap.

With a bag of fresh meat and rib-bones Mulga headed for the kitchen while Bindi started the Land Rover and drove back to the yard to move the remains of the carcass. Meanwhile, Mulga cooked their first meal of fresh meat for almost two weeks. Bindi returned, and, gathering dry clothes, headed to the shed which acted as a wash- and bath-house. He had a shower in the big galvanised iron tubs, with the bucket of water on the pulley rope above. In the kitchen Mulga had potatoes and pumpkin boiling alongside sizzling steaks. After Mulga had showered they sat around to wait for

Sandy, so they could all enjoy their first decent meal in days. As they waited they ate juicy rib-bones cooked on top of the stove.

When Sandy returned it was almost dark; the tilley lamp was burning brightly. After he had cleaned up they sat down to what they considered a feast: steak, potatoes, pumpkin and gravy. As they sat around their table, the drums they used as chairs felt like thrones and the strong black tea they drank from enamel mugs could have been champagne in crystal glasses. They joked and laughed about the hard times of a few days ago. The buster Bindi had, the charging cleanskins, the near misses and close shaves that could have been fatal. They could laugh at these things now the tension had lifted; now they could relax. The cattle were safe, the rain would leave no evidence. Mulga suggested they should send old Sugar-Bag a bill with all the hours of overtime they had spent mustering his cattle, eighteen hours a day for weeks. They swore again they had done Sugar-Bag a favour by mustering his country and branding all the cattle for him—even if it was the Red Hills brand they used. They decided to wait to see what the daylight would bring. If it was fine they would brand, castrate and earmark the cattle. Happy, contented and tired, they went to bed.

Next morning the rain had ceased. Empty clouds drifted south pushed by the fresh morning breeze. They cooked more steak and gravy and began sorting the meat, filling the fridge with steak and roasts, putting the salted meat into bags which they hung up to be cured by the brine. As the sun tried to break through the clouds they headed for the yard. Most of the unbranded cattle were too big to scruff, so they decided to brand them all in the cattle crush. They started a fire in a hollow log. A slot cut near the top held the branding irons, the handle resting on a wire between two pegs to keep them from falling out of the fire. As the flames rushed up the inside of the hollow log, with the branding irons catching all the heat, the fire fed on the dry inside of the log. No need to stoke it or chop wood all the time. So they sharpened pocket knives, checked dehorners and earmarking pliers as they waited for the brands to heat.

Then the job of branding, castrating and earmarking began as they stood in the packed crush. Bindi stamped on the brand irons, now red-hot, while Mulga earmarked and Sandy, reaching through the rails, grabbed the balls of a cleanskin bull. With a couple of swift nicks and slashes of his pocket-knife he desexed them before they realised what had happened. As the cattle came through they fought and struggled in the crush, sometimes charging in the forcing pens.

Steadily they toiled all morning. As the sun rose higher it became hot and humid. Broken clouds still hung around. The ground, wet and squashy before, became boggy and sticky. As the men climbed the rails of the crush to dehorn the cattle or earmark they began to sweat and curse. Once they stopped for five minutes for a smoke and a drink of water, another time the log burnt out and they replaced it from a stack heaped against the yard. By midday they decided to rest. They had laboured for six hours and decided they had more than half the herd branded, so they headed to the shed for a meal and a rest.

Looking beyond the yards they saw small puddles of water everywhere in the creek, while along the horse paddock fence the small red claypan was like a miniature lake. As the sun shone down it glistened and sparkled around the edges. A flock of cackling galahs flew down to the water, a magpie chortled from near the windmill and around the carcass of last night's kill. A hawk and some crows fought and cawed and whistled as they feasted. In the sky they fought each other; circling high they would come swooping down upon another bird as it tried to make off with the spoils. As the men watched, waiting for their own steaks to cook, they were reminded of the aerial battle scenes they had seen in war movies. Only here it was no dog fight in the sky: it was a bird fight. They soared high above, gliding round and round then with wings folded back they came swooping down like dive bombers on their enemy—any bird that had a piece of meat, no matter if it was the same species. Out here nature's law was survival of the fittest.

The men, tired, hungry and muddy, ate their meal, then rested for a short while. They returned to the yard, lit a fire and were soon toiling steadily again. Filling the crush, emptying it, then hunting up the cattle until at last they knew that only one last crushful of cattle remained. The last lot was forced in and christened with the brand of Red Hills station, and as the last beast left the crush the three men gave a mighty cheer, their task almost complete. All the cattle were safely mustered, yarded and branded. With about two hours of daylight left they saddled up and let the now almost starving cattle walk out of the yard to the grassy flats where they dropped their heads to eat hungrily. Mulga returned to camp to cook more steak and potatoes while Sandy and Bindi headed the cattle into a holding paddock. Just before sundown they rode home.

That night, clean and full of more fresh meat, the three men sat around the table. The only remaining thing to do was to scatter the freshly branded cattle through the Red Hills herd.

In a few months' time no one would know where these cattle came from. The only thing that mattered now was that they wore the Red Hills brand.

Mulga and Bindi did not work for Sandy full-time. They helped him with mustering, fencing, droving and many other small jobs, coming and going as they pleased when they were not employed by other stations. They would come to Red Hills to rest and break-in horses. Weeks ago when they had left town with Sandy they told people they were going to fence and repair yards. They had planned the muster well in advance. The rain that came in the last few days was a bonus: everything had gone right for them. They would now be paid so much a head for the cattle they had branded.

As they sat around the table drinking tea they tallied up their wages. They had cleaned up almost four hundred head of unbranded cattle for old Sugar-Bag from his unmanageable herd. They reasoned it would be much easier for Mulga Downs to muster now that they had lightened the herd. To Mulga, Bindi and Sandy, cattle running wild and unbranded belonged to those who could catch and brand them. The three men discussed the pay. Sandy added up three weeks' wages for the men for "fencing." This he would pay by cheque in case of any trouble and note it in his account books. When they reached town he would pay them the balance in cash. It was Sandy who stood to gain most in the future. The longer he held the cattle, the bigger and fatter they would grow and the more money they would bring. He had agreed to pay Bindi and Mulga four pounds each for every clean-skin they gathered: sixteen hundred pounds.

Bindi, always careful with money, had already spent some of his pay buying horses from Sandy, as well as an old ute. Mulga, as always, decided he would spend his money on a trip to the city, on booze, women and racehorses. As soon as the roads dried out, he would head south for a few months. Sandy talked about building a house with a huge veranda; one day he would marry and raise his kids here. Bindi had the same plan to marry and raise his kids on his tribal land, part of which lay on Red Hills. But to Mulga women were like the cheques he earned: hard to get and easy to lose. . . .

The years had passed quickly for Sandy, now the owner of two stations, Red Hills and Seven Mile, which he had made his home. Seven Mile had improved vastly since he bought it. The herds that roamed here were quality cattle, they always brought top prices at the sale yards and Sandy's horses were well known throughout the West. Comet, now an old horse, still roamed on Red Hills where Bindi was employed as boundary rider. All the work was now done from the head station. By now Sandy was a wealthy man and lately he had started to take things easier, although he still worked in the mustering camp and mended fences. Mary helped with the book-keeping. The big old fallen-down homestead they had moved into years before was now renovated and restored, the other building freshly painted. The place was a show-piece.

Sandy had everything, it seemed—yet he would always look towards the distant hills and mulga forests of Mulga Downs. He wanted to own the big cattle empire where he, Bindi and Mulga had duffed the cleanskin cattle that gave him his start. Although cleanskins still roamed close by on Mulga Downs, Sandy had no need now to build up his herd. He had all the cattle he could graze on his stations. Some evenings, as he sat and sipped his whisky on the big wide veranda, there was still that dream of yesterday, to own all he could survey. And Mulga Downs was part of that. Maybe, he thought, it will all be mine someday, a cattle empire indeed. By now Sugar-Bag had retired, his position taken over by someone equally inept. Mulga Downs continued to deteriorate and the cattle herd became even more run-out, but with cattle prices high you could make profits with cattle of any description. Yes, Sandy would welcome his chance to bid for Mulga Downs.

But for now his thoughts turned to his two children away at school on the coast, young Sandy at agricultural college. Might as well give him some book learning, Sandy had decided. It was something he himself never had and not much missed. He reasoned that no matter how much book learning you had, it was wasted without practical experience and commonsense. But at least young Sandy had completed his bookkeeping course and could help with the books when he returned home.

Sandy now drove the latest model car when he went to town. His hat brim, once turned up as he raced through the scrub, was now turned down. His stockman's outfit was replaced by tweeds and polished shoes when he visited town. He had grown stouter over the years. He often thought of Mulga and of Bindi, who still worked for him at Red Hills. Sometimes he heard news of Mulga from drovers passing through. As often as not he would be miles away, still on his wandering quest. At other times, when Mulga was in the district, he would call and ask for work—there was always a job for him. He'd been offered a permanent job as head stockman but had turned it down. Not for him resting in one place, he told Sandy; he wanted to be free to come and go where he pleased, in the city or the bush. Sandy decided he was like the red dust that would never settle in one place for long.

Sandy remembered their nights camped out, when they talked of every subject. It was always Mulga who asked unanswered questions and went on searching for answers. Maybe, he thought, Mulga would find his answers one day and settle down, unlike Bindi, who would never wander far from his tribal land. His roots were planted deep within the soil. As Sandy thought of Bindi, he wondered what would happen in the future. Already land rights claims were being granted to the true guardians of the land, the tribal elders. Within a few years the pastoral lease on Red Hills would expire. Would it be renewed as a pastoral lease, he wondered. He was pretty sure Bindi would lodge a claim to the country as part of his tribal lands. Sandy was sure that both Mulga and Bindi knew about the lease on Red Hills and would have talked about it between themselves. Mulga could act like a real bush lawyer when he wanted to. Secretly, Sandy was pleased to think the land would probably be handed back to the traditional owners. He was sure Bindi would have a valid case to support his claim. It was like some silent understanding between them that Bindi should one day own part of his heritage, a piece of his Dreamtime land.

Sandy realised that Aboriginal rights had come a long way in recent years. He realised, too, how far he had come in the same time with the help of his two Murri friends It made him think more deeply about what he really wanted. He had a wife and children, two stations, plenty of money . . . It was then he realised that above all he wanted to own Mulga Downs. Then he would be truly satisfied. Just as Bindi would be contented to be granted part of his heritage. As for Mulga, Sandy knew that neither the boundary fence of his cattle empire nor the extent of Bindi's tribal empire would be big enough for him. Mulga's boundary would not end even at the state border. It went far beyond . . . his interests covered the whole world.

At this point Sandy's thoughts strayed to Anne, Mary's cousin, who had come from the city to help Mary when she brought home their daughter. Anne was now married to the head stockman on Seven Mile station and had two small kids of her own. When she first arrived, Sandy noticed that she had taken to Mulga; he'd hoped she might be the one to stop his wandering way of life and make him settle down. Mulga had stayed around for a few years, then one morning he'd told Sandy he was off to somewhere or other—and that was the last Sandy saw of him for a couple of years. When he returned, he stayed only a short while. Sandy often wondered what happened between Anne and Mulga—he'd been sure they would marry. But now she was married to another.

Mary herself seemed happy here, helping with the books and running things around the house. They hired a cowboy to work around the house. Sometimes old Ten-Eighty or Dasher were employed as cowboys to help Mary with the garden and the chooks until their skin cracked, then they would head for town. Mary was boss around the house, and got on well with the workers. Her main concerns were her fruit trees and flower garden—her pride and joy, like an oasis in the desert. Sandy had never discussed with Mary the thought of buying and owning Mulga Downs. She'd been happy at Red Hills and seemed happier when they bought this place here, where they had reared their kids before they went off to school. He had many fond memories of this place, fonder ones still of Red Hills, where it all began; with himself, Bindi and Mulga, then Mary and the kids.

On the table by his chair was a letter from some graziers. They wanted Sandy to stand for the local council elections. He grinned as he read the letter. They wanted an honest, upright, hardworking man to speak for them. At least they got something right, he mused, he was hardworking. He poured himself another drink. So much had happened over the years. They had gone so fast; from the big old tin shed on Red Hills . . . those were the hardest but the most carefree days. Soon young Sandy would be finished college and one day he would take over. But still Sandy felt the desire to own Mulga Downs. Now, as he studied the graziers' letter, he wondered if he should stand for election. At least then he might get the dirt road to his stations graded more often, if nothing else. Over the years he had not been too interested in politics, but now, with a degree of wealth, came change. He was no longer the battling young poddy-dodging cocky straggling to survive and make ends meet and improve his herd. With expansion and wealth came a stronger desire to hold onto and increase his acres, and with that came the inevitable desire for power. Once, like Mulga and Bindi, Sandy had been a Labor supporter; now he supported the Country Party. When he visited town these days, he drank in the carpeted lounge of the hotel bar, attended meetings of a dozen local committees and donated to all the worthwhile charities. He got on well with stockmen and station owners alike. He had a reputation for feeding and paying his stockmen better than at most other stations. He would never be the real toff or abuse his newfound status in life. He was still called "Sandy" by everyone, unlike others of his ilk who liked to be called "Mr," even those who only managed stations. Such was the social structure of the bush.

Always, when driving to town, Sandy would pull up and ask drovers along the road how things were, if he could get them something from town. He'd talk a while about the country, where the good grass and water were. Yet when droving mobs passed through his land, he always made sure the mobs did not stray from the stock routes and eat too much of his grass—after all, as he'd once told Mulga, they were not the drovers' cattle. They might belong to some big absentee landlord living abroad. Remembering his own early droving days, he always sent one of his stockmen to see the drovers through his boundary gate and made sure they gathered none of his cleanskins, or a bullock for a killer at the journey's end. Yet when drovers wanted to spell horses on his place he would let them use his paddocks. Not many drovers owned stations. Most ran their horses on Crown Land stock routes and had to pay heavily for the privilege of doing so when droving was over for the year.

As Sandy sat on the veranda Mary appeared and told him the cook wanted some meat. They would have to kill tonight. The stockmen were camped out, branding, which left only him and Ten-Eighty around the house to find a killer. So Sandy gathered knives from the meat-house and found the cowboy. Soon they headed out for the meat in the truck, a rifle held in place by two pieces of hoop-iron bolted above the dashboard. When Sandy went for a killer, he always drove towards the Mulga Downs boundary. Today, as they searched for a killer, a dozen times Ten-Eighty pointed out cattle that would be good to eat, but always Sandy drove past them, saying "We'll find a better one soon."

For an hour they searched. Ten-Eighty, who was getting annoyed, said: "Bloody long time to find a killer." At last Sandy pulled up at a place where about ten head of cattle stood in the mob. He reached for the rifle, took aim and fired.

"Missed the bastard!" he yelled. A fat old cow fell to the ground—"No, you got one," said Ten-Eighty as they drove up to the fallen beast. Taking a knife, Sandy cut the spinal cord behind the head, then, cutting a strip from the brisket, plunged the sharp blade in deep. The hot blood came gushing out.

As they waited for the beast to bleed, Ten-Eighty, standing near the rump, noticed the brand. Never real bright, he shouted: "Hey, this is a bloody Mulga Downs cow!"

"Yes," said Sandy, "I told you I missed the one I aimed at. This one was standing behind it. We may as well eat it now, no good wasting good meat." And as they began to skin and bone the beef from the carcass of the neighbour's cow, Sandy recalled how he, Mulga and Bindi had once discussed the habit of a lot of station owners of eating only the neighbour's beef. They'd even heard tales of men being sacked because, sent out to kill, they had shot the station cattle instead of the neighbour's. That day Mulga had told Bindi the only reason Sandy never shot his own cattle for meat was because he was so fond of them. They were all pets, and he just couldn't eat his pets. Besides, other people's cattle always tasted better. Now, as they butchered the neighbour's beef this day, Sandy made up his mind to stand for council election, while Ten-Eighty deplored his ability with a gun, aiming at one beast and hitting another. Bloody useless bosses, thought Ten-Eighty, can't do anything right, should have done the shooting myself.

Talking to the stock and station agents handling the sale of Mulga Downs and adding up his assets, Sandy realised that to buy Mulga Downs he would have to sell off Seven Mile station. It would be difficult to sell Red Hills at its real value since the lease on the station was almost up. But with the sale of Seven Mile he would have enough to achieve his dream.

Unlike Mary, who loved the Seven Mile homestead, Sandy would have no qualms about leaving here and moving to Mulga Downs. The only thing he regretted in connexion with Seven Mile station was that he'd never been able to discover how it got its name. He knew it must be seven miles from somewhere—but *where?*

Once they moved to Mulga Downs, Sandy realised, he would have completed a full circle in his life. In future, it would be he himself who would have to protect the vast, unfenced pastures and the unbranded herds that roamed on Mulga Downs from the poddy-dodgers—including Bindi and his mob.

Within a month he found a buyer for Seven Mile. Mary was at first very reluctant to leave the house and garden she had come to love, to return to Mulga Downs as mistress of the big house—where all those years ago, when she first came to the bush, she had served and waited on old Sugar-Bag and his jackaroos, the "marsupials" as they were called back in those days. Gradually, however, she accepted the move. For Mary, too, the wheel had come full-circle.

While Bindi fought for the return of part of his tribal lands just beyond Sandy's northern boundary fence, far away in the city Mulga tinkered with the keys of an old typewriter and tried to imagine what he would write about . . . He was the only one of the three friends not completely changed by circumstances, except for his greying hair and the inevitable advance of age. Sometimes he lived in the city, sometimes in the bush. In the days when the three of them used to argue about everything that came to mind, or after they'd witnessed some funny episode in town or in the bush, Mulga would often say: "One day I'll write a story about you and all the things that happen." But none of them had taken much notice of him. For no one had ever seen Mulga with a pen or writing paper in his hand. They had never seen him either write or receive a letter. Always, when relaxing, he would have a book or perhaps a month-old newspaper in his hands.

However, on a recent visit to the bush, he had come to stay overnight at Seven Mile. Sitting in the station office talking to Sandy, he noted the latest computer equipment, installed with much urging from young Sandy. Then he spied a couple of old typewriters gathering dust on top of a filing cabinet. "You've no need for those now," he told Sandy. "Can I have one of them? I really might try to write something, now I have the time." So Sandy had given him one of the battered, dust-covered machines. Maybe, he thought, Mulga would write something at last, after all those years of threatening to do so . . .

PART FIVE

Urban Life and Dislocation

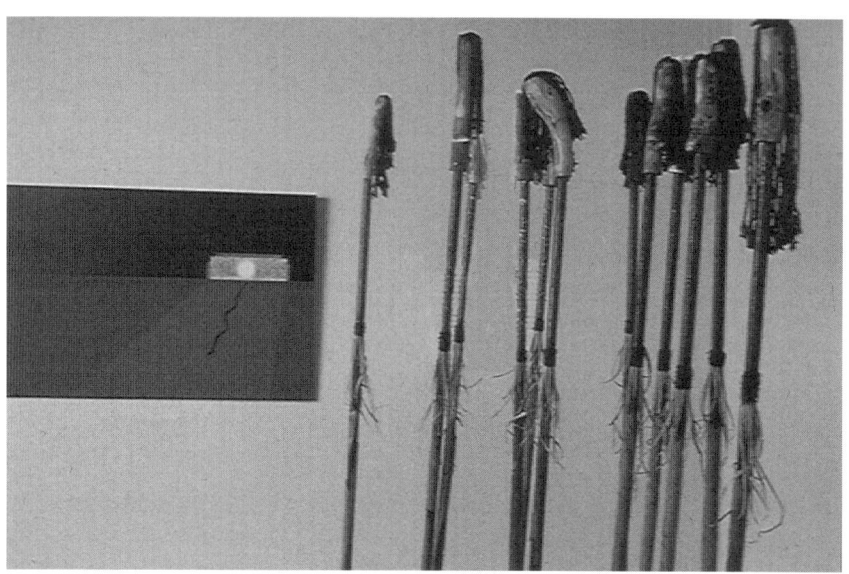

Darryl Pfitzner (Milika), *Same Story, Different Places*, 1997, sculpture exhibition with wall piece *Vision*, 750 x 1200 cm. Courtesy of Unley Museum, Unley, South Australia, and the artist.

"White man's vision"

ERROL WEST

White man's vision
Koories' nightmare, what do you know
you're not there!

Feel the earth; you touch my flesh!
Its only meaning in your quest is the
acquisition of a dollar, white man's vision
Koories' nightmare, what do you know
you're not there!

Aboriginal children, black and white
are the victims of our fight 'culture culture'
Where is your shadow?
You cleave my heart, my bone, its marrow,
White man's vision, Koories' nightmare,
What do you know
You're not there!

The blood of ages runs in my veins
Yes, my family knows the pains of cultural
devastation, just imagine—devastated by a
wormwood culture—yes your major society is the catalyst:
the vulture

Lots of drunks and hunger too
I wonder what it means to you—
you're responsible for its presence perpetrated
at a pace which is designed to eliminate my race
White man's vision, Koories' nightmare,
What do you know
You're not there!

Kids with dirty noses know the effect of the catalyst—
Even their appearance faces your condemnation,

These kids see their hollow future—
No, they are not the fatalists,
White man's vision,
Koories' nightmare
What do you know
You're not there!

Bitten

JACK DAVIS

I have been bitten by bugs
fleas scorpions
kangaroo ticks
almost by a snake
Had sandy blight
Bruises on my feet
through walking
Been hungry
Drunk brackish water
Had barcoo rot
But the worst of the lot
is to be bitten by the man

Suburban Heroine

KEVIN GILBERT

She ironed the dishes
hoovered shirts
polished carpets
scrubbed the hurts
rinsed the mattress

hosed the fire
lit the roses
tried to hire
baby sitters analysts
marriage counsellors
drug addicts
valium mogadons and pot
scraping out her daily lot
neighing braying mind decaying
rushing onward to her plot.

The Black Drunkard

KEVIN GILBERT

It only hurts when I'm sober
(my flagon is mostly full)
And I bury my head
In the sweet clean grass
Beside the rivers cool.
I muster all my dignity
To walk, if walk I can
To the pub on the corner of High and Main
To fill up me flagon again.

It's a high, hard road when I sober up
I'm a bull with an outraged pain
I fill me flagon as quick as I can
To cover me eyes again.
It only hurts when I'm sober
That sneer of contempt in the eyes
Of whites in the street as I pass them
Their hypocrisy and their lies
They claim that this land is 'God's country'
If so, then it's 'vacant', 'to let'.
He ain't lived here for two hundred years

Ever since the whites came, I bet!
Their preacher stands down on the corner
He's shouting 'Repent and be saved!'
He turns his head in disgust when
I grin, disbelievin' and wave
It takes more than merely repentin'
To stop our kids starvin' today
To stop them being hung up and crippled
Because of the whites and their way.

It takes more than just bible bashin'
To save all the souls that you hurt
With your greed and your cant
And your land thievin' slant
And those kids that you've stamped into dirt.

It only hurts when I'm sober
The haggard face of my gin
My kids with their bellies all swollen
Trachomaed, legs spindly, starved thin
An' our 'house' a tin shack by the river
No sewerage, no wages, no work
'Cept pickin' peas or red cherries
Where white bosses pay less on wage lurks.

It only hurts when I'm sober
The fact: you've no honour as men.

I blind out that pain through my flagon
I'll try not to get sober again.

Drumsticks

Margaret Brusnahan

Christmas dinner and the kids looked glum,
I had been dreading this day would come.
Twelve kids waiting in the dining room;
Those two little drumsticks would go to whom?

I tried to be cheerful, explained and begged
That this poor old turkey had only two legs.
The rest of the bird seemed to them a waste,
It was those confounded legs that had the best taste.

I tried to convince them the wings were the best,
Surpassed only by the succulent breast.
I could see that I was getting nowhere,
I'd let them down, said their icy stare

They finally ate and went out to play
While I set about clearing the table away.
I knew by next year I'd need to produce
More than two legs; they'd accept no excuse.

Then like a flash my brain came awake,
I smiled as I planned my next year's bake,
I'd give them legs, I would indeed,
Instead of a turkey I'd bake centipede

Excerpt from *Bridge of Triangles*

John Muk Muk Burke

The leafy town was mostly on the south side of the river At its centre was the Empire Hotel, the important looking post office with a clock, and, around the side streets a couple of brick towered churches. The biggest church though, the Church of the Good Shepherd, stood back from the main street a bit and just down from the Empire. Back in the previous century the townspeople had cleared the land and made their wide streets in a grid pattern. The river and the trees, those great solid river gums, were much as they had been forever. Once, before the invaders came with their sheep and bags of wheat seed and working men to dig canals, the trees had grown right across the land and kangaroos and emus were plentiful. And people had lived amongst the trees and hunted on the plains forever.

By the time the boy, Christopher Micky Leeton, was born up in the hospital which stood on a rise beyond the flood level overlooking the town, the most common animals, apart from the sheep on the cleared landscape, were lizards and the raucous grey and pink galahs. Huge eagle-hawks floated high above the paddocks but many of them had been shot out because they could easily carry off a new-born lamb. Ancient goannas lumbered through what little remained of the bush and the area is still known for its huge bull ants. Some of the relatives of Christopher Micky Leeton still lived around the area too. Chris was born and no doubt at that moment the bull ants were streaming over the red earth and the pink and grey parrots were freewheeling against the deep blue sky and the public bar of the Empire was host to those who never questioned their belonging as they drank their middies. Some of the boy's uncles might even have been kicked out on that day too, all those years and years ago.

From the beginning he was an exile. He was pushed into this world with its immense fiery sky. The sky was an enormous hill and it seemed he'd just come over the brow and was near the river and the trees to see if he might belong there for a time. The traveller looked at that place and thought pretty early that perhaps he might not belong there. For beyond his sweat and cigarette smoke mother he saw from the earliest days the vast sky-hill falling away, away, away, and it glowed fiery white with glowing torn orange-peel edges. The woman smiled and frowned—smiled and frequently frowned with wisps of brown hair and smoke rising into and across the vast sky which framed her face. The sides of his frame were wicker and smelt of sour milk and dirty wool and the faint shitty memory of other kids. Sometimes the frame swung into darkness and the great sky-hill swept away and he felt loss—he cried long for that great open plain of sky which had so recently and yet so distantly existed. Back in those days when he almost certainly knew more of the other world than this.

His mother was Wiradjuri and of the rivers. Her own mother, the Old Granny, had dwelt amongst the trees. His mum's father had been white and had given his name to the boy before spending his last six hours on this planet at the Empire Hotel. As old man Mick wandered back from the town he fell in his drunkenness into the swift black canal and drowned his watery death. But then as now the shining world kept spinning with its hills and streams and when the next morning it turned again into the sun and the waters were innocent and silver once more, you know what? The Old Granny painted her face and skipped to the Empire to weep for the change his going wrought and sat in the pub with her mob and the old man's mates. Lots of them would slip into canals and rivers and fires on other terrible nights too.

But the boy knew nothing of this except the coo-ing and frowning over his wicker frame. The Old Granny painted her face with great red lips and cheeks and hung shiny metal chains that looked like gold and silver all about her thick dark throat and wore many rings that might have come from Christmas crackers and curtain rods. Her sound and smell of stale sweet sherry floated sometimes across the great sky-hill and welcomed the child and he tried to feel the welcome.

The boy quite possibly was the first of his mob to speak the exile. It was strange that those who seemed furthest away from their roots were the ones who searched the hardest to find them again. Chris early knew that he was possibly the weakest link in a chain. He had to ensure he was not the last. He looked beyond the painted faces and bright patches of colour to the softly shining home he'd left. He knew that the Old Granny walked in this world: he knew that his mum walked in this world: and finally he knew he had stumbled into a shadow world of sorrow—he did not, did not, did not—he couldn't feel what it was he wasn't except that a joy and longing came together when he saw the sky-hill falling away, away, untouchable and left behind.

He had been carried to a world of fire and smoke. The Old Granny and aunties and his mum all creased and laughing, cradled him in their brown, warm arms. And carried him into other worlds of fire where many smoking faces passed him along a line like a bundle. Of course he didn't think that till later.

Everything came later—there was only the feeling in the beginning of the period of exile. The feeling and the smell and the taste. Aunties spooning Farex, the Old Granny poking her ringed finger into his mouth. Sweet bread. And brown warm breasts of Mum and aunties flattened on his face and urgent in his mouth. Everyone coaxed him to stay in the world and this world stretched off into the dust outside the lace windows and beyond the fringe of straggling oleanders.

Eventually the boy walked in this world of fire. The shadows of this shadow land grew sharper. He found little bits of fire which had fallen into the cool parts and lay there, for him. Had he brought them with him? He could reach into where the springy sharp twigs touched the ground and find the cold orange flowers on their tangy stems. He ate them all until he knew his aloneness again. Eating, shitting, playing, cuddling—were instruments of forgetfulness. But he could never really forget his sense of unbelonging.

Under the sky of fire he ran towards the enormous sky-hill past the springy oleanders to where the trough, half filled with black water had bright reds growing round the concrete. He could rest his face against the rough grey concrete and smell horses. Here were shiny little flowers—reds the three-year-old child named them. The reds were all on fire, standing in the shade of the trough like bright little suns. And so he held out his hands but they stayed cold. He raised his little snotty nosed face above the trough of slimy water and checked the distance. Away, away were the moving shadows which kicked up all the dust and made the distant crying. But this great fear couldn't get you because the long white fences and the tall power poles moaning in the wind trailed off straight and lonely until they reached forever. And that was where the big sky-hill came down to meet the road.

He thought he nearly knew why all the reds were cold.

The boy lay down into this world The stretched out sky quickly lost its shining and the wind rattled the loose boards on their nails Soon the blackness was complete.

He called the shapes to their dancing and they left the great sky-hill and came in through the window and danced for him on the elevated edges of their cave. He willed them to take him to their burning smoking mountains where he would join in their wild and sacred dust stirring. He felt the heat. Surely it would happen? Nearer and nearer they came and shrieked and pointed. Dancing. He saw their eyes—red: he saw the bodies dry as dust and strangely white like smoke. Surely it would happen? The wind buffetted outside and the cave was closing in. Yes. No. Yes. No. Yes. Two huge bird-like beasts were cawing somewhere near the floating curtain and a fat goanna formed where the lino lifted in the swirling air that swept beneath the house.

And then the mornings. The rain still lashed the window and the room glowed with a dampened whiteness. The vast sky-hill loomed away across the streaky world into the immense and it rocked into its emptiness and silence before the house awoke.

His mum's name was Sissy and way back then she pushed the pram past the hedges of oleanders and the privet shrubs. The smell of leaves and flowers and dust floated in the thickened sounds of the solid rubber wheels and people breathed and smoked. Sissy walked with her lovely sister Rose and the twins. She stopped now to shove the sour smelling blanket under the boy's chin so he couldn't move.

"You fuss too much Sis. Give him some air for Christ sake. You'll kill him like that."

"He's sick. I don't know what's wrong with him but he's not right. It's sumpin'."

"He's got sumpin' bloody funny 'bout him I reckon."

Rose dressed herself and the twins smartly and only some of their clothes were second-hand. By skin and bone and hair the women were clearly sisters but Rose's bloke Clarrie had money enough for his missus to carry herself with cheap style and was mostly able to avoid St Vinnie's. So Rose dressed herself like a queen in a play and always used lace hankies and people only knew they were sisters when they got close enough. That's what Rose thought.

Rose thought herself to be someone and believed she belonged in the great big world. Red lipped and tough, she had plans and they were enough for the rest of her life. She was a woman who drank cream sherry in the saloon of the Empire (sometimes even with Clarrie), and smoked Craven A's, not rollies. Sissy thought her sister to be beautiful—just like a pearl she often said, especially after the terrible event. But Sissy's own face was lined with early anxiety and a kind of seeking after something more—some place where she could belong. The unknown hurt was sometimes helped by the beer you could buy at the Empire. Her face fought each day and she felt like an exile too. Behind her deep-set eyes overhung with ancestral brow she seemed sometimes to remember with a child's optimism just enough of an early happiness to keep her going. But mostly a kind of resignation showed in her appearance, her straggly hair and downturned mouth. It was alright for Rose, she'd got a bloke with a bit of dough behind him and she could drive off to her own place with all those rooms she talked about any old time in that flash red car they'd driven into the bush in. But she wasn't jealous, it was just that Jesus knew she deserved a break after all she'd put up with. And Jack—useless bastard, had no get up and go even though he always thought he knew best. Sometimes enough of the child ebbed for Sissy Leeton to say she'd show him. She'd get up and go herself. With Rose. Rose had been in Sydney years now—Jesus—must be five at least since the war. Well, she'd heard enough. She'd be buggered if she was going to stay stuck here with Jack. Sure, Clarrie might have a few bob but so would she one day too. She'd show them, just wait. But then, all that time ago she still pushed the pram along its rough track to the town.

Sissy saw the other women with their mob of kids filing along their own dusty track that led up from the river. She saw their bare feet swirling up the dust around their ankles and saw the babies perched on bony hips.

These women were off to town too. Sissy noticed the slowing down of the other women, there were five or six of them stretched out in a line by the river. They were a group. Their great black eyes seemed only to look at the ground. Their hair was thick and knotted. Sissy felt her hand tighten on the pram handle and she moved a bit faster. It was as if there was some sort of agreement with this other mob not to meet at the bridge but Sissy did not want to think why this might be true so she quickly said, "They haven't even got bloody shoes."

"They haven't got anything because they won't get off their black arses and work," spat Rose and she smoothed her skirt with her brown hand.

"They don't get much chance either," said Sissy and there was a tired self pity in her voice.

"They're a pack of thieving bastards—you speak to Clarrie." Rose's voice was angry and self righteous.

Sissy laughed; after all they were sisters. "Well, you tell Clarrie to get a proper car—with a roof next time. Anyway, you don't know if they took his bloody beer."

Rose saw that her sister was smiling. "Well I hope they enjoyed them, that's all I can say!"

The two women smiled warmly.

"Might go down the Empire and have a few myself after I get my stuff," Sissy laughed.

They came to the white rails of the bridge and the pram wheels fluttered over the splintery wooden slats. Chris was awake in sweaty heat. From within the hooded frame the great shining sky-hill was knife cut by the railings of the bridge. He longed to reach out and touch the solid sky which seemed so close. But it swept back furiously fast and he fell back with rapid breaths of sickening green shallowness and the opportunity was gone. It was away, away—and he could only see the flickering orange border of his real home.

Way back then on that Autumn day when the wind was picking up leaves and heaping them against all the fences and the wicker pram was still of baby use before its wheels sped billy carts and Rose's pleated skirt transformed the boy's sister Mary into a princess, the two women came to the church. There was a big painted sign. "The Church of the Good Shepherd." St Vinnie's was next to it.

Sissy sensed the change.

"Are you too bloody stuck up now to come in then? Well I'm not!" And she pushed the pram savagely to the shop.

Rose sat on the brick fence nicely and took out her Craven A's. The leaves were blowing round the Kiwi whitened shoes on her vinegar brown feet.

Sissy lifted her son out of his pram and they went into the shop. The place was stacked with other people's junk and clothes—arranged orderly on counters and hangers. It smelled of old paper and dusty glass cups. The shop lady had displayed china cats and dogs, leaping fish, salt and pepper shakers with "Greetings from Sydney" stamped on them. They should have been with the wooden-handled egg beaters and chipped willow saucers and dull meat grinders but the tight haired woman probably thought that such nice things should stand with the "ornaments."

As Sissy rummaged through the jumpers and old shoes Chris found a stack of framed pictures, very dusty and chipped. There were about six altogether but only one he liked. He clutched it to himself. Here was something he knew—here was something he understood. Here he saw and recognised something. He felt the sharp little lion's feet on the corners of the tin metal frame, saw the crack across the bottom right hand corner of the glass. His picture of home. It had been snipped with scissors carefully from some magazine in an act of re-creation by hands perhaps now still forever. Faded pastels formed into a misted flatness impossibly far away—away. Somewhere above high streaking clouds was an eagle—soaring—although the boy did not know what to call the bird, and a winding track led away. The land showed no people. Years later he would know why he had wanted this picture. The missing people would return. One day. One day.

"A strange thing for the boy to want. Whatever can he see in it?" The lady waved a small toy and smiled with her teeth but not her eyes at the child's mother. Her glasses glinted. She was doing good in her full apron and tight hair and her smell of soap.

Sissy said, "How much is it?" Contemptuous.

The lady smiled, genuine. She tried to give the toy to the child.

"This," said Sissy, touching the picture with one broken nail. She put a heap of coins and a crumpled note on the counter. "How much is it?"

The boy rubbed the picture on his jumper. He felt a link. Like something would one day be complete again.

The woman and her child gathered up the clothes and shoes she had bought and walked out into the weak sunshine. The stuff was thrown into the pram and the boy walked. A huddle of women with dusty ankles waited for Sissy to turn towards Rose before they too went into the shop. Rose stood some way off with her back to the church. The boy and Rose's two were dropped off at Mrs Ladell's for the afternoon and the sisters headed directly to the Lounge Bar of the Empire. . . .

Rose's bloke Clarrie always belonged somewhere else. He was never really with Rose in her life. Perhaps that was why she ended up the way she finally did.

Yes, Clarrie Thompson was nearly always away but he burned in occasionally to give a kiss to his two boys and a wad of money to Rose. Then he burned away again in his red convertible. Sissy called him shifty and sly and told her sister to leave him. He had something to do with horses and it was this that occasionally brought him down from Sydney.

"Let's piss off to back to Sydney, and I'll come with you this time. We're not giving up our lives for this! I reckon I might belong there." Sissy flicked her hand at the kitchen where the two sisters sat drinking tea and smoking. "I sure don't belong here."

Jack was fettling for the railway and was away for two and three weeks at a time. Sissy used this freedom to smoke and dream and urge Rose to tell her of a future somewhere else; the big smoke.

"Just think Sis—I'll get a job; a place of me own. Imagine, Sydney. The kids can go to school and I'll get a job. In a shop or factory. There's millions of factories there. And the sea. Take the kids to the beach. Manly. I remember Manly."

Sissy's future was constructed from the best of her past. Thus her future was fairly restricted. Good times. Someone else will help. Always. Like when she'd recovered from diphtheria. Train to Sydney. Ferry ride. Ice cream. Big house by the breakers. Wonder. Magic. Brown arms in the white surf. Long way off—long time ago. Tomorrow. Soon. And Rose had it all already. Apparently Rose belonged in Sydney—why couldn't she?

She didn't see the bare light bulb and the shit coming up the kitchen sink or the shared bathroom or the kid from the next door row of flats being carried out under a green sheet because he'd hanged himself, or the ice-cream truck that always went past watched by her big eyed kids with Sydney's Christmas heat unparched, or the mad woman hosing her onions under an umbrella as the sub-tropic rain of Sydney eventually belted from the sky, or Rose in her grave after all the screaming and the newspapers. That was all to come.

But now they sat in the kitchen rolling cigarettes and drinking tea from a chipped enamel pot, pouring the strong brown liquid into flared cups with roses but no saucers. Floral cups with no saucers promised much. One day the saucers would come. The boy picked up this message. Promises for the future started to undo his memories of the other world.

A child insinuated itself into the kitchen crying of unfair play in the oleander backyard.

"Don't come running to me with your bloody squabbles. Joe, you're s'pposed to be looking after the little kids. If you can't play together then play by yaselves."

The backyard was his dreaming. Under oleanders and privet were six days of playing. A collection was made. "Play by yaself then."

Small sticks, bits of glass, old tins, broken bricks, stones and small rocks. A mixture of stiff clay was made in a tin. He cleared an area of ground with a flat bit of wood. Strong uprights were driven into the earth and walls built up with smaller sticks stuck together with the clay. The roof was easily made from a flattened jam tin bent to form a gable. Paths and gardens were demarcated with pebbles and fences were made with sticks. Just like Grandma Leeton's place. Broken lilac and oleander were urged into the ground for trees and sometimes ran in a shady line on both sides of a path. It was the best game in the world but then, he was only a little kid. That was years before. Of course it could not have all the stuff of Grandma Leeton's house: the pretty cups with saucers, the shiny tiled bathroom and rose bushes and big china dog called "Man's Best Friend" which guarded the funereal passage which had a heavy stained-glass door and brown velvet curtains where it turned under an arched trellis. Grandma belonged in such a real and beautiful house. Funny thing was, Grandma Leeton never seemed to touch any of the beautiful things in her beautiful house.

The boy could lie in bed at night and picture his little house standing there in the dark. All safe it seemed even if the big rains came and the wind howled. Or when the white moon merely glinted on the roof and turned the lilacs silver. His fingers itched to shape it all and he never knew, not ever, if he liked the building of it better or the knowledge that he would always knock it down and start again. Whatever, it was always a going back—never forward. Back to that which was nearly lost. A long time in the dreaming and he would finally come to that other ritualistic reconstruction of a deeper now-ness; to that which came not from Grandma Leeton but from the Old Granny herself. That black ghost. A flat plain. Love cannot be walled up. . . .

The Sydney days at Rose's became weeks and Clarrie was getting sick of everyone. Sissy had been led by Rose's two boys to the low cream painted school and enrolled her four kids on the first school day after the family arrived from the bush. She fidgeted and spoke in low little whispers in the school office when answering questions about the birthdates of her kids and where they'd been to school before and everything. But the bespectacled lady was helpful and had a kind smile and the only thing Sissy had to do was sign her name. She did this slowly and rested her free hand carefully on the enrollment forms. Keith was led off to the infants in shuddering sobs and Joe went off to the big school and Chris and Mary were put into different classes.

No one seemed to notice Christopher Micky Leeton, not even the teacher very much. He was given a free-standing table and a chair with a curved wooden seat to himself. Sydney seats he thought of them as. All the seats in the room were like that. The kids scraped them about and had different haircuts and seemed smart and probably had TV's. He saw a few of them furtively glancing at him. A couple smothered giggles into their hands and he thought he heard them say something about his hand-me-down clothes. He looked out the window at the grey scudding sky and the few birds. Sydney did not have many birds he decided.

The teacher seemed not to care if the boy did any work or not. Perhaps his mum had said he was only staying a few days or weeks.

Routines at this school were different from the one he'd known back in the bush. Here the huge crowd of kids had a big assembly every morning and the teachers sat up on a stage. Songs were sung very loudly and uniformed kids carried flags to the platform and stood there holding them until the assembly ended. Even prayers were said. The Leeton kids had barely begun to adjust to these new requirements when Clarrie kicked them out of Aunty Rose's place.

The first the kids knew of it was when Sissy, for the second time, came to their school and took them out long before home time. The only thing he really liked about that school was that if you put some money in a brown bag first thing in the morning it came back late in a box with a pie and a cream bun in it. Chris had never eaten a cream bun before. And the only school work he ever remembered was when the teacher drew with his hairy hands a map of Australia and marked where first Captain Cook arrived and then Arthur Phillip had settled the country.

"But what about the people who already lived here?" Chris had said.

"Well, they didn't really live here. Not properly—not like us. They just moved away a bit further into the bush. You've got to understand, they just wandered around the place—there was plenty of room for everyone. Now let's get back to how the first people in the new settlement set about clearing the land and building their houses."

Something disturbed the boy deeply. Sitting in a strange room surrounded by strangers a vague recognition that something of enormous importance had just been said, but he couldn't identify just what it was. It was somehow connected with the accepted convenience of the teacher's explanation—the dismissive tone and the necessity to now get back to a discussion of things that really mattered.

A vivid memory of a fire by a great flowing river on a night when the moon sailed across the wintery sky, flooded his mind. No, something was wrong here, not just in this room but with the whole world. He looked out the window and the sky seemed not to reach away to forever but to crouch down low over this room, this school, this suburb and the whole great sprawling city.

"Christopher Leeton, will you go to the office please?"

Chris could hardly remember where the office was. Sissy stood outside the headmaster's office looking more angry than worried this time. The headmaster was standing beside her, looking not unrelieved.

"Well here's the last of them. Goodbye Mrs Leeton, and good luck."

A quite new car with a lady stood waiting just outside the schoolgate and Sissy gathered up her kids and led them to it They all squeezed in and they were driven off by the lady who chatted all the way about furniture arriving later—although it wasn't much it would do—and she hoped that

that would be alright—but it should be—and they would soon settle in—it was only temporary she was sure and anyway there were lots of families there with children and it wasn't too bad all things considered.

The car joined a wide arterial road and stopped frequently at lights which changed colours and there were people crossing the road while all the other cars and trucks stopped too. They drove past a very long building with two huge wrapped lollies on the roof and under bridges that had trains going over them. And Sissy said, "Jesus, I don't know if I like Sydney. It's a bit bloody busy for me." Chris looked at the lady driver and wondered what she thought of a mother who spoke like that. The boy was learning that the world was very big and that not everyone was like all the people he knew best.

Even Mrs Ladell spoke differently from his mum. And Grandma Leeton never said bloody or Jesus. The teachers at school never spoke like his mum either. Words fascinated him. Why did his mum sound so different from the rest of the world?

The lady just smiled and said, "Yes, Sydney's like that. Never mind, we're nearly there."

The land was quite flat and the road was wide and busy. There were buildings everywhere, big ones with triangle shaped roofs all along their length. Along the side of the road some people walked; old people mostly, with dull coats and hands in their pockets. One old man was waiting at a light and the car stopped so he could cross with his little fox terrier. The man had grey stubble on his face. He was a Sydney man. So, Sydney had old people and dogs too, thought Chris.

"There" soon came into view.

"Here we are. Doesn't look much from the outside—but it's not bad once you're inside—and when you get your furniture all arranged and everything..."

The lady smiled as she edged the car along a muddy track which curved and followed a line of grey power poles to a long building which carried the memory of dull green paint. The flimsy walls were weatherboard up to the window line, then fibro. The windows were small and some of them were open, swung out from either side. Chris saw that power lines hung down and connected to the end of the long house.

"Is that ours, is that ours? Isn't it big. It must have lots and lots of rooms."

For the first time in Sydney the kids seemed excited.

"It's bigger than I thought too," said Sissy with a puzzled look on her face. She went to the back of the car and lifted the large suitcase out. "Jesus that's heavy."

"Well, let's go inside then, shall we?" and the lady picked her way over the muddy holes to a door of green boards. Stepping up two small steps she put a large key into the key-hole and turned it. There was also a grooved brass knob which rattled as she gripped it.

"Well, you go in. I'll be off now. Your furniture should be here soon. Well, ah, goodbye."

Leaving the key in the door the lady carefully weaved her way over the puddles. She wore high heels. She hunched her back and her head shrank into her neck as she walked away to the car in her cheery red suit.

Sissy stepped into the house. The four kids crowded around her. They stood in a large room with walls that went only partly to the roof. The windows were tightly shut and there was an unused stale smell. The kids hurtled across the wooden floor boards exploring the place. That didn't take long. There was one large bedroom and a smaller one.

"Aw, it's not very big," said Mary, with a look of disappointment. "Where will I sleep?"

"I'm sleeping here!" announced Joe, as he stood under the only window in the long room. "Then I'll be able to get out the window!" He'd already thrown the windows open and was pivoted on his waist across the sill.

Meanwhile Chris and Keith were exploring the front room They delighted in the enamel sink with its dull terrazo draining board. Chris turned the single tap; cold, discoloured water sputtered out and eventually cleared and flowed. It smelled like no other water Chris had ever smelled.

"Look Mum, look—a tap inside—a tap inside."

"Don't waste water youse kids."

High up in the roof was a single bare light bulb. It was operated by a long dirty string trailing down. They took turns at pulling the cord until Sissy told them off for wasting power. These words caused a ripple of excitement to run through all those kids. They took up the admonition with each other for the sheer joy of the words, "Don't waste power youse kids—don't waste power!" They now lived in a house where you could waste power because it had this mysterious power. Chris looked at the dirty string and was full of wonder. He looked again at the tap. That furphy at Waterbag Road had been the training ground for careful use of water. But power, this was a new idea which would take some getting used to.

The walls were simple divisions made from sheets of fibro and in the bedrooms the painted framework could be seen. The kids continued to investigate—tapping on walls, pushing the windows open, checking the lights in the three rooms over and over.

"Where's the lavvy?" asked Keith.

"There's another key here—it must be outside," Sissy said.

The combined bathroom and lavatory was at the end of the long block and was shared by each of the four flats. It smelled of rancid soapy water and mould and other people. A water heater with an inverted funnel for dropping paper and sticks into its interior stood at the end of the stained and chipped tub. Chris remembered the shiny bath at Grandma Leeton's gloomy house—the bath where once the old lady had scrubbed him till his skin hurt. That was the only proper bath he'd ever had. He wouldn't rub so hard if he had to get into this tub. The excitement grew as each new discovery was made. Only Sissy looked worried as the incomplete family sat about the front room; three kids on the floor, with Joe perched on the terrazzo sink and Sissy on the step rolling a cigarette. They could do nothing else till the furniture arrived.

"Can we get a TV Mum? It's got power," said Chris.

"We'll see son, we'll see."

A ute loaded with the furniture edged its way as close to the flat as it could get. Two men unpacked the pile of stuff and carried it inside. There were three single beds and one double, all with stained kapok mattresses; a dressing table with many small ornamental looking drawers; a wardrobe with a cracked mirror; a kitchen table and five chairs of a scratched dark green colour; a collection of mismatched crockery, and a cardboard box of cutlery and cooking gear. The flat already had an electric stove but there was no fridge There was another box with sheets, pillows and thin grey army blankets.

A single bed was set up in the front room for Mary. Another went into the long room under the window for Joe. It had jangly black knobs decorating the rails at its head. The double bed, which had many more and larger jangly knobs, but of brass, was set up in that room for Chris and Keith. The remaining single bed went into the small room. Sissy would sleep there. The boys had the dressing table and Sissy had the wardrobe.

"You and me can have this one Mare," said Sissy.

Joe took great delight in arranging the furniture in the boys' room. He used the dressing table to divide his bed off from the two smaller boys. The family had never used sheets so it went unremarked when Sissy hung these at the windows. Her dream of living in a flat in Sydney had started.

All she had to do now was find a job.

The fragmented family began to shape this new beginning with the little routines which map out lives. Sissy cooked sausages on the electric stove. The trailing cords became for the kids merely things which worked the lights. Despite the meanness all about Sissy set her jaw and told herself that everything would be alright—alright.

The Leetons had been allotted this flat by the Welfare. The flats were, strictly speaking, for immigrants, but an exception had been made for Sissy. She was treated as an emergency. In fact there were a number of Koori people scattered about that sprawling, regimented, ramp-connected collection of huts. But Sissy would have nothing to do with them. Her determination to make it by her own efforts had no room for the memories of the life she'd left far far behind. Sure, she'd write to the Old Granny—Harry could read the letter to her and Paula. But they were all down there and she was going to make it here—in Sydney. No, she'd left all that struggle and suffering behind her. If only she had known what struggle and suffering lay ahead.

Not a dozen miles away the crashing waves of the ocean beat against the tall cliffs and surged around the rocks as they had done for thousands of years, utterly beautiful. Softly quiet, the thick bush held the twinkling glow of campfires. And then the gaolers had arrived. And the bush had rung with the torment of men and women in irons as the trees were felled and the ground dug up. One by one the twinkling lights went out—never, ever to be re-lit. Until in dumb imitation Sissy cautiously fiddled with the electric element to cook a few sausages.

The night was not silent like at Rose's. Here was a spread of humanity all doing human things. Children crying, adults swearing, television sets urging their messages, pots being banged, dogs barking, older kids tearing along the ramps shouting, and all the thousands of sounds and smells blended together into a common mass with a common purpose—a new beginning in a new country. Even after the lights were out and only a glow from the street lamp outside Joe's sheeted window shone yellow into the long room, the noises didn't stop. While Chris lay in half sleep, disturbing, strange sounds—human sounds—flowed easily through the thin fibro walls separating each flat. This was the closest he had ever been to strangers.

The boy was being re-formed, like soft clay under the feet of the city: pushed into shapes by others who passed and pressed into his flesh and soul in the darkest of nights. And when the light came in the mornings he would be twisted into something quite unrecognisable; no longer known as a bush boy—one of Girlie's mob—part of her family, part of the old gnarled river gums and part of the broad flat river over which those gums had leaned forever. The worst part was that the boy had only begun to get a notion of how the world was seen by others. Now this view threatened to overwhelm and smother him. Intuitively he feared that the smell and taste and promises of this new world were foul, shallow and ultimately treacherous. He moved closer to Keith's warm back and felt the rough wool of his jumper. . . .

The boys were entering a phase where the Koori contact with their mother, their daily reminders of their origins, the connections, tenuous though they had been for Chris, who was the one who sought them, were about to be denied. The invasion continued and for them it gained intensity. At Waterbag Road it was as if the Old Granny had indeed become a ghost. As if the great bulk of Paula were a chiasma which floated somewhere in the imagination of a heart which had partly died. And which threatened to completely die. The man looked at his boys and refused to see anything of their mother. The man was completely white. And so, in his ordering of the whole universe, were his boys. The older boy, Joe, with his stark reminding skin and hair, was gone. Where had he gone? When would he return? The man neither cared nor worried about these questions. Like a mistake in spelling he'd been rubbed out and rewritten.

"Don't you worry about that Joe. He's got nothing to do with your life now."

"What about mum?"

"Your mother's in bloody Sydney. She's happy. Don't think about her now. You're with your father now. That's all that matters."

"And Mary? I suppose she's gone away too?"

Mary had gone away. Taken buses and trains to distant, hot desert parts in search of her father and stability and love. In a wind-swept mining town she found him. A gambling drunken man whose stability was secured by a wet-topped bar of imitation marble. A man whose love was buried deep beyond bloodshot eyes which squinted hatefully at a world that had given him nothing. He clung to the slightly rusted chrome stool and teetered on an edge.

Mary was to spend all of her life searching for the Real Father. This child was to find many fathers. False all of them. Truck drivers wiping remnants of steak and eggs against dark blue overalls in smoky roadhouses; hair-oiled refugees from Europe scratching through the outback dirt in search of the big break; small men with fresh combed dirty hair drifting through caravan parks and social security offices.

Mary the mother of God, squinting under a peppercorn tree where pegged to a rope a sequinned dress dried on a Saturday afternoon. Mary who would learn to create and shape a sustaining myth of her own, which she glued up around her rented house like some latter-day filmstars to inspire her onwards and away from memory.

Children learn what they live. Christ is the head of this house. The unseen guest at every meal, the silent listener to every conversation. A friend is one who strengthens the heart. Don't give up when your luck is out. In resisting untruth I will put up with all suffering. I will pass this way but once. Peace—be still. A smile costs nothing but gives much. The eternal God is thy refuge and underneath are the everlasting arms. Be patient—God isn't finished with me yet.

"Youse kids ask too many bloody questions. Now get your boots and polish them for school tomorrow."

Jack Leeton established a new routine for the boys. Outside behind the furphy stood a wooden box with an enamel dish of water. It was Chris's job to walk down to the dam every afternoon and reach into the still green water with the bucket. The water was carted back to the shack where it became the means of the new male family to wash itself. The bucket was set on the ground and water was dipped out with a tin mug and poured into an enamel dish, a cake of washing soap was next to the dish. A towel hung from a nail hammered into the supporting framework of the furphy. With his solid ways the man set about establishing habits and values which had about them a certain immoveability. There were potatoes to be peeled and washed so that the white flesh was without blemish. Every night. And wood to be split over on the woodheap which straggled across the yard next to the vicious blue heeler's kennel. The big kettle needed to be filled as soon as the boys arrived home from school. Struggling with its weight Chris placed it on the rough brick hearth of the blackened tin fireplace. He lifted it up onto the dangling hook and arranged chips of wood and slender sticks so that the man could easily light the fire when he came in from the paddocks. He came in from his labour with his work-worn hands.

"Don't let me catch you lighting the fire. I don't want the bloody place burnt down."

"I can light the fire dad."

"Don't be cheeky and quit your answering back. Listen and you'll learn."

And every so often the man would recite the legend contained in the circular writing on the end of the furphy from which the drinking and cooking water was taken. "There it is there, plain as day for youse to read." He pointed to the convex end of the wheeled water butt and read with solid satisfaction:

> Good better best
> Never let it rest,
> Until your good is better,
> And your better best.

"And don't forget it. If you live by that rule you won't go far wrong." The man's reading of it was mechanical—like a tired prayer.

The boy wondered how he would ever get good if he were never allowed to try anything. Even the kerosene lantern was out of bounds. At night the man would wait until the interior of the hut was grey and it was impossible to make out the lettering on the jam tin. Only then would he solidly move with the lantern over to the lino-covered table and raise the glass with the wire lever. The lamp gave its familiar metallic protest. The match was struck and applied to the saturated wick. It caught and flared. The glass, partly covered on the inside with black soot, was lowered and the yellow light caused shadows to dance around the walls of the shack. Tom Piper Apricot Jam. The table's shadow gently rocked on the concrete floor.

Over in one corner the man kept a circular incubator in which he raised chickens. This contraption had a kerosene-fed flame in its centre which warmed the cheeping fluffy birds.

"Can I hold one Dad?" Keith's eyes were large.

"Don't be so bloody stupid. They're not bloody pets. When they're big enough I'll knock their heads off and they'll feed us."

The world was closing in. The great sky-hill was being dragged down into dimensions controlled and manageable. The whole world was to be ordered about and contained. The great sky-hill was in danger of losing all its wonder and hugeness. It was in the man's safety that the greatest danger lay.

"Can I get a guitar Dad? Joe had a guitar . . . "

"Don't be bloody stupid. You can't play a guitar."

"I could learn."

"Don't be so bloody stupid. Howya gonna learn? You can't even play one. And besides, money doesn't grow on trees."

The logic was purely his own.

The man had bought a radio. In the evening he carried it out to the ute which stood in the lane. Methodically he lifted the bonnet and wired up the radio to the battery. The strident orchestra introduced the news. As the important voice finished its urgent speaking and began in a far more relaxed tone, "In just a few moments we begin our evening's programme . . . " the whole process was reversed and the wireless was carried back into the shed. "Don't want that rubbish on—waste of a bloke's battery." The announcer's voice died.

"Don't know what's going on with the world. Whole place's going mad. Man needs his head read for being alive." And so in the deepening night they would sit—two boys and a man. All of them waiting.

In the night a few crickets sang away off amongst the grasses and laneways. Around the group their shrill song pierced into the silence. And away and above it all if Chris listened hard enough, he could just hear the distant stars humming in the vast black immensity of sky.

"Where does it all go to Dad?"

"Where's all what go to?"

"Behind the stars?"

"Don't be so bloody stupid." The man looked at the boy and scratched his head. "I reckon you've been out in the sun too long."

Somewhere in his memory a flickering recognition of a young man in the leech crawling jungles of New Guinea asking a similar question as the open staring dead eyes of a soldier mate momentarily shone in the light of the moon as thick tropical clouds scudded overhead. But in a time long long gone. No, it won't do you any good. Don't ask, don't ask. What's the fucking point?

The man reached out his rough hand. He touched his shoulder. He added, " . . . son."

The wooden chairs on the dirt outside the shack sighed in the darkness. Then, strangely, the man started to softly sing a song he'd remembered from somewhere in that deep hurting past,

The strangers came and tried to teach us their ways
They scorned us just for being what we are . . .

Somewhere, in his heart, the man did know. He knew he had been used. He knew he was a user.

And so a pattern of days and nights formed. Days which held a promise at their close. A promise that tomorrow might be somehow, miraculously, better than today. That the all-consuming meanness of the life these people lived would transform itself into something wider, broader, lighter. Chris didn't know. While he held vague hopes for the future there was no plan. His mother, although finally taking off to the big smoke, had never included her kids in any of her planning. Likewise the man, his father, never spoke of the future. Never thought ahead except to worry that tomorrow would no doubt be bleaker than today.

"We're out of wood for the fire. Get over and split a few logs up."

"Jesus, that wood heap's looking a bit low—you been wasting wood again?"

"Get down the lane and scout around for bottles." The man would have run out of money. Half a ute load of beer bottles and soft drink bottles might bring in a couple of pounds, to get them through till he got his next pay. This towards the end of the long Christmas break.

"I s'pose there's not much bottles left lyin' round the lanes. I s'pose you bloody kids been down there and collected them already!"

"Right then, get your boots on and hop in the ute. And run a comb through ya bloody hair. What are ya, blacks or something?"

"Where're we goin'?"

"Just get in the bloody ute."

The man eased the ute down the rough lane. The red rutted road was fringed with the bleached grasses of a summer's ending. Slender gums cast deep shadows over scrubby saplings. The boy breathed in this landscape which was there—just out there, beyond this dusty ute with its three occupants cramped against the sweating leather seat. He pictured the roof of the ute, slightly dusty, with the sun, the heat, beating down on it; on the roof of the shack they'd just left behind. Over there, behind the darkening trees, the fence wire shone dully. And beyond the gentle hills curved away. And further—on the crest, were the rocks, massive boulders, blocks of whitened grey rising up from the cracking thistles and clumps of milk grass. Those rocks with lizard-green lichen that could be peeled back in small pitted sheets. And from the rise the shack, with the wood heap and the furphy and the waterhole, now black, now silvered by the sun, all viewed from above.

The ute travelled through the landscape. The man was retreating, groping around for some sort of strength to live with the awful knowledge of his own ignorance and powerlessness. Something to relieve the inexorable power of the forces which had shaped him. If only he could get through this day.

The boy too was retreating—escaping—surviving. He would survive by dreaming, by holding on to the, what was it? To say the land was too simple and not enough. The land, like him was always retreating—was always just somehow beyond. And yet what it was, came, emanated, began and dwelt in what the land really was. Or what he suspected it to be. But it, whatever it was, could never be known, nor seen, nor satisfy the pain of his need. Strangely, as with his father, there was no future. Who were the destroyers? What had the boy forgotten that might have carried him joyfully into the future? The man neither willingly lived remembering a past nor for a future. Nor in a present. His was the real tragedy. Not to have taken his youthful sex seriously—was that it? Was he just another in a long line of mindless rapers of land and those whom the land gave life? In what agony of secret guilt did the white man live? What was the war all about? It is certain that he never knew with his brain. His heart felt that somehow he was paying for the unknown evils of a system which turned relentlessly and was fed by what was ultimately a deep contempt for the earth and all who dwelt thereon.

Long after, when this ute was a rusting carcase in some backyard near a levy bank overgrown with sticking grass—then in some strange way the boy came to understand a little. That this man had eventually sensed the forces which had led them all to this present time and place. Chris could understand how the heart of the man came eventually to reject these forces. Nine words could never be enough to speak of the evils he came to perceive. And because he rarely used more than nine words he dwelt in silence and suffered for the part he had unwittingly played in putting his calloused hand to the wheels of human misery which those from across the sea caused to turn in every league of this invaded earth. Invasions are escapings.

"S'long time since we saw Ted. Run'll do the ute good. Charge the battery up a bit."

Ted was over in the next town.

The ute left the dirt lane and swept itself of loose dust and leaves as it geared up to the tarred surface of the new road which stretched forward into the summer day; between fenced paddocks cleared of most trees; across man-made culverts of concrete where reflectors flashed on the dust-white posts. Above, the arching blue-white sky shone like a new sheet of cartridge paper on which black crows drew their slow lines.

Ahead lay the town with its towering grain silos and dark green kurrajong trees; its squat long railway station; the verandaed shops with their corrugated iron side walls stained with ghostly aftershadows of advertisements for tea and ice-ream.

Chris knew that Ted was his father's brother and he could vaguely remember him as a young man who had lived with old Grandma Leeton in the big dark house in town. Now Ted was married and had a couple of kids and worked on the railway in this two-pub town. It would be good to meet his cousins and his new aunty.

"Me brother's married now. You call her Aunty Vera."

As the ute neared the tidy cream railway cottage Chris saw that there were two cars—one under an attached roof and another, shiny and well cared for, next to the trimmed hedge. Jack saw the shiny black car.

"Well, I'll be buggered."

"What's wrong Dad?"

"Be quiet, be quiet, nothing's wrong."

Ted came out from the house. "G'day stranger. Bugger me if it doesn't rain but it pours."

Vera came and lounged on her husband's arm. She squinted up at Jack. "G'day stranger. Bugger me if it doesn't rain but it pours."

Ted looked at his wife. "Hey, mind your language."

"Oh phu to you—just 'cause ya mum and dad are here."

Chris had thought the car was Grandfather Leeton's.

"Anyway, you better come inside. We're just having a cuppa."

"Thought I'd charge up the battery. Take the boys for a bit of a run."

Vera squinted at Chris and Keith.

"You must be Chris and Keith. Which one's Chris?"

"He's Keith," Chris whispered.

"What's the matter, cat got your tongue? Anyway, I'm your Aunty Vera. Come back to live with your dad, eh? Bit different here from the big smoke I bet."

"You'll be better off here too," said Ted, "as long as you behave yourselves. Father's gone to a lot of trouble to get you boys back. Hope youse appreciate it. You're lucky boys I reckon."

PART SIX

Hardships and Resilience

Robert Campbell Jr. *Aboriginal Change of Lifestyle,* 1987, acrylic on canvas, 81 x 108 cm. Courtesy of the Roslyn Oxley9 Gallery.

Hypocritic Sponsorship

GRAEME DIXON

This TRULY MAGNIFICENT
SPORTING SPECTACULAR
is so PROUDLY
BROUGHT TO YOU BY
cirrhosis of the liver
BREWERIES,
THE LAGER
THAT REAL MEN BUY!
In conjunction with
the COMPANY
THAT GAVE YOU
lung cancer cigarettes
And JUST FOR YOU
gambling folk,
THE STATE HAS SUPPLIED
FACILITIES TO BET
We'd also PROUDLY
like to remind you
that the MANAGEMENT
of these
AUSTRALIAN COMPANIES
have DONATED
A BIG FAT CHEQUE!
to HELP stamp-out
MARIJUANA DEALERS
and JUNKIE WRECKS
Because, with
DEEP SYMPATHY,
they realise
that DRUGS RUIN LIVES
of INNOCENT KIDS!
And this country
WON'T BE SAFE
till ALL FORMS

OF ADDICTION
have been rid!
Also,
they are opening
a TRUST FUND
in the not too
distant future time
TO AID A CAUSE
THAT NEEDS
PUBLIC SUPPORT!
A FREE
suicidal assistance
telephone line
And you women
in the audience
don't worry,
you've not been left out,
as they're starting
a CRISIS CENTRE
FOR THOSE LADIES
WHOSE DRUNK HUBBIES
knock them about
And also
YOU BEAUTIFUL KIDS
they have
A PROJECT
JUST FOR YOU'S
They will GIVE
two cents an empty,
so make sure your folks
DRINK MORE BOOZE!
Lung cancer cigarettes
have a SCHOLARSHIP
AVAILABLE
FOR THE FUTURE
All you
have to do
IS SMOKE
their teenage label

And finally
the MINISTER reminds you
that these
companies
HELP fill
state coffers
and the money
IS NEEDED
BY THE PEOPLE
NO MATTER WHAT
is said
by the COMMUNIST scoffers.

The Other Side of the Story

KEVIN GILBERT

I'll sell me moot for half a note
And a bottle of wine if wine you need
Or I'll try and hock me old red coat
To bring you'n me'n our kids a feed
I know it's sad, wish't it wasn't so
An' I know it's bad, preacher told me Joe,
That ya can't work now an' yer kidneys gone
An' yer liver swolled an' I'll sell me moot
For yer me man an' yer crippled now an' I understand
That our life depends on half a note.

Our life is tough in the river bed
At Alice Springs where our old bough-shed
Made of boughs 'n leaves 'n scraps of tin
Lets weather 'n dust 'n disease right in
While up on the street in the flash art shops
Struts the managers with their guts aslop
With the food from our children's mouth
And stealing it is when they say 'Good job'

And they give two bob for me man's art work
An' sell it for a hundred to a man down south.

I can't get me welfare cheque no more
Nor me 'dowment, the man at the general store
Gits me cheque 'n me 'dowment now
An' me man is crippled an' busted inside
From the sneers and the jeers at 'is manly pride
He useta work once but he got no pay
From the cattle station out Yulong way

No pay but tea, tea 'n flour
An' I'll sell me moot for half a note
Though it's shame an' I see a white man wrote
Our shame in the papers south
But whites killed the soul of me man, his pride
Couldn't take it and his mind ducked away to hide
Itself in its own despair.

Baal Belbora—The Dancing Has Ended

KEVIN GILBERT

Baal Belbora
Baal Belbora
the end the dancing has stopped
the warrior lies dead where his broken spear fell
beside the high pinnacle rock

Baal Belbora
Baal Belbora
his lubra lies dead on the slope
the mounted trooper who mounted and raped her
had slashed her black throat when she pleaded with hope
the child that she suckled
lies dead on the grasses
the grey quivering brains smashed out with cold steel

Baal Belbora
Baal Belbora
the dancing has ended now
ask me whiteman
how do *I* feel

We Are Going

OODGEROO OF THE NOONUCCAL TRIBE

For Grannie Coolwell

They came into the little town
A semi-naked band subdued and silent,
All that remained of their tribe.
They came here to the place of their old bora ground
Where now the many white men hurry about like ants.
Notice of estate agents reads: 'Rubbish May Be Tipped Here.'
Now it half covers the traces of the old bora ring.
They sit and are confused, they cannot say their thoughts:
'We are as strangers here now, but the white tribe are the strangers.
We belong here, we are of the old ways.
We are the corroboree and the bora ground,
We are the old sacred ceremonies, the laws of the elders.
We are the wonder tales of Dream Time, the tribal legends told.
We are the past, the hunts and the laughing games, the wandering camp fires.
We are the lightning-bolt over Gaphembah Hill
Quick and terrible,
And the Thunder after him, that loud fellow.
We are the quiet daybreak paling the dark lagoon.
We are the shadow-ghosts creeping back as the camp fires burn low.
We are nature and the past, all the old ways
Gone now and scattered.
The scrubs are gone, the hunting and the laughter.
The eagle is gone, the emu and the kangaroo are gone from this place.
The bora ring is gone.

The corroboree is gone.
And we are going.'

"Misty mountains tell me the secrets you hold, of men"

ERROL WEST

Misty mountains tell me the secrets you hold, of men
and women, the young and the old who graced your treed
slopes and from your sweet water streams drank to their
content. Are their spirits still occupying your beautiful form
as totemic beings ensuring your continued existence.

The Banjil soars high, surveying his possession, his eye as
clear as your sweet water and his body as firm as your mature
gum nut and cumbungi root, yet is his eye responsive to their
physical absence? Does he, also the hunted, long to see the
campfire's smoke, long to hear the songs and the voices of
both your aged and your little ones?

These mountains are lonely for their tread in both stealth
and joy to give up that which makes its heart beat for their
pleasure, their comfort, their presence, is her greatest gift.

As a grandmother who has seen successive generations from
her children's children, so has the mountain long time, loved
her children's children—but they are no more in visible
evidence to comfort her. Does she as a grandmother of ages
close her eyes and enjoy the living memory of her lifeline,
children whose stories and dances and songs made her heart
swell with absolute contentment.

In their absence, white men have occupied her pulsing breast,
not content with her natural beauty they have engaged in
rude plastic surgery on your most gracious nature; they have
divested you, in this they have scarred your silken

appearance. I watch the mists begin to dissipate as the sun's rays bear down on your gentle crown, I touch the leaves, flowers and the grass. They seem to be suddenly deluged with droplets of water—can I convince myself they are not your tears.

"I feel the texture of her complexion with both hand and heart"

ERROL WEST

I feel the texture of her complexion with both hand and heart;
I shut my eyes; still I cannot divorce the loving memory of her touch,
   her influence on my life.

To separate from my only reality is impossible, as long as I live—
   is that not a fatalist's view considering her future?
Mining, digging, drilling, a cancer attacking the essence of my life;
   in unity our spirits scream Stop! Desist!
We can bear no more your attack.

Under better law this assault could not occur—
my brothers and sisters would stand, a human wall, a barrier
   against this vicious attack—yet now, with almost none to
   defend her you rip out her heart, her spleen and liver—
   mining, digging, drilling, a cancer attacking the essence
   of my life

You destroy her lovely face and scar her gentle body—as we
   can see; to your disgrace—I shut my eyes; still I cannot
   divorce the loving memory of her touch, her influence on
   my life—

Songs of another time were sung—and so she had remained
   —I know not those songs or the singers to face yet with
   them I am entwined—
There are the songs anew, the answer in them lies, I take

nothing for myself, I wish to nourish and nurture—see
she grows in strength.

 ## Capitalism—The Murderer in Disguise

LIONEL FOGARTY

You know I'd like to tell you a story
But I'm afraid.
I won't use names.
I thought now what if I get out of this chair
and walk to the cupboard
get the gun
load it up
and shoot
any white person
that walk
pass this chair
and any black
that cry for them.
I thought
When they're shot
I get out my best knife
cut the heart out
then stuff it in their mouth
until it went down to the gut.
I thought
I must slice off the balls
and shove
in the eyeballs
with blood
spitting out of the nose.
I thought
I'll put it in the moiu
to smell the filth
of the white man's brain.

I screwed the neck around
until purple, green and white
lit the face.
I tightly moved my legs
onto his screaming belly.
A silence came
But my pain
was still the same.
My legs shook
Out of my reality
a pig killed my arms
He laughed and said
 'You black bastard
what did he do to you?'
I said
You make my fathers afraid
then give them a carved body
ready to shatter
a mind
held in drunkenness
fooled
and worn out.
You make my mothers afraid
so when she sleeps
an axe appears
covered in blood.

Look pig
what you do to our people.

Who cares
I'm locked up here
with no arms
no legs
but a body
and mind
really
my spirit.
But I'm not going to be afraid.

You don't make me afraid.
Beware, we'll be out of your prisons

I was afraid to write this one
real thing
but remember
Your Enemy
He's
Ours TOO.

This poem is dedicated to Jim Boy Edwards and ALL the brothers and sisters who have been fighting since the invasion of the white man, for our FREEDOM and IN-DEPENDENCE.

Need

JACK DAVIS

I need a bouquet of words today
To bind my heart
in interplay
To strengthen my will
to grind to grist
to lighten the dark
and the shrouded mist
to remove the mask
unclench the fist
To better the world
for tomorrow

Imarbara I Am—Generation of Existence

Lionel Fogarty

I am a living entity, you belong to me. I AM.
I am of earth and space
I am a son of the world
I am the religious law
I am the kin to all creatures
I am kin to this creation
The world is my nation
The earth is my mother
The black man is of this earth
The red man is of this earth
And the yellow man of this earth
But where is the white mad man's home
He has rape in mind to his own mother earth
I have to fight with the trees
I have to fight with the rivers and rocks
Dear mother earth have my love
Day by day
Withdraw the force a companion pain of you, to be part of me
Please mother I'm sorry and lonely for your natural cause.
I am the birds dat die
I am the snakes dat die
I am the sea creatures to die
Sure man, we am but why must we bang and blast here on this ground?
I'm your native here in captive
I'm your native ready in revolt
I'm the native to bring all
white human being to a new world
where you mother earth rule.
I know you can just take so much.
So I'm the land's sources of identity.
You mother earth provides for my physical needs
and my spiritual needs.
You are the holy and sacred and I'm the regeneration
of history and the continuation of your life
I'm the begin and dat where we all returns.

Excerpt from *Don't Take Your Love to Town*

RUBY LANGFORD

A Stranger in My Camp

Alexandria, the Gunnedah Hill

It was May 1960 when we arrived at Phillip Street, Alexandria, where Mum Joyce was living with Rita and Dennis and Kevin. She fell into my arms at the door and then we sat down and had a good cry. She was lost without Dad—they'd been together for eighteen years.

'I want you to have these things belonging to your father,' she said. It was his cricketing cap, I put my face into it and could still smell the Brylcreme, and every time I wanted to remember him, I'd smell his cap, his personality was so strong in it, it was just like he was there and not gone.

The other thing was his cricket trophy which read BEST ALL-ROUNDER H. ANDERSON and the date was 1951–52, the years that Billy and Pearl were born. There was also a hat-trick ball mounted on a trophy, Rita got that.

We settled in but with thirteen people in a two-bedroom terrace the tempers flared and Peter didn't like living in a mob scene. I spent a lot of time with Mum Joyce and it was like we were locked into our own world of grief for Dad, and Peter wasn't part of it. He decided to go and stay with his sister in Redfern.

I didn't like to stay with Mum Joyce and not help out, so I applied for welfare support. I'd get a cheque each fortnight but it wasn't enough. I thought if I could put the kids in the Church of England homes and go back to machining I'd manage better. I think I must have decided this in the numbness of shock over Dad's death.

The big head of the homes was a floor manager at Mark Foys in the city. I'd made enquiries and had an appointment to see him. I went up in the lift, my heart sinking as the lift rose, wondering how long it would be before I could afford to get the kids out again. I told him I was a qualified machinist and wanted to place my kids in the homes till I got settled. I'd give him the endowment and what I could afford out of my wages. He asked all sorts of personal questions and I told him everything. He said he'd give me a date, and that someone would come and pick the kids up.

The kids and I were sleeping on the floor on mattresses, Dennis and Kevin who were ten and eleven were sleeping with Mum Joyce in her bed and Rita was on the divan downstairs. At night my mind was in a turmoil and I came slowly to the realisation of what I was doing. The people would be picking the kids up in a few days and I couldn't bear it.

A wind was howling and blowing up the stairs, it was so strong it blew the bolt off the door. In my anguish I tossed and turned and was weeping as though my heart would break. Then I could sense my father's spirit, he was there, I could feel him patting my arm, comforting me. I fell into a deep sleep.

A few days later Peter was there with his sister's car loaded up with fruit and vegetables from the market. 'Go and get dressed up, I'm taking you somewhere,' he said. I was shocked but in a strange way pleased he'd come back. I put my best dress on and he took me to Newtown and pulled up in front of a jeweller's store. What is going on? I thought. Why's he being so secretive?

Next thing he pointed to the wedding rings and said to pick one. 'You and me are getting married today—' He had a big grin on his face. I didn't know what to do, I was dumbfounded. I picked one with orange blossoms on, and we had to go to Marrickville to the Schools of Arts to have the words said over us. The JP who married us introduced herself as Mary Louise Hills, and we asked the janitor and his wife to be our witnesses.

On the way home, to celebrate, Chub took out on hire purchase black-and-white television set and we took it home for the kids to watch. Mum Joyce and the boys moved to Wilson Street and sister Rita moved away with her boyfriend Podge, and left us the house. I didn't have to put my children in the homes after all. Peter was working and I landed a job cleaning in a printing place in Henderson Road where I live now, twenty-seven years later. My work started at five in the afternoon and finished at nine. Sam's sister, Brenda Leslie, came to live with us and she and Peter fed the kids at night.

We had just settled in and got the kids started at the school around the corner, Alexandria Public, when a letter came from Chub's father, old Jim Langford, saying he was sick and needed Peter at home. I wasn't sure what this meant. Peter was his youngest son, and maybe he just wanted him around. I knew from things Jim had half-said that he didn't think Peter should take on a woman with so many kids to other men, and though the baby, Ellie, was Peter's and mine, Jim didn't seem to take this into account, or the fact that Peter might have decided he wanted to help me bring up the kids.

I couldn't say any of this to Peter, and maybe the old man was really sick, at any rate we were soon on the road again. Brenda Leslie came with us, also her boyfriend Reggie Morris, who was Mum Joyce's nephew. We didn't own any furniture at this time. Chub took the TV back to the hire purchase place, and we packed our clothes into suitcases. We travelled all night and into the following afternoon in the Holden ute, Chub driving with me, Ellie the baby and Aileen in the front, and Brenda and Reggie in the back with Billy, Pearl, Dianne, Nobby and David. On the road, those flat roads going west through paddock after paddock of sheep and wheat, I thought Coona was like a magnet to me, always drawing me back. I was always in the thick of the city or at the edges of country towns in missions and camps, there was no in between.

We were tomato picking a few days later, the smell of ripening tomatoes all around us and the green viney smell of the bushes, and then we were apple picking and I was like a permanent Eve, eating the apple and having babies and walking around the orchard in a daze of good smells and backache. Brenda and Reggie had gone to live on the Gunnedah Hill with her mother (my first 'mother-in-law') Ruby Leslie, and we camped with Jim and Kassie in the workers' hut near a creek on the farm five miles out on the Barradine Road. Old Jim was picking tomatoes and apples along with us, he didn't look too sick to me and I realised he had wanted Peter home, and this was the way he'd gone about it. There was no point saying anything, we had work, the kids were happy and healthy, but I see from this distance now, it was another example of me being moved about by other people's needs and I would not have minded being settled.

When the work finished, Jim and Kassie moved back to old Joe's market garden and Peter and I pitched our tent on the Gunnedah Hill down from the Leslies. It was no trouble in fine weather but it leaked pretty bad in the rain. We looked around for work but things had gone very quiet, and then Peter told me he was going back to Sydney to look for a job. I didn't know then that it would be the last time I'd see him for years.

I was alone with seven kids and one on the way and no money for food. My camp was near the aerodrome, only used by light planes, and other people camped round about. Drunks would see my fire and come over but didn't bother me—if they got rowdy I'd say, 'Please go further away, my kids are asleep,' and they would. But I was scared and I slept with a butcher's knife under my pillow.

Harold Leslie gave me a camp dog, a cattle dog cross. She had a litter of six pups and when they grew up I had seven watch dogs.

I had to have a plan to live so I applied for the dole at the police station, and because I had no word from Peter I took out a maintenance order against him for non-support, then the battle began.

I'd put my endowment book in at Billy Woo's store and have it used up months in advance. I earned money scrubbing out his shop and when that ran out I gave him my wedding ring to hold for £6 worth of tucker. There go the orange blossoms, I thought. As far as I know the ring is still there.

Then I bought a dozen flour bags off Colin Neate the baker and some twine and a bag needle and opened the bags out and sewed a big fly for the leaky tent and put bits of tin round the side to stop the wind. When the dole came through we got a voucher each fortnight for groceries, value depending on how many were in the family, and another voucher for meat. This took care of the food, then to get it back to the hill I'd wrap it in my coat and carry it, or book a taxi. My next concern was to gather some things for the hospital, nighties, baby's clothes. That had me stumped for a while.

Back in the tent at night Billy had the kids on their knees praying 'Please Lord bless mummy to have all the things she needs, for our new baby brother or sister.' It made me proud to see their little heads bowed by the light of the lamp without a globe and the wind somehow not blowing it out and the kids' voices curving round the tent walls.

One night we could hear a big storm coming up and the kids were praying again, 'Please Lord don't let the storm blow down our tent, it's the only home we have,' and the wind howled and it knocked down pine trees and blew roofs off houses in the town and it blew all around the tent and never touched it. The light didn't even blow out and I felt kind of powerful then, that God was on my side if he existed, or at least the kids had the power to stop Mother Nature from destroying her own.

And all the clothing I needed came from nowhere, people gave things to me. Pauline Harvey came over with her father's station wagon loaded up, she had a double bed and mattress and a big cane pram, which she said was hers when she was a baby, and boxes of baby clothes and nighties, also a side of sheep and boxes of eggs and vegetables. I'd lived on her father's property before, and used to make skirts and blouses for her. So I ended up with everything I needed for hospital and then some.

A young bloke who said his name was Robert, not the full quid but harmless, came sometimes to help me carry water and cut wood. He wouldn't accept money for the work, so I gave him tea and damper with syrup. At weekends he rounded up the kids to go to the Dep (town dump) and they rummaged for toys.

One day he was digging trenches around my tent, drains to let the water get away when it rained. He kept going back and forward to the bush. I thought he had the runs, and didn't take any notice till he started to fall over.

I rushed to see what was wrong and I could smell metho on his breath. 'Robbie, who gave you the goom?' He pointed to the bush and said, 'Montie Chattie,' and passed out. I picked up the biggest waddy I could find and ran at the bushes. Montie took to his heels and ran like blazes.

I was still finding it hard to make ends meet. One morning I wrote to the Smitho's head office in Sydney and they sent some of the head catholics in Coona over to check me out and these people then brought boxes of clothing and food. I managed to buy another tent and I paid two young fellas from the mission to pitch it for me. The first storm we had arms and legs every where, in the space of two seconds FLOP the tent caved in on us and the scramble was on, me and the kids fighting to get out from under all this tarpaulin and laughing and grabbing each other's legs and falling over again. But after the fun I was wild and I went down to the mission, about two hundred yards, to see if I could find the helpful young men. But they'd shot through and later a few of the old fellows came and pitched it properly for me, pegged it down tight and put drain holes so the water could run away. Pauline came to inspect my new place and after a while she was teasing me about the new baby's name and threatening not to speak to me unless I called the baby after her. I mentioned that I had four girls and three boys, maybe the new one would be a boy to even it up, but Pauline put her nose in the air and said very sternly, 'This one will be a girl.'

Every day I went down to the mission and got through the fence to their tap and carried my drums of water back to camp. On the way sometimes I met old Ruby coming down from the shanties and one day she told me Brenda had had her baby, a girl called Regina. This child was first cousins with Billy, Pearl and Dianne. Ruby and I sat our water drums down and rested, halfway back up the hill, and talked about who was related to who around the place, which was half or step, which was full, and so on.

It took us quite a while, and when we had that sorted out we carried on our way. I was two weeks from my time and I went in to visit Brenda and Regina and felt lonely in advance that I'd have no man there to be glad of my new baby and I kicked the foot of the bed (without thinking) and Brenda said, 'Ow!'

When I went into labour Jackie Milligan took me into Coona hospital in his taxi and my eighth child was born a girl and I named her Pauline Ann. It was January 1962, hot, fine, and this was the fourth child I'd had in this hospital and it was Doc Frazer attending me.

Back at the camp I sent the kids to the Dep for drums to sit on, I was tired of having no lounge-room furniture. When I was well enough for walking I went to the Dep myself and obtained my laundry—a copper for boiling the clothes. At this time I also improved my method for carrying water—I had a forty-four-gallon drum near the tent for my tank, and I'd been filling it by carrying eight gallons at a time from the mission tap, four gallons in a kero tin in each hand. Now I made myself a yoke with wires, I put a towel on my neck then the yoke and this was easier on the stomach muscles. I couldn't take it too easy because I had to cut up big trees and drag logs home for the fire. Billy was now eleven and Pearl ten, and they helped with the lighter work.

My tents started to look like a home. In one I had two double beds and one single for Bill and a cot in the corner for Pauline. In the other I had a table and four chairs I bought when I received some welfare money, and a kitchen cabinet for food and crockery. My toilet consisted of three pine trees growing in a triangle, which I nailed hessian around, a seat pan the council collected once a week, and an umbrella on a limb in case it rained.

Once a month a welfare officer came to see me, to check on the kids, and he was surprised, he said, to see everything spotless and the kids off to school each day on the mission bus. By this time Pauline was five or six months old and when she was bathed and fed I laid her outside the tent under the shade of a tree to sleep, with a mosquito net over her. I was arranging the net one morning so it didn't drape on her face when I heard a Hello behind me. It was the welfare officer again. I offered him a drum to sit on and stoked the fire to make tea. I wondered what it was about this time, he looked serious.

'I want you to get in touch with the Aboriginal Protection Board,' he said, 'because I'm gonna recommend you for housing land in town. It becomes freehold in ten years, what d'you think?'

'I'll be pleased if you'll do that,' I said, and straight away while he was talking I had fantasies about getting a roof over the kids' heads and having taps, and floors. Full of excitement and plans I wrote the letter but not long after a reply came that I was refused, because I was a woman who had eight kids and no husband to support me and was only surviving on welfare and endowment payments and what I could earn washing and ironing in town.

Pauline took sick with gastroenteritis, flies everywhere and on the hill sandflies. I took her to Doc Frazer and he said she was OK, and then in the middle of the night I noticed she was dehydrating, her eyes were sinking inwards, so I wrapped her in a rug and left the kids asleep in the tent and carried her to town, about two miles, and at the hospital the sister called Doc Frazer and he came straight away and said quietly, 'It's a good thing you're an observant mother.' He admitted her to hospital where they kept her for two weeks to make her well. Doc Frazer gave me a lift back to the hill as I told him I'd left the others asleep in the tent.

About a month later one of the kids from the mission caught up with me carrying my water back to camp, and said Doc Frazer wanted to see me. I went in to his surgery and sat down, not sure what it could be about. He said, 'I've had a private investigator track your husband down. He's with a sideshow next to Cadbury's chocolate factory in Tasmania. You go and tell the police this information, Ruby, and we'll see what they can do to get some maintenance out of him.' I thanked him and when I was walking to the police station I realised he must have paid the private eye out of his own money, I felt pretty grateful about that.

The police told me I'd have to pay to have him extradited back to face maintenance charges, so I said, 'Look, let him rot in hell,' and walked back to my camp.

At night when the kids were asleep I started to write, and that made me feel happy. I entered a NADOQ (National Aborigines Day Observance Quest) writing competition. The subject was what you would like to become, and I wrote about doctoring. A while later I received notification that I'd won the quest. My prize was one guinea, and I was very happy to have it though the prize for this quest today is an all-expenses trip overseas. There you go.

On a hot morning I was washing clothes in the big tub and glanced up to see a tall man going by on the road up to the Leslies'. I thought it was Sam, he waved, and I waved back. A few days later I went up to Brenda's to borrow some camphorated oil and she introduced me to the tall man, whose name was Lance Marriot. He patted me on the head and called me Shorty. I slapped his hand away and stormed out, saying, 'Don't manhandle me,' forgetting the camphorated oil I'd come for.

Later in the afternoon he came down to the tent and apologised to me. He reached in his pocket and took out the camphorated oil, and I made tea and we yarned. He soon had me laughing and got my axe and offered to cut me a heap of wood, and I was grateful for the help.

We became good friends and in the night he brought his guitar down and sat by the fire and played. The kids from the mission heard him and came through the fence and over to our fire one by one appearing out of the shadows and one by one they'd go home to bed, and when all mine were asleep, we'd sit and drink tea and yarn half the night away.

He came from fruit-picking country at Wentworth, near Mildura, from a family of seven, one girl and six boys. He'd lost his mother and his youngest brother through cancer. His mother was an up and coming tennis player in her day and she was part Aboriginal, and his father was a Pom from Shropshire who was a head chef at Heidelberg Repatriation Hospital in Melbourne for many years, and before that in the merchant navy.

Lance said he was married (to a Koori) and separated, he'd left home as a boy when his mother died and hitchhiked around doing bush work. I looked at him while he stared at the fire and talked. He had a Koori nose, broad shoulders and a long thin body like a runner. Dark eyes, dark hair, big bony knuckles from street fighting. He told funny stories, he liked to laugh.

I didn't know then I would live with this bloke for eight years and have a son with him. All I saw was a stranger in my camp, someone who'd helped by cutting me some wood, a laughing sort of man at a fire surrounded by kids and singing:

> I fell in love with a Mexican girl—
> night time would find me in Rosa's cantina
> the music would play and Fillina would whirl
> Black as the night were the eyes of Fillina,
> wicked and evil while casting a spell—

and Lance sang this song looking past the kids at me, he serenaded me and I was in love again.

I was happy living on the Gunnedah Hill. They nicknamed me the bush lawyer—anyone on the mission needing forms filled in for endowment and pensions came to me. I was renowned for winning one guinea on the subject of doctoring and now I was the local writer.

But later on I became sick from all the gut-busting and heavy lifting I had to do and I developed a hernia. Every time I coughed my navel popped out and eventually Doc Frazer told me I needed an operation, but I'd have to go to Sydney to get it done.

Lance and I were living together now, that serenading with the guitar had done the trick. When I told him what the doctor had said, we discussed it and decided to move to Sydney. Lance had been doing bush work and we had some money saved.

The day we were to leave I called my seven camp dogs to me and stood there with them for some time. There was no one who would feed them and I couldn't leave them to starve, and just as I was deciding what would have to be done, Nerida Chatfield, my old friend from the days I'd lived here with Sam, turned up, having come from Wreck Bay to the mission to visit her relatives. She flung her arms around me and hugged all the kids. I introduced her to Lance and then told her about my operation and the dogs. Lance looked at the dogs, then at me, then mimed firing a gun and I nodded. Without a word he went off to the Leslies' place to borrow the rifle, and while he took the dogs over in the bush and put them to sleep and dug holes and buried them, Nerida was helping me dress the kids and cut sandwiches for the trip. I would spread margarine and hear a rifle shot, do up buttons on a dress, hear a rifle shot, spread Vegemite, a rifle shot. It was pretty hard.

I gave my tents to Brenda and Reggie and they bought my camping gear off me—beds and cabinets, chairs and table, the camp oven (which I thought of as a friend, my old faithful). I stood looking sadly at the only home I'd had for my kids, and wondered if I'd ever improve on it, then Jacky Milligan and Morrie Hunt arrived with their taxis to take us to the station.

When I bought the tickets we were still short, and the train was waiting for us. I yelled to Jacky and he backed up. I gave him my endowment book, signed, and got the rest of the money off him, and I gave him my address to post it down to me. Saved again by the taxi-banker. I hugged Nerida hard and told her where we'd be in Sydney, we herded the eight kids on to the train, and we were on our way to Sydney again. . . .

We were in the Empress one night, Neddy and me and her brother Tommy T. and B. T. Leslie, and we were partying on and when it was shut up time we were going to Neddy's daughter's place in Carey Street, Marrickville. We walked up the hill from the Empress and there was a bus that said St Peter's Station so we jumped on. Neddy's son, Dan, had joined up with us. What we didn't know was the bus terminated at the station.

I was drunk and singing loudly and Danny said, 'Sing it Shirley Bassey' and I was letting it go. We were the only ones on the bus.

Neddy was up front with her arm around the driver, trying to con him up to take us to Carey Street, but he said he couldn't. It started to rain. We got down at the station and B. T. was carrying the beer in a carton and it got wet. The cans tipped out and rolled down the street and we were chasing them along and rounding them up. Up pulled a cab and we rode along singing in the rain.

One morning early after our run of the Cross, we had an Islander girl, Manya, with us. We caught a taxi and she said, 'I know a place that's open now, the Yugoslav Club in Elizabeth Street.'

We'd no sooner sat down and bought a beer, when the police raided the joint. They grabbed Gert, the little one, first. They were hauling her off and she called out, 'Don't take me without my titis,' so they came back and grabbed us.

Neddy, Manya and I were shown into the van. Next we were herded into the charge room at Central Police Station. We were put in a cell with the other women. So drunk we started singing at the top of our voices. The police drivers joined in. Then we turned on a go-go session. Gert was in the corner at the wash-basin crying, 'I've never been in gaol before ahh, ahh,' and I looked at her and Neddy and burst out laughing. 'I haven't either,' I said and we couldn't stop laughing. When the police walked past our cell we wolf-whistled even though we couldn't see them. Manya said, 'My husband will kill me.'

They kept us four hours to sleep it off. When we fronted the magistrate, we'd all given bodgie names—I was Ruby Marriott, Neddy was Mary Ford. Gert gave some name and forgot what it was, so when the name was called we elbowed her.

We were getting our property from the office and the sergeant said, 'You've got a good voice, where do you sing?' I said, 'The Empress Hotel,' and we left feeling ashamed of ourselves for being pinched for drunk. At home Bill said, 'Mum, where've you been? I've been ringing up the hospitals, I thought yous were in an accident.' We told him we'd been in the cells and he burst out laughing. 'Hah, look at the gaol-birds!' We didn't live it down for months.

In February 1970 we were just getting back on our feet after the shock of Pearl's death, when Neddy asked me to go to Wollongong for the weekend. Her daughter had a Housing Commission home in Dapto. I agreed, thinking the break would do me good, so after giving the kids instructions I left them in the care of Dianne and Steve and Billy who were only teenagers but well able to look after the kids, or so I thought.

We arrived at Dapto and she asked me to go further down the coast to Wreck Bay, as she wanted to show me where she'd lived when she left Coonabarabran years ago when her children were little. She took me and showed me where she lived on the mission there, then we visited Huskisson. We went back to Dapto only to find the police waiting for me to tell me that Jeffery had been abducted from a park in Newtown. Then I was frantic.

Neddy's son drove us back to Sydney. It was a Sunday and the traffic was banked up—it took us three hours to travel fifty miles. I listened to the car radio, it was even being broadcast there. They said the police were concerned for a three-year-old boy who was taken from Newtown Park and no trace of him could be found. I felt dead inside. I'd just lost Pearl, now this, my baby was missing. I never stopped praying all the way home that he'd be found unharmed.

When we arrived in Sydney I had them take me to Redfern Police Station. I burst out crying while I was explaining that I was the mother of the missing boy, but then they told me he'd been found and was safe. The police told me to go home and they'd bring him—he was with Dianne at CIB headquarters.

Back at the house, I let into the kids and screamed at them, 'What are you doing to me? All of you couldn't look after one little boy!' I was so furious I screamed and swore badly at them, then we were all crying together. I loved them so much, and the struggle to raise them was beginning to tell on me.

About an hour later, Dianne and Steve arrived with the little fellow in a police car. I was so relieved all I could do was hug him and cry.

After a while I was told the full story. This is what happened on that day. Bill had a car and he took our kids and went over to Georgina Street to pick up my sister Margaret and her kids to go to the beach. On the way back he dropped our kids off at Portland Street and because the car was full he didn't notice young Jeff was still in the back with Margaret's kids. He let them out in Georgina Street. The car was mucking up so he lifted the bonnet to fix it and didn't notice Jeff taking off with the other kids to play in the park across the road. Bill fixed the car and drove home.

When they noticed Jeff was missing they reported it to the police so Bill, feeling bad, went into the Clifton Hotel for a beer. He was just lifting the beer to his lips when he heard Pearl's voice calling 'Bill—', and he looked around towards the door. Her spirit was beckoning him to go with her. She was warning him that something was wrong. Bill said he left his beer and went looking again.

It appears there was this bloke, a new Australian who had no kids of his own, who took Jeff from the park. The man lived only about four doors from my sister's place. When Jeff was found the police took him with Dianne to CIB headquarters. He wouldn't answer the police when they were trying to find out if the bloke had hurt or interfered with him, so they got Dianne to sit him on her lap and she asked him, 'Where did you sleep, baby?' He replied, 'I slept with a ghost, my sister Pearl slept with me.' So there she was, still looking after him, even when she was dead.

Not long after this Nob was let out of Daruk and came home on the train. He was wearing his diso suit (discharge suit) and was taller and quieter. He talked about what it was like in the home and we told him our news. He wouldn't hear mention of Pearl's name, he'd taken it very bad. I remembered the picture of him the day of the funeral, stepping out of a police car handcuffed and sitting handcuffed in the church, then being taken away again. I was so glad to have him back and soon he settled in.

Bill and Nobby were very close. I'd see them getting dressed and combing their hair to go out and I'd say, 'Where are you two going, all slicked up?' and they'd say, 'Chasing girls.'

'You'll go bald chasing gins against the wind.'

They laughed as they went out, arms around each other's necks.

Dianne and Steve decided to go ahead with plans for the wedding. Somehow we still thought of it as a double wedding, we couldn't put Pearl out of our minds. When we talked, we tried to make the wedding how she would have liked it too. Greg came in and out, hardly speaking. The date was set for 2 May 1970.

Money was scarce so I rallied all the mates to help with sandwiches and Bob McDonald was out the back with a boiler full of eggs, cooking them on the open fire. We had no gas. Neddy and Gert wrapped Alfoil around sandwiches and packed them in cartons. Mum and my sisters from Beaumont Street made cakes and savouries. Aunty Beryl made angel food cakes. Steve sold raffle tickets to get his suit and Dianne hired her gown. A girlfriend of mine did Dianne's and my hair, and Bob escorted me to the wedding.

The church was just off Elizabeth Street, Waterloo. The minister paid Pauline twenty cents to run up and down to the corner and tell him when Dianne arrived. We walked to the church and our dog Judy followed us. When Judy saw Pauline going in to the church to tell the minister, she ran inside too.

Then Judy wandered in and out among the wedding guests till Dianne appeared at the church door. She waited till Dianne stepped in, then she followed her down the aisle. Judy took up a position near Steve and the ceremony began. When they went into the registry to sign, Steve tried to shoo Judy away but she wouldn't go. Then the minister tried to shoo her and she lurched forward and bit him on the hand. Outside, when Dianne and Steve were getting into the wedding car, Judy put her paws up on Dianne's shoulders and licked her face side to side 'like she was congratulating me,' Dianne said later. (All the wedding photos had Judy in them.)

We drove across to the Foundation in George Street for the reception. The women had put up streamers and balloons and vases of flowers all along the tables. After the toasts and a small speech by me, Max Silver and his band Black Lace struck up and we danced for a while.

Bob and I were left to straighten up after the reception, along with a few others. No one had mentioned Pearl. It was Dianne and Steve's day. But we'd all noticed Judy, the brown and white fox terrier, in every scene.

We joined the wedding party at the Clifton where the Mad Scot Bronc had put his wallet over the bar and the drinks were flowing. The bride and groom were floating on cloud nine. I think, as I remember back, that everyone we came in contact with was floating.

Back at Portland Street I gave Dianne and Steve my room and I slept on the divan. It was a windy night. Next morning at breakfast Steve said to me, 'Did you hear anything last night?' I looked at him. 'Pearl was at the bedroom window,' he said. 'The wind was blowing and the curtain was whooshing. Then I saw her face at the window, smiling and throwing kisses.' Nobody said anything. We kept eating.

A few days later Dianne was passing the girls' bedroom and looked in and caught a glimpse of Pearl's legs, then her feet. In the girls' room there were bars on the window, this house used to be a bookie's joint. A week later I was laying on the bed near the window to have a rest and thought I was dreaming when I saw Pearl's spirit blowing kisses to me through the bars. I was so startled I sat up rubbing my eyes, then she was gone. Blowing kisses as if to say 'Happy Mother's Day,' then gone.

Not long after that the house in Portland Street was to be sold. The owner gave me $150 to move quickly, so the kids and I scanned the papers and found a place about half a mile away. Number 13 John Street was a two-storey place with two bedrooms and a balcony. The street ran directly onto Botany Road and the kids went to school around the corner at Waterloo. We couldn't have a dog so I took Judy to have her put down, and it was one of the hardest things I've ever had to do.

I always had a houseful wherever I went. It was a means of survival. My brother Kevin and his wife and brother Dennis stayed with us, they slept in the lounge or dining room and Neddy shared the upstairs bedroom with me and the girls. Dianne was with me too, as Steve had gone to New Zealand with the All Blacks football team for three weeks.

Eight months after Pearl died, I woke up one morning and the boys said, 'Come quick Mum, brother Bill's having a fit.' I rushed into their room and looked after him till the seizure was over and he went into a deep sleep, which always followed a fit. I slipped an old dress over my nightie and went downstairs to have a smoke.

The kids had gone out to play, Neddy was away and Dianne and Steve were at football, so were Kevin and Deirdre. I turned the TV on and was thinking how quiet it was, the house so silent.

Then all of a sudden there he was there in front of me asking for a smoke. I said, 'You OK son?' He answered, yes, and left the room. I turned back to the tele and watched for a while. It was Saturday, *Bandstand* was on. I couldn't get over how silent the house was, when suddenly something said, 'Go out there.' I got up and went to the dining room, then on to the kitchen. I pushed on the door of the bathroom.

That's where I found him, slumped over the bathtub. I guessed what had happened, I screamed, 'Billy!' and pulled him out and gave him mouth to mouth but he was gone, he was blue-lipped, I was too late.

Ten minutes it took for my son to run about eight inches of water into the tub and bend down to wash a pair of trousers. He'd taken a fit and fallen headfirst into the water and drowned. If only the plug wasn't in, I thought. I kept saying, 'Oh my God, not again. Not again.' I was hysterical. He was gone, my Bill.

Nobby came in then, and I told him what had happened. He seemed to be staring straight through me. Not able to believe it. He came into the bathroom with me. Bill had kicked off one of his shoes in the struggle. We stood still for a while. I said, 'Don't leave your brother there.'

He picked up Bill's body and put it on a bed in the dining room. I could hear him crying. He took off Bill's other shoe and covered him with a blanket. He ran out crying and I didn't see him for days.

When the family came home I told them straight away, before they could get started on the football news. They stood there in twos and threes, shock registering like waves across their faces. Bill? they said in soft voices, as if he couldn't really be gone, they'd just spoken to him this morning about a boat, he was going some where in a boat.

I ran out into the street crying and then I turned one way and another like a crazy dog looking for something, it didn't know what, nothing, nothing was there, half-whimpering and half-hysterical I ran up and down the street and turned in circles till one of the neighbours came up and said, 'Ruby, what's WRONG?'

One of the neighbours rang the city Coroner's Office and they sent a car to take Bill to the morgue.

Just then Terry came in and said into the silence, 'Right, where's Bill, we're going out on a boat today, he's late.' I burst out crying. 'Your mate's dead, they just took his body away.'

'Ah Mum, don't joke like that.'

'I'm not joking. Why do you think I'm crying?'

Soon after, Terry left the house in tears too.

I buried him on 27 August. They kept his body for a week, I couldn't rake up a lousy $55 for grave-digging fees amongst my family and friends. In desperation I rang Bob McDonald and he showed up with a cheque for $100 and we gave it to the funeral directors, with the promise I'd pay the rest when I received Pearl's insurance.

I thought of the specialist we'd been to, the brain wave tests. He had no tumour, yet he was dead at eighteen years of age. Pearl had just turned seventeen. We had to walk past one to bury the other. That day we followed the pall-bearers up the hill, and Bill was put in the ground forty yards up from where my father and my daughter were. It was a sunny day. An ordinary day. Birds flew over and people wandered in and out among the graves, bending to place flowers or pull up a weed. I looked at the row of date palms near the front gate and a low brick fence, then I turned and looked out at the sea. Nothing made any sense.

After Bill died I couldn't hear anything. I stayed in bed for five days and Neddy and Gert looked after me. I saw them come into the room and go out, but I couldn't hear anything. It was like I was in a huge fog. Nobby came and took me out the back to the toilet and waited, and brought me in again. There were no outside noises. Bill's spirit had me locked in. I stayed in bed. People came into the room, I could see their lips move but I couldn't hear the voices. I stopped eating. Gert and Neddy sent for my mother.

I could hear my mother. She told me to go out to the grave and talk to him, and tell him to leave me alone. I knew if I didn't get out of bed it would be the end of me.

Gert came with me down to the bathroom where I'd found Bill dead. We shut the door and turned the light out. I called to my son in the lingo, I told him to leave me alone, 'What about the other kids? I have to look after them too. Do you hear me, Bill?'

Then I said over and over the words my mother had told me, '*Nunyars jarjum, ningana,*[1] you're making me *jung*,[2] I have to live for the other jarjums too, so leave me alone, you hear me, Bill? *Ningana*.[3]'

There was a loud noise. A heap of stones had fallen onto the roof, loud as hail. I knew he'd heard me then, so I went back upstairs. Now I could hear people talking, could hear the sounds of life, children playing and cars out in the streets.

When I could think again my mind went round on rails. Why why why why why. It was a hurt I thought I'd never recover from. Later it seemed to me as if God had looked down and said, 'Here's a woman battling and struggling to raise her family, I'll take a couple to lighten her load.' . . .

SHE'S VERY IMPRESSIVE, MARY

Allawah ('Sit awhile'), Granville

I was working with my editor on rewrites of the book, and keeping my eyes open for anything relating to Kooris and writing. I'd read Charles Perkins' autobiography, *A Bastard Like Me,* and James Miller's *Koori, A Will to Win.* Now I read Mum Shirl's biography, a book by Margaret Tucker called *If Everyone Cared,* and then *My Place,* by Sally Morgan.

There were ads in the paper for the Second National Playwrights' Con-

---

1. *nunyars*—my, mine, *jarjum*—child
2. *jung*—bad
3. *ningana*—don't do that

ference, where they'd be talking about black issues and writing, and workshopping the plays. I wanted to go, thinking I would learn a lot from this, but it wasn't possible at the time.

One afternoon I was cleaning up the newspapers and I saw a headline EVERYONE SAID THEY HAD THE SAME DREAM. Another heading mentioned SACRED ROCKS. I knew Aunt Millie Boyd had been made Keeper of the Rock in Bundjalung-Githebul country near Nimbin.

I sat at the table and spread the paper out.

> Millie Boyd, 86, has always lived at Mulli Mulli mission, near Woodenbong, just below the Queensland border.
>
> An elder of her Githebul people, she is known tribally as a 'cleverwoman' . . . She is the spiritual custodian of Nimbin Rock, an Aboriginal sacred site shrouded in mystery, superstition and death.
>
> Whites who have visited the site have experienced a series of accidents not dissimilar to events that befell Lord Carnarvon's team of archaeologists who opened the tomb of the Egyptian king Tutenkhaman in the 1920s . . . A classroom of schoolchildren who went on an excursion near the site all experienced the same dreams that evening . . . There have been other events which no conventional white logic can explain.

It turned out the kids had 'Aboriginal dreams' about goannas and snakes and spirits. One boy dreamed of a warrior, 'a big fellow with a shield and spear. It was as if he was guarding the rock. It scared me. I had a sense of overwhelming power.'

Millie wasn't surprised by the story of the dreams. 'That's given to them by the spirits,' she said.

Other people have seen the warrior spirit. One man was sitting on a hill facing Nimbin Rocks when the warrior appeared. 'He was looking away from me and he turned and smiled. There was a silver and blue quality about him.' A Thai Buddhist monk, who was staying with a friend near the rocks, said that one morning when he was meditating he saw a white light shining out of the top of Cathedral Rock. Nimbin gets its name from Nymbunje, the Wee-Un or cleverman who is buried near the rock. The area is traditionally male-only, but the spirits are worried the old ways will die with Millie's generation.

Three clevermen who died in the past few years made her the Keeper of each of their sacred areas.

Millie is a high priestess of Aboriginal culture, and with other cleverwomen and men is the equivalent of the white world's highest university-educated people. A professor of anthropology has compared the cleverwomen and men with the great yogis of Tibet.

Millie has an apprentice, Lorraine Mafi-Williams. The women had never gone to the male-only site till concern over rainforest logging in 1982. Lorraine said the rocks were so sacred that clevermen who went there for initiations brushed the soil from their feet before leaving.

When Millie took the journalists from the *Sunday Telegraph* to the area, 'She would sing out in dialect to her mother and grandmother who belonged to that territory and who, she says, are living there in spirit. She told the Spirits we were coming and asked for protection for herself and us.'

Then there was some news about people from the Richmond River Historical Society at Lismore, where I'd written for information on Grandfather Sam and Uncle Jim Morgan. They had lots of records about Bundjalung and Githebul people. A woman called Marjory Oakes, a collector of Aboriginal history, had learned the Bundjalung language from Lyle Roberts, the former custodian of the rocks. She had written, 'The district is alive with spirit beings . . . only white people pretend they don't believe in them.' Mrs Oakes had known about the Nimbin-Lismore area. Her friend Marjorie Henderson knew the Evans Head area. 'In 1962 she began agitating for the protection of what is now the Bundjalung National Park.' This was the park I'd pointed out to Jeffery when we were coming back from Rita's. The paper said there are many Aboriginal artefacts here and a 'clever cave' where the wee-uns held ceremonies.

'Mrs Henderson says numerous people she has taken there have heard Aboriginal voices . . . Aboriginal cleverpeople claim to have power over the elements . . . Mrs Henderson believes this since working with the Keeper of Goanna headland at Evans Head, Mary Cowlan.'

The hair was standing up on the back of my neck. Here was information about a culture I had lost when I came to Sydney. Only it wasn't lost. There was a direct line from Uncle Ernie Ord to the woman singing in the lingo at Yamba, calling the porpoises in, to people like Aunt Millie Boyd and Lorraine Mafi-Williams and Mary Cowlan.

Mrs Henderson had said that Mary Cowlan can talk to the wind. 'We have sat on top of the hill there and the weather changes and storms blow up.'

The main thing was that political action could come from such powers. The Bundjalung area was now protected as a National Park. The traditions of the rock was being handed on. Logging of rainforest was (as much as possible) being prevented.

I sat there for a long time thinking about the difference between city knowledge and bush knowledge. What happened to blacks in cities, particularly to people like Nobby, made me despair—and then I would find something like the story of Aunt Millie Boyd and I would feel connected again, not just to my Bundjalung origins but to positive forces happening now, to these people who carried the culture and kept it strong, who were concerned with ecology and spiritual health.

White people had given us all kinds of technological comfort, but the tribal ways still need to be strong. I thought of the difference between white people saying 'I own this land' and blacks saying 'We belong to this land.' I looked out at the street and the tall weeds in the railway yard opposite. The phone-lines, the traffic. And I wondered who had been the custodian of Henderson Road, Alexandria. The Eora tribe. Eora country was at La Perouse but it reached this far into the city, to Redfern.

In Botany Road in the old Winn's building is the Eora Centre, next door to the CES. You can do courses there in painting, dramatic arts, music, photography. It's an off-flow of TAFE.

A few days later Annabella rang to say that Nobby's request for bail had been moved up to 18 December (1986). I had an appointment that day with Mack the Knife, my surgeon Doctor Graham, to be assessed for more surgery on my mountainous stomach. I rang and cancelled, and sat down to write something in support of Nobby.

On that day we took the lift to the thirteenth floor of the Supreme Court in Macquarie Street. We asked if we could get a clean shirt to Nobby. While we waited for his solicitor from the Aboriginal Legal Service to show up, Anna and I decided what each of us should say.

Then we decided to sit in on a few bail applications, just to see how the magistrate was reacting. Out of five cases he only granted bail to a Vietnamese thief. The other were drug traffickers and dealers.

Court adjourned for lunch. Nobby's solicitor came in and said we were on at 2.30.

The room was large. I could see Nobby looking very dignified in his navy suit, sitting between two gungabul.[1] He looked strained but when he saw us he waved and smiled.

Then the charges were read out by the police prosecutor, a beautiful blond woman in her middle twenties. She read out all the times Nobby

---

1. *gungabul* —policemen

had escaped from custody, as far back as the children's homes. All his record was read out.

I held my breath. Why was all this coming out *now*? He'd served six years for this same charge (shooting at a police car) fourteen years ago. Ironic. Futile. He was being judged on a record he'd already served time for.

Then Nobby spoke. He'd had a nervous breakdown, he said, and thought if he went away 'I'd be able to get myself together and come back and face the music when I felt better.'

'Where did you get the gun?' the magistrate said.

'A mate gave it to me to protect myself,' Nobby answered, ' —in my condition I didn't know what I was doing, I wanted to die. I was grieving over my brother David's death. My family found me laying on his grave, he's buried with my eldest brother Bill. And later I was found by the police, fighting with a man in a prime mover.'

He told how the police had not taken him to the psychiatric centre, but kicked him on the road and bashed him at the station. 'I came out looking like the Elephant Man, my face was so swollen.'

Later he said, 'I realise I need help and I want to have counselling.'

'You saw a psychiatrist in Maitland,' the magistrate said.

'Yes. But he only stayed half an hour and all he did was look at his watch. I'd been in custody nearly five months and that half hour was it.'

'What's to stop you from doing this again in another fourteen years? With your psychological problems you might snap again and I wouldn't feel good if I let you out in the community again. Bail refused.'

I tried to interject but they wouldn't hear me. As they were taking Nobby away he turned and said, 'They still won't listen, Mum.'

'Hang in there son, we'll win one day.'

Anna had given a good account for him, but to no avail. I was so angry I yelled out, 'I wonder if a half-caste will ever be given a chance—or will white Australia ever understand—'

I left the court in tears and didn't bother to bow.

I had been reading in the newspapers in National Aboriginal Week (27 September 86) that finally a Royal Commission would be held into the treatment and deaths of Aboriginals in police or prison custody.

We have known for years that police in some country towns can be as brutal as they like to Kooris, and get away with it. People who try to protest and get help are persecuted or run out of town. In some places they herd old blackfellers out of town like they were dogs. I have witnessed this.

I had been checked out for my second operation and was booked in to hospital for 27 March. Aileen came with me and stayed while I was operated on, and she came to visit nearly every day.

They cut thirteen kilos from my belly and sewed my muscles back in place. After the gut-busting work I'd done I was now really gut-busted—the scar ran from near my kidneys right around my stomach to the other side of my back. I looked like I'd been sliced in half, and I thought of the Bodiless Woman at the sideshow. There were 180 stitches and 86 metal clamps holding me together.

I was there for a month. Horse and his family came to see me, and all my kids except Nobby. The doctor said I was likely to feel depressed and under stress for the next six months.

At home the nurse came to change my dressing every day. I felt weepy and low, though I was glad to be home amongst my books and Land Rights posters and the family calling in. Neddy came to visit and we swapped our latest stories. She'd applied for a Housing Commission place at Wreck Bay, the mission where some of her kids lived. She asked me how Gert and James were. And she'd stopped drinking.

I was too unwell to work on my book, so I read and researched. An alternative network magazine called *Maggie's Farm* had an article called MISSING LINKS—A SEPARATE REALITY, about Aunt Millie Boyd.

> Continuing the *Maggie's Farm* series with Aboriginal shaman/storyteller Lorraine Mafi-Williams of the Bundjalung tribe in northern NSW. The following is an interview with her teacher, elder/custodian Aunt Millie Boyd, 89 years, of the Githrabaul Tribe.
>
> Lorraine asked her to explain about totems.
>
> 'Wherever the old tribal Aborigine was born that place was their totem. What's in the water, what's in the mountain, was given to us by the old tribal people . . . our totem is the goanna and the bullock.' (Aunt Millie later explained the spirit of the bullock totem 'wandered in' from a distant tribe. It is suspected it might be a buffalo, an Amerindian totem.)
>
> 'Is the Willy Wagtail bird also a totem in your family?'
>
> 'Yes, that's our messenger, brings us messages. But when the Williams who married into our family die, you see, the main totem will be goanna. If we see a young goanna dead we know we're going to lose young men

or young girls, that's how our totem comes and lets us know things.'

'And when you're sick yourself do you send your spirit—'

'We send our spirit just like a fog travelling in the morning. Just like that!'

I lay in my bed wishing I could send my spirit somewhere so my body could heal. The drain was messy, I felt low and mopey and had no energy. I read on.

'... Are there any "clevermen" still living in this area?'

'Yes, there is one cleverfellow" who is Githrabaul.'

'What's his work?'

'Everything. If he wants to travel a long way his spirit can go. He travels in the form of a giant bee—'

I must have gone to sleep then, and my dreams were full of the wings of the giant bee ranging across the hills of Mulli Mulli, Woodenbong, Box Ridge, Yamba, Lismore.

When I woke up I read about a woman years ago who was a master of jumping long distances.

'Her name was Denargu and she lived up in Blue Knob (behind Nimbin),' Lorraine said. 'Denargu used to sing out to the wind, call the wind. She could travel on the wind the same way a tornado picks up things. No matter where she wanted to go she could be there in an hour.'

Aunt Millie: 'Even when her husband was in the tribal wars she would sing out and call the wind to turn the other tribe back from the foot of the mountain.'

The paper's interviewer said, 'A line of fire across the mountain in the rain?'

Lorraine: 'You see Mary W, the one I told you about, even now she can whip up a good storm. She's very impressive, Mary, she's the one that drowned all the bulldozers down at Goanna Headland when they tried to peg it out for development. They were going to put a tourist resort ... '

'So she's the custodian of that place.'

'She's no lady to play with, old Mary,' Lorraine said.

I slept again. I seemed to be able to sleep for days ... I could read, and think about these things, but I had no energy for other activities ... The operation and a series of stressful family events had laid me low. I went back to sewing class a few times but then it took another day to recover.

I managed to find another solicitor for Nob. Her name was Kathy and she seemed genuinely concerned about his case. She went to Long Bay to see him, and engaged a barrister. They said that he should not be in gaol, and they'd work for free.

They prepared his case, I wrote a letter for the judge and a psychiatrist wrote a full report. On the day, Kathy came for Jeff and Shelley, I wasn't well enough to face more court.

'He'll be out by Christmas,' they shouted as they came in the door with Anna. I made a pot of tea.

'The judge took into consideration,' Anna said, 'that he'd had a breakdown, that he should never have been taken to the cells, that he was bashed. We showed pictures of the house. I spoke for him too. I said he was a good man and a good worker.'

He was given a three-year sentence for the charge of firing at the police car, with an eighteen-month non-parole period. By August he had already done twelve months. He was to get remission for his work in gaol, for the courses he'd done, for playing football.

On 4 August 1987, Kathy rang to say he would be out by 17 September. 'Surviving culture,' I thought, 'I hope Nob survives.' It was a great relief to know he'd be free.

I was in and out of hospital during this time for chest infections and other problems, no one seemed to know what was really wrong. It was four months since the operation and some sort of long, slow recovery was taking place.

At sewing class I'd heard about an Aboriginal hostel in Granville for people who'd raised their families and didn't want to become live-in babysitters for their kids. It was the first of its kind.

I moved there on 11 August 1987.

The place was called Allawah, meaning 'sit awhile.' It was a huge house with rose gardens and stained-glass windows and a hallway big enough to swing ten cats. I had a room of my own and a sunroom off that for a study.

Six or seven other people lived there—I'd known them all at various stages of my life and they all had their stories to tell. It looked like someone had pointed me in the right direction if I wanted to do more writing. I felt at peace here. Not hemmed in.

I unpacked my books and bought a typewriter (my other one had packed in), a desk and a filing cabinet. Outside my window a hibiscus opened its buds and the noise now was not traffic but birds.

One of the men was an actor, and the next morning a car called to take him on location. Word had got round I was writing a book, so there was teasing talk about how if they didn't look out this place would turn into an artists' colony.

Someone had left the *Telegraph* and a copy of *Land Rights News* on a coffee table so I took them to my room to lie down and have a read. On the centre page of the Land Rights paper was a photo of a woman talking into a microphone. This was Helen Boyle, who had gone to Geneva to talk to a UN working group about the deaths in custody. She was chairperson of the committee who had put out the leaflets of case studies I'd read.

Every time I picked up a paper the numbers had gone up. The committee had 101 deaths in custody recorded, and feared there were many more. Fifteen this year so far. Averaging one a fortnight. Underneath there were lists of national actions that people could go to.

White journalists were now picking up on the issue and making fairly radical statements, particularly now the Bicentenary year was coming up. People felt something had to be said. In the *Telegraph* an article called 200 YEARS OF INDIFFERENCE talked about how the white race 'have learned nothing, and lack the maturity to be a nation . . . ' It was honest and well-written and I sat to write and thank the journalist for this article. I read it out to a few people around the house. Then I typed another one out real deadly and sent it to him.

On black Friday, 13 November, Nob was released from the Bay after fifteen months, pissed off and ecstatic. Something had finally gone right for him. A good solicitor and the Shadow Attorney General as his barrister, and both had worked on his case for free because this imprisonment had been so unjust and we had no money. Some white people you couldn't knock, but you had to find out who and where they were. We were very lucky this time. Fingers crossed this would be the end of Nob's career of doing time.

The next week I had a phone call from the All Blacks asking if I'd make twenty dampers for their football presentation dance. My reputation for dampers was still around. Mrs Christian and I used sixty pounds of self-raising flour, four large tins of Sunshine Milk and water, with half a pound of table salt. This time I had mod cons and a big kitchen. I'd never used a

Kenwood Chef and the first damper came out so hard the general opinion was to take it outside and bury it, so we hoied that one. The others were fine and on the big night we went to Souths Juniors at Kensington—Brenda Leslie and her old man Nicko, Mum Ruby, Aileen and me.

Max Silver and his band Black Lace were playing the All Blacks song 'We keep the ball in motion/Just like a rolling ocean' and later they played 'Midnight Special' and the place was jumping.

My manuscript was almost ready for the publisher. I knew when I finished this book a weight would be lifted from my mind, not only because I could examine my own life from it and know who I was, but because it may help better the relationship between the Aboriginal and white people. That it might give some idea of the difficulty we have surviving between two cultures, that we are here and will always be here.

PART SEVEN

Communities

Elaine Russell, *Inspection Day*, 1994, acrylic on canvas, 94.5 x 120.5 cm. Courtesy of Boomalli Aboriginal Artists Cooperative, Sydney, New South Wales, and the artist.

Maturna-Jarra-Kurlu Kujalpa-Pala Wangkaja

PANSY ROSE NAPALJARRI

Yamangka kapala ngatinyanu-jarra nyina wanta-kujaku.
Kuja-kapala nyinami, wangkami-kapala-nyanu yapa-patu-kurlu
Nakamarraju ka kuja-nganta wangkami Nampijinpa-kuju, 'Yuwa,
nyangunpa-jana ngula wati-patu kujalpalu rarralykajirla
kilji-nyayirni warru yanu?' Nampijinpa-ju-rla yalumanu,
'Yuwayi, manu kuja kalu tarnngajiki warru parnkami
rarralykajirla-juku, wapanja-wangu. Kala yangka ngalipa
kuja kalarlipa tarnnga-parnta wapaja nyurruwiyi.
Wankaru-ku-wiyi-rli-jana ngatinyanurlu manu kurdanyanurlu
wankirri mani, ngularra-ku ngayi wati-patu ku, kuja kalu
tarnnga-parntarlu waru kanyi rarralykaji'.

Nakamarra-julpa-nyanu wangkaja kuja. 'Ngularra-rlangu
karnta-karnta kuja kalu warrarda yani wati-patu-kurlu,
yangka kuja kalu-nyanu kalinja palka mardarni.
Mimayirli-jiki-rli-nyanu pakarnirra, pakarnirra kaji yapa
jinta wapamirra yalyu-wangu. Ngula karnta-karnta, kulalpalu
wati jinta-kurlu nyinayarla, walku'.

Nampijinpa-jurla Nakamarra-kuju wangkaja, 'Manu yangka kuja
kalu pama-kurra warrarda parnkami. Pama-wangu-rlangulu
nyina. Kujangku-juku kapurlu nyanu kulu-ku, kulu-ku mani,
warlalja-jarra-rlangurlu. Kapulu-nyanu tarnnga-kurra
pakarni'.

Nakamarraju wangkaja, 'Karnta-karnta-rlangu kulalpalu
kurdiji-kirra yantarlarni, walku. Parlpirrpa-rlajuku
yungulu parntarrimi, wirntinja-wangu. Yii . . .
punku-wati-nyayirni, ngurrpa kapulu kujajiki nyina'.

Ngulajangkaju Nampijinpaju karrinja-pardija manu
Nakamarra-ku-rla wangkaja, 'Yani karna ngurra-kurralku.
Ngakarnangku nyanyi jukurrarlu'. Nampijinpaju
ngurra-kurralku yanu wangkanja-warnuju.

"Two women sit in the shade away from the hot sun"

Pansy Rose Napaljarri

Two women sit in the shade away from the hot sun. As they sit, they discuss the behaviour of others in their community. Nakamarra says to Nampijinpa,
'Did you see the way those young men drive around so fast in their car?'

Nampijinpa replies,
'Yes! They never walk around, not like before when we used to walk everywhere. For their own sakes, their parents should tell them off not to speed around like that.'

Nakamarra reflected,
'And those girls who go out with the men all the time. You know, those men who are already married. If they have a fight over a man, let them fight till one woman walks out without being hurt. Those girls, they never stay honest to their husbands, no!'

To Nakamarra, Nampijinpa says,
'And those men who always go out to drink grog. Why don't they stay off the grog? That's why they fight a lot when they get drunk. They even fight with their own relation. They might kill each other.'

Nakamarra says.
'And those women should come to corroboree instead of bending their backs playing cards. They should dance whenever there is a corroboree. Oh . . . it is so dreadful they should be so ignorant!'

Nampijinpa stands saying to Nakamarra.
'I am going home. I will see you tomorrow.'

Nampijinpa goes to her own camp.

Fashion Statement

Lisa Bellear

Raybocks and reebans
And jeans with holes
And photographic chemicals
That leave a pattern
Of blotched bleached
Benign dreams

Henna your hair
If you dare
The smell
Of leather

Give out energy
Strong powerful
Black women's energy

Look at those
Wudjella women
Wanting a piece of
My womanist energy

Fantasising fanatically
On how we are women.
Are oppressed and in
Our oppression we are
United

Thanks tidda girl—
My wudjella sister
For your thoughts
And love and whatever

But I'm in love
With my Koori community

I'm in love
With Black women

Henna your hair
If you dare . . .

Double Standards

MARGARET BRUSNAHAN

I lived with people as a child
Who were well-respected folk.
To the public eye well bred and mild;
It was obvious when they spoke.

They gave their money to the parish
When collection time came round;
Nothing was too much or lavish,
They both felt duty bound.

But back at home behind closed doors
They really showed their form.
They said to me, "Obey our laws
Or you'll wish that you weren't born."

To use their bath caused great concern—
They said I must be clean—
But so they wouldn't catch my germs
They scrubbed it with kerosene.

I never sat with them to eat;
I knew my place of course,
A turned up fruit case for a seat
Out on the old back porch.

The times they spoke or smiled at me
Were few and far between.

I think that they were born to be
Just hard and cruel and mean.

No one doubted sincerity,
So their name was not defiled.
They were pillars of the community
But they couldn't love this child.

Civilised

MARGARET BRUSNAHAN

I don't believe you, people say to me,
When I tell them that I am part Aborigine.
I'm part Irish too, I venture to say,
And their eyes light up in a peculiar way.

They say, "My dear, if you hadn't confessed,
There's no way in the world I would've guessed.
So why don't you play the black part low,
Tell them you're Irish, they'll never know."

They think that being black is a sin;
They don't want to know the person within.
I've thought about it but I couldn't hide
The me that is black, the me inside.

My forefathers killed, that's true I know,
But that was so many years ago.
Killed in tribal fights, and land protection.
They'd never heard of Government Election.

My other half, the half that is white,
They've been educated, they know what's right.
They read the Bible that says Love Your Brother;
They're so damned civilised they're killing each other.

One Way Street

JACK DAVIS

It's a quiet one way street
this street of ours
though two tiny tots
across the road
let us know they live here
Parking has its limits
and we play draughts
each day
vying for a parking lot
A guy who has a crazy laugh
a yuppie type
lives almost opposite
Our cat a tortoiseshell
guards his piece of turf
and keeps the other cats at bay
But most days it's a quiet place
to dwell in
is Little Howard Street

Pissing in Parks

LISA BELLEAR

It's 6.30 am or 5.35 pm
The dog and the dog owners
Are pissing in parks
And I'm dodging the shit
And the piss and the
Glass and the needles
And I photograph a blade
Of Grass, the solitary

Piece that has not
Begat doggie do
And I'm planning to write
To local council,
in protest of curfews imposed
On kids in the streets after dark

Give me gangs and teenage wankers
And old people who
Unearth the flower beds
To brighten their uneventful lives
In an uneventful culture
That doesn't give a fuck
About their elders

Eh give me teenage Ninja turtles
And gummies that spit and yell abuse
At the casual passerby

But dogs and their owners
Who piss in parks, who
Kill the grass . . .

I've sent that letter to council

Fellow Being

LIONEL FOGARTY

An' we aborigines in humanity.
The pulses of the red sun give a beat in aboriginal people.
The kissing of winds to trees are the love between aborigines.
Even the water we drink is the pure tears aboriginals share.
We wisely in our humanised aboriginal homes are united under all one
  colour.
The aboriginal is the bread of man's rich land.

We are the rocks of ages and purpling skies.
Look at every scenery in bush you will see an aboriginal face,
    body and spirit.
The aboriginal is not owned by any human being on earth.
Our presence is the flesh of fresh new worlds.
We are music that floats into a wonderful note to all ears.
An aboriginal is nature's soil, you pick it up, hold it in your hand and
you will feel our growth in the ground.
We are the gods of man in this land but then we are not humans.
Yet we are part of your kind now hey.
The earth above is our spirituals.
And now if you speak our tongue, don't mean you are native.
The sea, hills and lakes are in our hearts and minds.
The universe is belonga to dem big spirit creator.
Oh, now man you go out there to find out more of us. who down here.
Well listen to that fish talk and you will know we ate it the other day.
And if you talk to a bird of paradise you find they are people, same with
all creatures here, we aboriginals come from them.
If you feel the heat of the sun, you feel us.
If you see and feel the light of the darkness then you have just
    touched an aborigine.

Excerpt from *Unna You Fullas*

GLENYSE WARD

REAL SOLID AND NEAT

Another change which we couldn't quite take to grips, was the coming of teachers. A lot of the girls and boys from the earlier times didn't worry about it so much, because they knew about teachers, they'd already been to schools. They were taken from those schools and brought to the mission by their parents, or with the help of dedicated Christians and white Native Welfare Supervisors, on the grounds that the kids were better off growing up the good Christian way, and our people's way of life was no good.

   Most of the newcomers had also been to schools, where they were taught by whitemen teachers. So it did not come as a shock to them so much as to us, when we were told in the dining room one day by Fr Albertus that Sister Petra would no longer be teaching us. She was going to take up a post in Perth.

Our new teacher would be arriving the next day, a Saturday. That would give Fr Albertus enough time to show him around the mission on the weekend and he could meet us kids on the Monday. We were to call him Mr Pitts. Father hoped we would be on our best behaviour. A two-storey building would be added to the fathers' dining room, to be used as classrooms.

"Next veek anozzer teacher iss arriving from Pers. His name iss Mr Foley and he vill be taking zer smaller grades until zer new buildings are ready. For zer time being he vill teach in zer girls' recreation shed." This was a corrugated iron shack not far from the rubbish tip, used by the girls in winter for play and to relax in.

That night we sat on Banner's bed.

"Hey, you fullas, I wonder what this man teacher gunna be like?" said a puzzled Thelma. We'd never had a man to teach us before, apart from the priests giving religious instruction.

"I hope he is kind and don't hit us like them sisters." First Sally, then Ruby spoke up. She had not long arrived in the mission. "Where I come from is a little country town in the wheatbelt and me and my cousins went to a school where we had a man teacher."

"What was he like?" we all eagerly asked. Ruby sort of screwed her nose up in the air, shrugged her shoulders and in a deep-drawn audible breath told us how she and her cousins were always in trouble with that teacher.

"We never liked him, because he let them white kids call us black boongs and niggers."

"What does that mean?" Being so innocent and vague, I didn't know what she was talking about. Ruby looked at us.

"Choo, Sprattie and you other fullas, don't you know what nigger and boong mean?"

"Nah." We smiled at her in a real simple way.

"Well all you fullas are niggers and boongs."

"Hey, how come?"

"Well, because . . . " Ruby fiddled with the corner of the sheet, which was hanging over the side of the bed, " . . . that's a sling-off word used by them white kids at school for us people who are dark."

"Choo." We looked at one another, we'd never heard of that before.

"Now you girls know, for later on."

It sort of never really sunk in, as I listened to Ruby carry on about her teacher not listening to her or her cousins, how they used to belt the white kids up for calling them those names, and their teacher always took the white kids' side. Banner scoffed.

"What? I hope our new schoolteacher not gunna be like your one, Ruby."

"Nah, I don't think so. He can't be like that, because we are all dark here."

"Hey Banner, just make up, if this new one hit you, what will you do?"

"Thelma, I'll wait till he turns his back, then I'll run up behind and hit him over the head with a piece of wood and knock him out, so he can't move, and then I'll knock piss out of him. He'll be blacker than you, Thelma."

"Choo." We all killed ourselves laughing.

Saturday morning came, with excitement and whispers in the air. The dining room was like a beehive. Us kids didn't take long in gulping down our bread, milk and sugar, which was all mixed together in a huge pot made up in the kitchen. Whenever Sr Gertrude was on duty she would stress to us that back home in the little German village where she grew up, her parents fed her on bread and milk every morning and it was good for us too, as we'd all grow up to be healthy and strong girls.

Sometimes she would soak our bread with buttermilk, which we loathed, especially for that first meal in the morning. I would rather have faced a bowl of sauerkraut. Whatever we were having for breakfast, be it semolina or bread and milk, it would be washed down with a plastic cup of white sugary tea. That was also made in a big pot. Sister would pour out the tea, making sure none of us got more than the others. Sometimes one of the kids would be slow at eating or drinking, and we would think nothing of helping ourselves to their last drop.

After the meal, we all stood beside our places, which was a regular thing after and before our meals. We'd recite with Sr Ursula our thank you prayers to God for the meal.

On this day, before we could start, Sister raised herself up and down on the heels of her black shiny laced-up shoes.

"You all know that today iss a special day, because our new teacher vill be arriving. Fazher will deal viz zer boys. I vant all girls to carry on viz zheir shobs as usual. You all know your Saturday duties. Vhen zer new teacher arrives, I don't vant any of you girls coming out of zer building oontz running up to zer car oontz staring. If I see any girls hanging around zer car vhen zer new teacher arrives, which I think he vill be arriving after dinner, zhen zhere vill be trobble!"

While she spoke, the two fore-fingers of her right hand tapped the left palm, and her darting eyes pierced straight through us. My stomach squirmed when I saw her in one of these moods. She had a habit of pinpointing a person out in front of everyone, and I'd get real shame, whether it was me or not. Her loud voice echoed through the dining room.

"You ringleaders know who I mean vhen I say you vill be strictly punished if you disobey my orders. Glenysen Sprattsen, Banner, Zhelma, Lynn, Sally, Florry and Poppy, do I make myself clear?"

"Yes, Sister." I could tell the others were sniggering at us. We murmured our thank you prayers, "We give Thee thanks, Almighty God, for these and all the other gifts which of Thy bounty we have received, through Christ Our Lord Amen."

Everybody went to their various jobs. Banner, Thelma, Lynn, Sally, Florry, Poppy and myself cleaned the dormitory. This was a spring cleaning day, which meant all of us had double jobs. We had to change all the sheets on all the beds, and take the dirty washing to the laundry. We took turns carrying it away in big wicker baskets. Then we washed the entire walls. Then we waxed and polished the floor.

Our group didn't mind working in the dormitory because we mucked around quite a lot. When it came to polishing the floor, we would take turns pulling one another around on old jumpers, to put a shine on the floorboards. That was after having rubbed the wax into them on our hands and knees. Besides, we could see clearly out the windows if any visitors turned up.

All morning we kept peeping out during the work. In one way we were glad to have a different teacher, not that we could say anything against Sr Petra, but it would be a change from getting our ears pinched and being pulled from our seats by our cheeks.

The midday meal came and our teacher had still not appeared. Us girls were back in the dormitory, straightening out things, getting ready for Sister's inspection. Jessie, who was a new arrival, came banging on the door.

"Quick, you girls, open up, there's a car coming, quick!"

"It must be him," yelled Banner, running to open the door. She slid the bolt back. We used to lock the door from the inside to keep out other girls and to give us time to stop any mucking around if Sr Ursula came to the door to check on us. We would find some excuse to tell her why we had locked the door.

"Get in here," Banner grabbed the excited kid by the hand and flung her inside. We nearly fell over one another getting out of Jessie's way. Not waiting for her to catch her breath or say any more, we pushed one of the double-decker beds up to the window. Our spick and span bed-making looked like a bomb had hit it, as we pulled and struggled with one another for a good possie to look out the window.

Every time a visitor came to the mission we would get really excited, and if we weren't jumping all over their car, we'd be peeping out the windows of a building like animals in a cage. The light and dark blue two-tone Holden pulled up outside the fathers' and brothers' monastery. We could see everything from where we were perched on our bed.

"Look at those boys all standing round the car." It was Banner's wild tone. "That's not fair, unna you girls? Them boys think they great."

"I reckon they are spoilt, they get petted up all the time by them nuns and priests." Sally dug Banner in the side.

"They got no shame! That man can't get out, they baulking him. Besides, they are in our way, we can't see what our teacher look like." Banner had the best position at the window and stared out at Teddy and Jimmy standing right at the car door. I could see Fr Albertus coming out of the monastery. Thelma gasped.

"Baalay, look out now! He gunna make them boys scatter."

We all fell silent, pressed against one another, putting up with the discomfort. Father walked over to the car, gesturing and calling to the boys to move aside. The car door opened.

Our teacher got out, and we noticed that he was tall, well-built, strong and good-looking. He extended his right hand to Fr Albertus, who gave it a good shake, but with his left hand. Father's right hand was tucked away inside the black sock, in the pocket of his brown khaki trousers.

Father ushered up the boys, pointing them out as he introduced them. Again the teacher held his hand out. The boys hung their heads in shame, scraping the dirt with their feet as they put their own hands up weak-way, for the new teacher to shake. Us girls killed ourselves laughing at their antics.

"Choo, choo. Them boys look winyarn. They got no koondang."

The boot of the car was up and the teacher placed his cases on the ground. Father organised the bigger boys to carry them away to the monastery, where he had prepared a vacant room. Then the two men walked across to the buildings with the rest of the boys crowding around them.

"Baalay, quick, Sister coming!" Thelma sang out, so we jumped off the bed and two of us pushed it back quickly, while the others made the covers on it straight again. Sister walked in to a nice clean and shiny dormitory with everything shipshape.

The weekend passed. Although we never officially met the teacher until the Monday, we did have a good look at him in church on Sunday, when he strode up to receive holy communion. Us girls stared at him cruel. He was bald in the middle part of his head but around the sides his blond hair was thick and wavy. He had clear crystal blue eyes and stood expressionless in his pew. From what I saw he looked hard and stern, but then in those days I thought almost everybody looked like that.

Religion was different in those days of the Latin mass, there were no smiling faces. It was a sin to laugh and talk in church, everyone was so serious and reverent. I thought, he might be different when we get to school. After mass we were back in the dormitory changing out of our tunics into Sunday best dress.

"What you reckon about him?" Thelma sang out, "Were you watching him in church when he went up for communion?"

We didn't get a chance to answer. The working girl we called Silkie overheard us talking. She came rushing in and sat down on the bed. We all froze because we thought we were going to cop it.

"Listen here, you kids! I don't care what you think or say about him . . . " She had this real sheepish grin all over her face as she grasped one of the girls round the waist in a cheeky way and sat down on the bed. " . . . from what I saw of him, I reckon he looked real solid and neat."

Then she burst out giggling and bent down and gave me a hug, as I was sitting there on the floor in front of her! She stood and picked up the hem of her dress and twisted it round her body so that when she twirled herself round and let go of the dress, it all spun out, and we saw everything from her legs up to her bloomers. She went chuckling out the door.

Our minds were so innocent, we never said anything, we carried on getting ourselves dressed for breakfast. It seemed real strange to see Silkie acting this way. Most of the time she walked around strict and stern like the nuns. Very rarely on occasions she'd do things out of the ordinary, like sneaking off for swims with us in the dam. All these changes going on around the mission left me with a frightening confused state of mind.

A New One to Us

The following Friday we all had to go over to the bigger classroom, to join the older kids, so Mr Foley led us over and jammed our class in the front of the room. We all stood quietly, with Mr Foley's eyes glaring down on us.

Before Mr Pitts delivered his speech he bent forward from the waist in a peculiar way, with his hands behind his back, like an emu stalking out something shiny on the ground. Then with a sudden lifting motion of his head and in a deep voice he bellowed out, "Good morning, boys and girls!" We all answered back with a singsong, "Good morning, Mr Pitts."

I happened to glance at Banner. I could see she was trying hard not to laugh because he looked so funny. Thelma dug me in the back, making it very hard for me too. Mr Pitts walked with long slow steps, his arms folded behind his back. Up and down, up and down in front of the classroom, where we were all standing.

"Every second Friday, we are going to have what they call an Assembly. The school I have come from held Assemblies, so we shall do the same. Assembly will be every second Friday."

Us kids had never heard of the word, it was a new one to us. We stood looking at him like stunned mullet. He had stopped dead in his tracks, with his left hand resting on his hip.

"Do you all know the meaning of the word Assembly?"

"Nah," we all chorused in our giggling, smiling way. The smiles soon disappeared. Mr Pitts' right hand furiously stroked back the long strands of his blond hair, that normally lay over the front balding part of his head. He rushed over to his desk and picked up a long, springy rod. His blue eyes were intense as he cut the air with the whistling cane.

"Now, I will ask you all again, and you are to answer me in a proper manner of speech!" He thrashed the cane down past the right side of his body. "This is one thing that I am going to change in your school, and I am sure Mr Foley will be doing the same. We are going to teach you all to speak proper English, none of this 'nah' business when you are being spoken to or asked a question. You are to say 'Yes sir! No sir!'

"And another thing. What does this 'choo' mean? Last week when I held up one of my paintings, during our art lesson, all I could see were these grinning silly faces all saying, 'Choo, choo!' You don't know how stupid you all look and sound.

"Another word I do not want mentioned in either Mr Foley's class or mine is the word 'unna.' What sort of language is that? Unna! A sort of language that has to be stopped. I will get very annoyed if it is said in my presence. And if I do hear it, maybe a few reminders from my friend here will refresh your memory." The cane swished as he held it out and turned himself around so that all of us had a clear view. "Do I make myself clear?"

"Yes sir." We all spoke together.

"Now, as I was explaining to you about our Assembly, we will be gathering outside the classroom every fortnight for discussion on different topics. For your information, Assembly means to gather together and talk about things. Discussion will be followed by singing. We shall sing songs about Australia. And now I think we will just run through some of the songs that you already know. Could one of you boys come out to the board and write the names of the songs you have been taught by Sr Petra?"

Teddy stood up and strolled down the aisle to the front. Mr Foley ushered his class to the back of the room to make way for Teddy and Mr Pitts to use the board. Us girls thought Teddy was a showoff. He was in Grade 7 and thought he knew everything. He was so sure of himself as he slouched on down the aisle, with his hands in the pockets of his grey knee-length shorts, thinking he was great because all of the girls were looking at him. There was a smirk on his bony face as he stood by Mr Pitts in front of the blackboard.

Then Mr Pitts grabbed him by the front of his collar.

"You walk down the aisle properly, with your hands out of your pockets, and don't put on the smarty-pants act with me, is that clear?" Teddy's bold character turned to shame as Mr Pitts jarred him up. We could see his face going funny.

"Yes, s-sir." Mr Pitts let go of him. Teddy stumbled back and clung to the teacher's table to stop himself from falling over altogether.

"Now get yourself over to this board and write the songs down. There's plenty of chalk, get on with it."

Mr Pitts stormed over to the corner and picked up a peculiar shaped object. It was wide at one end, skinny at the other and with both sides curved in at the middle, with a case-handle to it. All eyes turned away from Teddy, who was shaking like a leaf as he tried to write a song up on the board. We were curious to know what Mr Pitts had inside this strange box, which he opened up. It was lined inside with purple velvet and clipped to the underside of the lid were two long curved brown sticks which seemed to have elastic stretched along them, going from one end to the other.

Then he lifted from the box a brown object, hollow and made of wood, with thin wires all in a row, running up to some knobs at one end. Mr Pitts lifted this object right up to near his ear and pressed his cheek into it. Then he unclipped one of the long sticks and rubbed the elastic part of it up and down on the hollow wooden object, making the queerest noises. We had never seen or heard anything like that in our lives and all burst out laughing, especially at the expressions on Mr Pitts' face.

We were so busy laughing we didn't notice he had stopped making the noises and was standing there furious. A complete silence spread over the room. Mr Foley was holding his shoulder and shrugging it. Mr Pitts spoke almost in a whisper.

"What is so funny?" No-one dared to answer him.

"I think you are the most rude, arrogant lot of children I have ever met."

He Might Come in Here

At the end of the following week, our teacher said he was taking us mushroom picking, because his friends were coming from Perth and they loved mushrooms. He would only take a few of us, three boys and three girls. I loved gathering mushrooms, but I dreaded that he would choose me.

He picked Penny, one of the new girls to our school. Then he picked Gina and then me. Three boys were to come with us, Jimmy, Brian and Billy. Mr Foley told us all to go over to the big redgum tree. He was driving home to get changed. We were to be waiting there when he returned. We weren't to worry about buckets, he would bring the buckets.

I liked Penny. She was tall and lanky, a highly strung girl who often told me how she missed her baby brother. He was still back home in a country town, south somewhere. She had asked her mother if she could bring him with her next year, after the holidays. Her mother had said it was bad enough letting the priest talk them into sending Penny away, let alone her brother. She had said, "Home is where Mum and Dad are."

Gina was another girl who had only recently arrived at Wandering. She was plump, always laughing and joking, that's why I got on with her. Both Penny and Gina shared my feelings about Mr Foley. They came running behind me and pulled at the sleeve of my jumper.

"Sprattie, where you going? We supposed to meet sir and them boys at the gumtree remember?" The rest of the kids had gone out to the fields to play but I was walking slowly down to the bathroom.

"I feel sick, I'm not going."

"Choo, come on Sprattie, you always loved picking mushrooms. He gunna get wild if we not there."

"Don't worry about me, you two go ahead and if he ask where I am, tell him I'm too sick to go." Next I heard their footsteps following me into the bathroom. They got on both sides of me.

"We don't want to go either! Let them silly boys go, never mind if we get into trouble." So they said but they were frightened.

"He might come in here and find us."

"Don't be silly. I been here longer than you. No man's allowed in the girls' bathroom, not even the priests or brothers come in here." We all sat back on the bench and laughed about the boys, thinking they must be in Mr Foley's green panelvan by now, speeding off to the paddocks by the dam, where the mushrooms grew.

"Can you fullas picture them sitting in sir's pretty car, winyarn-way."

"I don't fancy sitting all squashed up with the boys in the back of that van. Our Lady's Truck is the best, hey? No other cars can beat it."

Our conversation was interrupted by the banging open of the wooden door. Mr Foley pounced on us, dug his hand into our necks and sent each one of us flying out of the bathroom.

"Are you girls deaf? Didn't you hear my orders? When I say or tell you to do something, you had better do it!" Too shocked to say anything, we walked over to his car, with a shove in the back from him every now and again to hurry us along. The boys were already in the panel van, sitting bunched against one another to make room for us.

We climbed in slowly, shameful-way, careful not to show anything personal of ourselves. Mr Foley stood there pulling his shoulder. He made sure that we were in the car, huddled in a bunch, before he slammed the door and stormed around to the driver's side. He started the car and took off, catching us off guard. We suddenly ended up on the boys' laps. Deeply shamed, we quickly got back to our normal position and clung to one another as the old car sped along a dusty gravel track.

There was no division between the front seat and the back of the van, so we could see ahead. Every now and again I noticed Mr Foley glancing through the rear vision mirror at us. It made me feel no good inside and I concentrated on the scenery of trees and hills flashing past. I changed my position to sit upright with my legs out straight, facing the boys, who also had their legs stretched out. I tried to keep my feet from touching theirs.

The boys thought it was a great joke to see us in this uncomfortable position. They could sense we were unhappy, which gave them all the more reason to poke fun by pulling tongue at us when Mr Foley wasn't looking, or pressing with their feet when we swung around a corner.

All the time they looked at us putting a brave face on, and knew full well that if we were anywhere else other than sitting in the teacher's car going flat out, we would have dropped them right on the spot for what they were doing.

We kept driving till we came to a clearing with paddocks on both sides of the track. Mr Foley leaned back suddenly and shouted, "Which is the best spot?"

"Wandering Brook, sir, not far from here."

The boys all spoke at once, blocking our view as they knelt forward, crowding over the back of Mr Foley's seat to give him directions. We sat listening to their jabbering.

"If you just go a little further sir, you'll come to a big gate. You can drive down to the big dam and park there. We find lots of mushrooms there, unna you girls?" They all looked behind at us and we nodded our heads. The car came to a standstill and we were glad to get out and stretch our legs. Mr Foley gave us the buckets and told us to go get mushrooms.

"You boys go in that direction. I'll come with you girls." Our hearts sank. We just put our heads down and walked off slowly, all the way making sure we didn't get out of sight from the boys. Mr Foley kept following us around. Every now and again he would find a few mushrooms himself and come over to drop them in our buckets, making sure he either brushed one of us on the arm or came really close. We were relieved when we had a bucket full.

At the back of the van, waiting for Mr Foley to open up, Gina bent down to pick up her bucket of mushrooms.

"Hang on, Gina, I'll give you a hand with that." The teacher closed his hand over the top of Gina's as she grabbed the bucket handle. I could sense Gina's alarm.

We were into our early teens and still naive about many things. The boys used to watch the teachers' attitude towards some girls, and watch us girls too, sly-way, sniggering and carrying on silly-way behind our backs, saying how the teacher must be mardong for us, and we were jirruping for him. On the way back the boys sat smirking and grinning. Yet for once in my life I never minded the boys teasing us, I could put up with that better than getting those sickly looks from Foley.

There were no smirks back at the mission that evening, as we walked past their tables to get our tea. I was relieved but I also knew that the reason they didn't smirk at us was because the nuns were there. Over the weekend Jimmy, Billy and Brian were teasing us in the paddock about the mushrooming and Mr Foley.

"Choo Penny, he love you, shame!" And all the boys started laughing and singing out to us, "Shame you girls, you must be solid."

We had separate playing grounds, joined by a fence. Whenever the boys would see the girls in the paddock, they'd automatically run to the fence and start cheeking us, and this younger girl Trina shouted back, telling them to shut their mouths.

"Billy Rice, Brian Leathe and Jimmy Neal, you fullas tight on your own. We don't want that ugly-looking thing. Gurn, you come over here, we'll make yous jump, unna, all you other girls?"

By this time a few more girls stopped playing games and came over to join with us and ask what was going on. Trina told them how the boys were teasing us about Mr Foley dragging us out of the bathroom. We walked away from the fence because we saw Sr Ursula coming towards us from the convent with one of the big girls, who was Trina's cousin. Trina broke away from our group and ran to her cousin. So it was that Sr Ursula got wind that we'd disobeyed Mr Foley and hid in the bathroom, instead of waiting at the gumtree.

Over the weekend we heard nothing more about it. We were getting dressed for school on the Monday morning. Gina and Penny came over while Banner was combing my hair.

"Hey Banner, what if us girls was getting dressed like this and our teacher walked in?"

"Oh, I wouldn't know what I would do but I do know one thing, you wouldn't catch me in that classroom after, I don't care what happens, they can flog me all they like, it wouldn't matter, I am used to it, what would you two do?"

Gina and Penny said that they would tell their mothers and fathers when they went home at the end of the year.

"What would your mother and father do?"

"They'll come here and knock them teachers flying, they not frightened," Gina pouted her lips, full of confidence. "Mum got a brother and I seen him having a fight with three big rough wadjalas down the street outside the pub, because they was gunna mob dad's cousin."

Suddenly a voice made us jump.

"Glenysen Sprattsen, Gina and Penny, stand where you are. You other girls can go and line up for school."

We three stood in fear as Sister went over and waited for the last girl to go out. She shut the door of the old tin bathroom and turned to us, her face scarlet.

"You girls tell me vhat happen in zer bazhroom zer ozzer day. One of zer big girls told me zhis morning vhat's going on." My heart sank, for I was expecting to be hit. Words came stumbling out of my mouth.

"Sorry, Sister, I never listened to Mr Foley. He told us we had to go mushroom picking with him. I didn't feel like going because I wanted to play a game of rounders with Banner and them other girls." I thought to myself, any excuse is better than none at a crucial time like this.

"Zhen vhat happened, girls?" Sister wasn't even interested in my excuse. Still trembling, I went on to explain how I got the girls to come toilet with me and how we sat down on the bench. I looked over to Gina and Penny for support.

"Oontz vhy did you sit down on zer bench, girls, knowing full vell zhat Mr Foley vas vaiting for you?"

"Penny had a splinter in her foot and it was hurting her, so me and Gina was getting it out for her."

"Lift up your foot, Penny. I vant to see zhis splinter."

Taken offguard, a bewildered Penny turned her back towards Sister and lifted her left leg from the knee, with her left hand holding her foot back, so the sole was turned up. I stood in front of her to give support and she clung to my shoulder to keep her balance. I could feel the fingers of her right hand digging in as she glared at me. This was how we turned the soles of our feet up for inspection of stone bruises, cuts and cracks to our heels, which we often had because we did not wear shoes.

Knowing full well the condition of Penny's foot, I ignored her eyes and bowed my head to join Sister in looking for the splinter that wasn't there. Sister's two fingers kept prodding hard into Gina's foot.

"I can't see zhat zhere iss anyzhing wrong viz your foot. You komm zhis afternoon to zer Dispensary oontz ve can bazhe zer foot in zer tob, zhen ve vill know if your splinter iss still zhere, or not!"

Penny gladly put her foot down and stood up straight, while Sister walked to the basin, turned on the water and rinsed her hands. Then she reached into the long sleeve of her habit and pulled out a white hanky which she always had tucked away there, to wipe her dripping hands. The look on her face was serious and her voice stern.

"Vere any of you girls really sick? Vhy did you behave in zhis manner towards your teacher? Glenysen Sprattsen, you haf been here zer longest, you know zhat zhere iss a punishment for disobedience oontz you are setting a bad example for zer new girls zhat come here." She put her hand up under my chin to lift my bowed head up. Her piercing eyes burned down on me.

"Tell me zhis, girl, did Mr Foley come in zer bathroom to get you?"

I got a sudden bout of nerves.

"Yes, Sister." I couldn't stop blinking.

"Did he see anyzhing of you girls, vere you getting change?" Feeling real shame, I said softly, "No Sister." She released my chin and my head dropped down again. Quick as the wind, her voice came soft and kind.

"Ach, girls, if you vere feeling sick, vhy didn't you tell zer teacher, zhat vould haf solved all zer problems."

"I kept telling the teacher all morning my belly was aching but he wouldn't listen to me."

"Girls, zhis iss enough talking. You may go to school, and not a word to anyone vhat ve haf been discussing."

Only too glad to escape, especially without a hit, we bolted out of the bathroom shack like wild horses. The next weeks in the classroom, we three girls found ourselves doing extra duties. Mr Foley seemed to have us in mind whenever a job came up.

What Is the Matter with You Lot?

The year with Mr Foley was up for Florry and me. Some of the girls and boys went back home. They left the mission altogether. Banner and Thelma had left school to work with the nuns, helping out in the kitchen. Never mind, we still had Poppy and Lynn when we joined Mr Pitts' class.

By this time Mr Pitts was in his brand new classroom, a second storey on top of the little girls' dormitory. I was glad in one way that I was in Mr Pitts' class because my sister Sally was in the next grade and around me most of the time.

Mr Pitts started the year off by putting us in mixed groups, girls with boys, something we had to come to terms with. Before that we had never sat close to boys, we were kept segregated in the classroom. Now Jimmy, Billy, Florry and I had to sit together. When we were used to sitting next to one another, the girls and boys mucked around something wicked. One of our group was always dragged out of the desk and made to sit on the floor in front of the class.

I noticed the teacher's attitude was more furious on a Monday.

Sometimes I wondered what could be upsetting him so much? I would try double hard at my work, but seeing him like that I became nervous and made a whole lot of mistakes. For the rest of the day our bodies used to suffer from Mr Pitts' cane.

Fridays were different. One Friday morning he told us that after doing our sums we were all to follow him into the dining room. We just carried on doing those sums, we couldn't think about anything else. As usual he stalked around the room checking up on us.

So after sums we all followed in a line behind Mr Pitts, who was carrying that object of his in a case. He had told us it was a violin. We entered the dining room through the back door and filed to our usual places, along the neat long tables.

"All you boys and girls, I want you to shift the tables and chairs over to one side. Hurry up, and make it quick."

He laid his case on one of the tables, removed the violin and fiddled around with it, while us girls helped carry over the benches to make space. Mr Pitts told us to sit on the floor in front of him, while he sat on a table.

"Right, I suppose you must be wondering what's going on." He ran his fingers through his loose blond hair and flicked it over the bald patch. "Every second Friday you all know that we have Assembly. Well, now on the other Friday, we will have dancing. You are going to learn a few dances. These we call square dances."

Mr Pitts babbled on about how he would like us to dance at Assembly, and also when the school inspector came later in the year. We were to sing songs and do dances, just to show the inspector that we could do something.

Florry kept digging me in the ribs as Mr Pitts made himself comfortable sitting on the table, with his legs dangling. I thought to myself, if the nuns saw him sitting on the table like that! Would he get into trouble? When we cleaned the dining room, us girls would take a break and perch ourselves on the tables like that, with legs up and feet resting on the benches. If we were caught we'd get a flogging from the nuns. A table wasn't meant to be sat on, it was a place where people ate their food, and it wasn't ladylike for us to sit like a man, they said.

Mr Pitts' gruff voice broke my thoughts up.

"Very quietly now, I want you to pick your partners for the barn dance, which we are going to learn."

He turned his back on us. to get his violin ready, and we all excitedly ran for our best mates. I grabbed Florry's hand. Other girls grabbed their mates and the boys did the same. Teddy and Jimmy were partners as they came over and stood beside us giggling and messing around us.

Mr Pitts turned around, as we stood there smiling winyarn-way, holding hands with our mates. His face abruptly turned red and he slammed down his bow. We heard it hit the table and thought he had broken it.

"I said take your partners! For a dance! And that means boys with girls, like this—" He tore around the room, grabbing girls and distributing them. He shoved me by my shoulder over to Teddy and put our hands together. He continued on like that, putting girls with boys, till everyone had a partner. Choo, I never felt so ashamed in all my life.

This was the first time that we ever learnt to dance and hold hands with a boy. Talk about koondang. Mr Pitts played some quick music on the violin, and we just all stood there staring at him, not knowing what to do. I looked over at Thelma, standing there holding hands with Jimmy. Her face looked really stiff and embarrassed. I gave her a grin. Mr Pitts stopped playing.

"What is the matter with you lot? I have never met such a dumbstruck mob in all my life." He put the violin down. "Right, you boys, go to that side, and you girls come to this side. Make enough room, so you can skip down the middle."

We all formed a line, girls on one side, boys on the other, facing our partners.

"Now, when I start playing the violin, I want you, in pairs, to take your partner and skip down the middle, to the end of the line. boys to their side, girls to theirs. Clap your hands to the beat of the music. We will go through this routine a number of times until you have all had a turn, and until you all get used to it!

"Then on the following Friday we will learn another step, because I can see it's going to take me a long time to teach you lot anything that will stick in your thick brains."

He turned suddenly and walked over to my sister Sally.

"Now we will go on to one other step. Before I start playing, this is what I want you to do."

He grabbed her by the hand.

"Choo! Choo! Waadow" We all shouted. I could see Sally feeling shame as he walked her to the top of the line.

"Right, you get your partner by the hand like this. Sally, we are going to skip down the middle. All you other lot start clapping."

He looked so funny skipping that Sally was too shame, she just ran beside him and disappeared back to her spot. We all burst out laughing, thinking it was a great joke. Mr Pitts walked to the front and turned on us.

"Haven't I told you before about this silly attitude you all have? That word 'choo, choo!' That expression is driving me mad." He raised his hands in the air and his big blue eyes poked out. He looked funny. Some of us kids couldn't control our laughter and still had our hands covering our mouths.

"1 am warning you now, I am not going to warn you again. If I hear stupid sniggering and going on, I won't hesitate to thrash the living daylights out of you. Glenyse Spratt, Florry Jacks, you can wipe those silly grins off your faces. or I'll wipe them for you."

We clammed up, and he lifted himself on to the table in a sitting position, then swung himself around and stood on the table top, in his shoes and all.

"Right, I can see you all from here, so look out. He lifted the violin to his shoulder and was about to play when a voice sang out. "Ohhh waa!" We all looked around to see where it came from. Poppy was standing there with her hands over her mouth. By the look of things I think she didn't mean to sing out.

"Right. I want the person who sang out to come forward."

All our eyes were on Poppy as she went to the table with her head down and stood in front of Mr Pitts. Still standing on the table, he glared down at her.

"Poppy Turner, what's this 'ohhh waa' business?"

Poppy rubbed her foot on the floor.

"Put your head up when you are being spoken to."

She lifted her long face up and her black eyes shone out.

"You are not allowed to stand on the tables. Sister always hit us."

"Well, is that right, Poppy Turner? So she should hit you, you are an arrogant mob, cheeky and very rude. And another thing, Poppy Turner, what gives you the right to speak to a person in authority such as me? Do you know what authority means, Poppy Turner? Answer me!" We could all see sir was steaming, his face was red. "Nah," Poppy said in her shy way.

"Well let me get this through your thick skull. I am your teacher, and nobody, nobody, tells me what to do. If I want to stand on the table, I'll stand on the table, and I don't want a snotty-nosed brat telling me otherwise!"

With that outburst, he jumped down from the table and took the waddy in his hand. Everywhere he went he took that waddy with him. He grabbed Poppy by the shoulder, swung her around and gave her a few cuts across her legs.

"Any more outbursts from you, Poppy Turner, and look out. That goes for the lot of you." He climbed back on the table and dancing lessons continued in a state of gloom for the rest of the morning.

At night in the dormitory when the lights went out, we were all on Poppy's bed yarning about our teacher, which seemed to be the usual topic of late. Banner wanted to make herself more comfortable and leaned down hard on Poppy.

"Ow, Banner you hurting me." As Poppy pushed her off, Banner started laughing.

"Don't laugh, her legs are sore. She got belted from Mr Pitts today," I told her. Banner grabbed Poppy.

"Sorry sister, I didn't know about that. I didn't mean to laugh at you, you all right now?" Poppy pulled her legs over the other side of the bed so nobody would hurt her again.

"Never mind," Banner said, "me and you will be together next year because you'll be a working girl, and you won't have to worry about him any more."

WHEN THE FIGHTS STARTED

A couple of months went by, our group just biding time in our world of uselessness. One Monday morning Mr Pitts added more confusion to our minds. He ordered all the fair kids to pick up their books and stand out the front of the class, while the darker-skinned ones had to help clear one side of the class for the fair ones.

He explained that he could do so much for the fair ones and besides, they were a lot brainier, and he had already wasted enough time on the darker ones. He had no great labour picking anyone from our group, because we were all dark. Jimmy, Billy, Florry and I walked slowly backwards and forwards, helping the others like Sally and Poppy to shift their books over to the desks on our side of the room.

Again I had this horrible feeling in my stomach as I glanced up at the line of fair kids standing there waiting with their piles of books in their hands. Megsy gave me a superior look. She was a newcomer. I never liked her ever since she landed at the mission.

I could see that Sally, Billy and Jimmy were wild. They made out they accidentally dropped a book, and slammed down a desk lid. Even when everyone was seated, fair to one side, dark to the other, we couldn't relax. My mates had sad, wondering looks. Mr Pitts was explaining.

"This will be the seating arrangement till the end of the year."

The fair ones were sitting up like proud peacocks. That's when the fights started amongst us kids outside the school. Us dark ones wouldn't talk to the fair ones, because they walked around the place thinking they were king pins and better. At breakfast one morning I overheard Megsy giving my sister cheek across the dining room table.

"Pass me the spoon, darkie."

Her skin was real fair, just about white. I shouted from my position .

"Gurn, who do you think you are? You just as black as us, unna Poppy and Florry?"

"You think you white but you just a poor black thing like us," they sang out in support. Megsy stuck her nose in the air.

"Shut your mouth. Glenyse Spratt. you got no right to talk to me about being black, look at you, you're not black, you're purple!"

"Ohhh waa, did you hear that? Get up and punch her, Sprattie. I wouldn't let no-one talk to me like that," Poppy whispered.

"Nah, I'll wait till after breakfast and get her in the bathroom, I'll make her piss."

"Gurn, don't tell us you're frighten of her, Sprattie?"

Megsy leaned over the table with her lip pouting.

"I'd like to see you try and hit me, because see this fist?" She held up her clenched fist, "It'll punch your black mouth in and knock you silly."

By this time, with all the arguing going on around us from the other kids, I saw red and slid down my chair, stretched out my leg and gave Megsy a hefty kick in the shins.

"Ouch, you bitch!" She jumped out, picked up her fork and threw it. Everybody ducked as the fork bounced off my head and I cowered in pain. She had made me bleed and all the time of my growing up in that home, I never felt so bitter and angry.

I picked up a china cup full of sugar off the table and with all my strength threw it at her. The cup split her forehead open, blood spurted out and Megsy started screaming. Now the whole dining room was up in arms. I just went mad. I jumped up and rushed around the table to hurt her more.

The full force of Sr Ursula's open hand made me see stars. She slapped my face to bring me to my senses and pulled me away from Megsy, who was crying hysterically.

"You go and vait in zer dormitory, Glenysen Sprattsen." She took Megsy by the hand and led her away to the Dispensary, leaving a couple of big girls to keep order in the dining room. My sister Sally and all my mates followed to the dormitory.

I sat down on a bed before I fell down. I felt really sick in my stomach. That was the first time I got into a real fight. At the mission any fight was a big thing amongst the kids. It was so bad in the eyes of the nuns that we could expect to be punished severely. They crowded around and Sally put her arm over my shoulders.

"Thanks, sis, for taking it up for me. Next time it's my turn. Don't worry about Megsy, she be quiet enough now, serve her right." Someone else squeezed my hand.

"Good job, Sprattie, you give it to her."

"Baalay, look out, Sister coming!" someone shouted. Everyone scattered except me. Whatever punishment was to be bestowed, I was ready for it. I started feeling sorry for Megsy and said a silent prayer, thinking I might have killed her.

"Glenysen Sprattsen, you know what you have done?" Ursie started with her lecture. I wasn't feeling too hot now. "You nearly killed Megsy. Vhatever came over you, girl? You vere never a violent person." Her softly spoken voice shocked me. Usually Sister's lectures were rough and boisterous, especially in a situation like this, after a fight.

"Megsy tells me you have been calling her names."

"I heard her calling my sister darkie," I said.

"Vhat iss zhis language, girl, darkie, vhat iss zhis meaning?"

"It means, Sister, that Megsy called Sally darkie and she said I was purple," I blurted out.

"Vell, ve have never have zhis kind of language here in zer mission, vhat do you suppose Megsy meant by zhat?"

"She meant that we are black-skinned and she thinks she's white."

"Ah, I see!" Ursie exclaimed in surprise. "How did all zhis business start?"

"Well Mr Pitts told us in school that the fair ones were good and he can't do nothing for us black ones."

"Ach girl, zhis explains zer whole situation about zer unsteadiness of you children lately. All right, vait here while I call Megsy in." She was standing outside the door. Megsy walked in slowly with a big bandage around her head.

"Megsy Bruce, Glenysen Sprattsen has told me how zer fight started and I vant to hear from your own mouth vhat Mr Pitts told you all in zer classroom." When Megsy had finished, Sister made us both to kneel on the floor and say prayers asking God to forgive us for fighting. She made us promise not to fight again and gave us a parting lecture that we were all equal under God's care, nobody was different. Then we made up and said sorry.

"Zhis time girls, zhere iss no punishment for you, but don't let it happen again."

We were so relieved that tears spilled from our eyes and I could not stop crying. Especially when all my mates came to see what our punishment was. We sat on the seat in the bathroom just letting all the emotions out of our distraught bodies. They kept passing wet towels to us, to wipe our faces with. Pulling myself together, I managed to tell them what I had told Sister, and what she had said. Like us, they were very surprised that we weren't punished.

A month later Mr Pitts behaviour was still the same towards us. The only change was that the fair ones were mingled in again. And we noticed that the nuns' attitude towards us was changing to kindness and understanding, which was a big shock to us girls.

Excerpt from *True Country*

KIM SCOTT

HIGH DIVING

One hot afternoon Billy, Liz, the high school kids, they all went for a swim. They went to High Diving, which is just down there behind the mission grounds where the river widens into a big pool before it slides among the rocks and into the rapids of Running Creek. They had to walk past the community office, and past the old people gathered there, sitting in the shade; Fatima, Sebastian, some others. Jasmine came out of the office. She decided she was going too.

The group moved in two major clusters, divided according to sex. The girls grouped around Liz and Jasmine, with Jasmine the main focus because she was of greater novelty than the teacher.

They laughed, they shrieked, they studied her earrings and hair. They asked the two women about boyfriends, husbands. 'Mr Storey hit you ever? What he like when he drunk?' It was Friday. Jasmine said she was annoyed with the office, with working there, with the people, the laziness and the fighting. These kids wouldn't be like that when they were working there would they? Oh no, no.

The girls held their guests' hands and put their arms around their shoulders. They led them past puddles and over the rusting barbed wire fence behind the mission. 'See that, Miss?' They pointed to a metal-framed corridor leading to an opening in a tall corrugated iron wall which also served as part of the fence. It looked like a cattle run, but much narrower. 'That's where people, us mob, older ones but, used to get food, line up for food.'

The boys walked twenty metres ahead. They threw rocks at the coconuts as they went past them, then at the mango trees, at birds, into the river. They spoke of cars, ninjas, of whether Russia or America would win a war, of Arnold Schwarzenegger muscles. They quoted whole lines of dialogue from the videos the camp was watching this week, role-playing with their voices. For their first few months here all teachers understand them clearly when they repeat lines from videos in American accents, but are puzzled by the local English.

Imagine, again, seeing all this from above, as if you were flying slowly, just drifting, quiet, way above them. They are walking along, walking along on a narrow two-wheeled red dirt track. Long grass in the middle of the track and long grass around them stretching to the rocks of Running Creek as they walk past it. You are up high so you don't hear their voices too well, just some little shouts, and the wind sort of singing, and the clank clank of the old windmill there. You are invisible, you cast no shadow. Their clothes are just spots of colours in the vast green which gets drabber as you go higher and see the land away from the river. There is the blue of the river near them, the big green of mango trees and the plantation in the mission. The kids are mostly tight in around those teachers. Black skin looks good in the sun, shiny. Then, nearly at High Diving, the kids break away and start to race to the river. They shed clothes on the run. They dive. They spear the water. They disappear and surface among the reeds by the bank. They climb a tree, and jump. They swing out on the rope there, and drop. They dive. Silent splashes, blossoms of froth, circles in the water. There're white patterns, different colours in that tiny part of the river where they're jumping and making bubbles.

'Aren't they beautiful people? Look, such big smiles,' said Jasmine as she and Liz sat on the bank. 'The boys are so spunky, aren't they, really?'

'I'd say they're all nice looking.'

'And the babies. So cute! Really! So cute!' Jasmine clasped herself with the pleasure of their cuteness.

Billy climbed up the sloping trunk of the great tree which leaned over the river. It was wet and slippery where the kids had been climbing it. He'd watched them virtually walk up it before he'd decided to do so himself. But it was so slippery, and high. He felt a surge of panic. He was bent over like a chimpanzee, using hands and feet. He wished he had claws to grip with. If he slipped here he'd bash himself on the tree, and then on the bank because he wasn't yet out over the water. And the tree kept sloping up and out. The kids behind were getting impatient.

'Okay, I'm an old man, remember?' He forced a grin.

'C'mon Billy, move along.' Liz called out to him.

He managed the grin again. 'Hey, I'm frightened,' he attempted to joke. His joke was taken. He hadn't realised the tree would seem so high. Liz was already far below. When he was a child he'd always dreamt of flying, but hadn't known about heights. He'd experienced vertigo one day walking around some cliffs above the sea. From then his childhood dreams included the terror of heights, of falling from cliffs into the sea, falling falling falling; then entering the water without a disturbance, and going down and down past curious fish that watched him, and the bubbles leaving his mouth for the light, shrinking, above.

He grasped the tree trunk between his knees and continued shinning along it as if it were vertical. The tree moved with his weight as he got to the branches from where the kids leapt. There, Beatrice grinned at him, and, levering her weight with her knees, made the tree branch spring and sway. He grinned back at her, wished she wouldn't. He sat with his arm firmly around a smaller branch and dangled his feet. Kids pushed past him, rocked and leapt, their dark bodies plummeting and exploding as they hit the water, making a moment's dark opening in the centre of a circle of white spray and bubbles in the water. He smiled with Liz, kilometres below him.

Sliding off the branch, he suddenly became incredibly heavy, the water at his feet drawing him. There was an explosion as he hit the water, but he was still intact, himself, and lightened. Brown water around him, bubbles. He swam up elated.

As he surfaced his eyes met those of Francis. Or rather, his eyes met Franny's thick-lensed spectacles, which reflected the river water itself and in which Franny's eyes swam like dark fish. Billy smiled, Franny nodded. Franny very rarely swam. His health was poor because of some trouble when he was very young. Now he smiled back, and Billy duck-dived into the dark water.

'What are they like at school?' asked Jasmine, still smiling at the cuteness of the youngest children, who were also starting to arrive at the river and leap into the water.

'Well, they're way behind most kids in schools. Not all of them, the best are maybe a weak average for their age. But look at the place. Parents don't read, there's none of that back-up at home. Why maths? What's science? You know. Some things, generalising, they seem extra good at though. Special strengths. Maybe like telling stories, joking, sometimes miming. And visual literacy . . . I sometimes wonder what we're doing here.'

The older boys swam with the river's drift, and took Billy with them. The pool ended in a clump of pandanus and rocks and became rapids. They climbed out of the river just before the head of the rapids and walked across logs and rocks.

The boys explained to Billy that, by swimming hard, you could get across the rapids to a large tree which hung over the river about fifty metres along the other bank. They demonstrated. And were swept away laughing at one another, looking back at him as their heads bobbed in the sinewed, sharp-edged water. It seemed the tree and they leaned together, and they clasped it, each boy stretched from hand to foot with the torrent, and sometimes hand-in-hand with another boy. They climbed the tree gracefully, they flowed up it, and leapt into a still and deep pool in its lee. They duck-dived back into the current to the edge of the pool and somehow, underwater, swam against the river back to the base of the tree.

Billy watched for a time. He entered the river and struck out for the other side, stroking as if sprinting but going sideways. He got close to the other side, and lined up the tree. The river buffeted him, pulled him under its surface, tossed him up, came into his throat, and then the boys grabbed him as he came to the tree reaching up with his hand and his head going under again. Teasing him, their laughter bubbling with the river, they pulled him to them.

They showed him how to move against the current underwater.

In the strange and changing sepia light he clasped the reeds on the stony river floor and pulled himself along with them. The dull roar in his ears, the sharp slippery reeds in his hands, his body stretched by the same current which pressed his hair to his scalp. Quite alone for those moments, calm and moving against the current, beneath it.

Then rocketing up into the noise, white light, the laughing faces greeting his reappearance.

They played hide-and-seek in the river and reeds. Sylvester would duck-dive and disappear. Long minutes later, in a stiller part of the river, Billy would hear a voice calling him, but would not be able to find the speaker until, there, Sylvester parted the reeds and Billy saw just his nose and twinkling eyes above the surface of the river.

Billy followed Sylvester underwater. In the yellow river light Sylvester pointed to passages under trapped trees, and where you could surface for a breath and not be seen because of the twisted branches and reeds knotted together.

Billy, his lungs straining, followed Sylvester as they pulled themselves along the bottom of the river. He watched the pale soles of Sylvester's feet as they waved, flapped, glimmered before him.

'You know, Sir, they call me crocodile. I was a crocodile.'

Billy returned to the pool with some of the younger children who'd come down to the head of the rapids. He picked his way across the boulders to the other bank and took them back to the still water, but allowed the older girls to join the boys in the rapids. After experiencing the competence of those he'd just been with, he could hardly disbelieve the girls' assurances that they were capable swimmers.

Jasmine interrupted Liz. 'What about Milton's kids?'

'Oh, they're probably the cleverest, school-wise, for their age. They're only young though, yet.' Liz said.

'Yeah, Milton'd only be in his late twenties. Spunky, don't you think? And his wife, Annie? They both seem impressive. Well educated, they seem.'

'Relatively,' said Liz. 'They went to private schools. Perth, Darwin, Broome. Maybe it helps to be sent away, have your world opened up. Like Moses. Almost like, maybe it helps to be taken away from your family and that. Not like they used to do, but . . . this place is so tiny, so insular and isolated. To go away is an education, important, and if you know you're coming back and still loved . . . '

Billy swam gently to the bank to keep an eye on the youngest kids. In this heat he felt he could stay in the water forever. Tiny children, five and six years old, emulated the older ones by leaping from smaller trees. Billy swam with a younger child holding his shoulders, floating behind. Little Louella, standing on the bank, called to him. 'Me too?' He held out his hands, and she leapt into them. He let her into the water, chest deep to him, and she struggled and spluttered. Someone called out from way up in the tree, 'She can't swim, Sir, that one.' And Billy, tardily realising this, grabbed at her and lifted her into his arms again. He taught her to float on her back. Tiny children climbed up into his arms, stroked his cheek, feeling the stubble there. They drew their fingers through his hair, pulled at his earring, investigated him; the difference in smell and touch between him and their adults. The similarities. They did the same with Liz and Jasmine. They dived off Billy's shoulders into the water, and he picked them up and threw them into the air so that they landed in the water, splashing anykind.

The young children swam in knickers or shorts. The eldest boys in their jeans. The older girls swam fully clothed. Jasmine and Liz came in and swam in their bathers and the little children draped from them as they did from Billy. The kids noticed the women in their bathers. All that flesh. Like swimming in your undies, the older girls said. That's what those people do.

When they all left the teachers came along last, shepherding stragglers. Some of the older ones—Deslie, Jimmy, and others—helped collect up clothes the little children had left behind. They sniffed them, and knew to whom they belonged.

Five minutes' walk and up at the camp they were hot again. Dusty, the smell of cow shit; and the rubbish trapped against the wire fences, blowing across the land, spilling from the bins. Jasmine agreed to come over for a drink with Billy and Liz later in the day. And, perhaps, dinner also.

In the office later that afternoon, after Jasmine had returned to work, Samson came in and sat on her desk. 'We go swimming some time, eh? I take you to a waterfall I know. Beautiful. Everyone that see it want to take photo. You wear your bathers that you do, with your cheeky bum, eh?'

At High Diving the river beneath the tree is calm again. The tree is still wet. The water still flows toward the rapids, and leaves fall and drift away, and bubbles break the surface now and then. Bubbles from the mud, or turtles, or little crocodiles maybe.

Visitors in Great White Boats

Milton and Billy went fishing in Billy's dinghy. 'This way.' Milton's arm pointed across the smooth ocean toward some land, vague in the distance. He sat at the bow, his shape dark against the milky turquoise sea and the traces of mist which remained above it, as yet untouched by this day's breeze.

They skimmed across the ocean. The outboard's roar was left behind them, and the aluminium hull amplified the skip and tap of the sea. A lone dolphin flashed across their bow, dark and swift, and flew, once, for a blinking time only, clear of the water, splashing them, before looping away into its own blue silence.

Milton knew a place around the headland. He was returning there, to that place, the one quite close to the rocks and red beach, but where the water is very deep. The old people used to walk there. Milton and Billy motored slowly to and fro across it, dragging silver lures. Occasionally the lures broke the surface. Great fish sprang from the deep, and silver arcs flashed past the boat. Sometimes a lure was hit clear of the water.

The sudden singing of a line as it tautened. The queenfish Milton brought in; it shot into the air shaking itself to free the lure from its mouth. Milton kept the line taut. The line cut the water as the fish swam deep, and it burned in his hand. Billy had silenced the motor. A tension, a singing line. The fish leapt again, it seemed in slow motion, and hung in the air for a moment, a template held against the blue hues of sea and sky with a crowd of silver droplets fleeing it.

Milton hauled it in, and the gaff pierced its armour of scales. Red blood spurted over the floor of the dinghy, and over their bare feet as the big fish thrashed among the stiff corpses of its fellows. They cursed each fish with joy, and with a tiny whispering fear as they saw the sun fade in each great, glassy, dying eye.

There were little suns all around them. They bounced from the knife blade, the aluminium of the dinghy, the ocean's surface as the sea exhaled. Little suns sparkling thorns. The sea breeze began.

Returning around the headland they saw the catamaran which brought the rich tourists. It was moored out from where they'd left the car. They circled it in the dinghy, not having seen it up close before. The few staff remaining on board came out and called down to them as they tossed around in the echo of their motor and the chop bouncing off the large hull.

Someone invited them aboard, so they tied the dinghy to the catamaran and were led through small upholstered rooms, treading the carpets in their blood-caked feet. They sat at the bar with the crew and shared a beer with them, and spoke in embarrassed belches. It was small and muffled after being in the spread of the sea, under the roofless sky, in their tiny resonating dinghy, yet they spoke beneath those low ceilings as if across a great distance. The tourists and some of the crew had gone into the village to have a look. There was a corroboree tonight, for the tourists. Milton had forgotten, Billy hadn't heard.

It's a good idea, that crew said, having the bus take the tourists into the settlement itself. Must be rough on the bus though.

They took the dinghy ashore, waving their thanks to the crew gathered at the top of the ladder. The catamaran looked more impressive from the shore with its white paint sparkling as it slowly turned on its mooring, its shape and size so novel along this coast. It looked so out of place, so pristine, and so, well, advanced that it could have been a spaceship.

Half-way back to the camp they came across the bus. The chassis at the rear rested on the ground, and the vehicle sat at an uncomfortable angle. It had become bogged, and Raphael, revving the motor and spinning the wheels, had broken the rear axle. The tourists sat huddled under the trees, like exotic and very ripe fruit, unable to survive the heat and about to suddenly decompose into this foreign soil. Only fading pastel clothing, a sandal or two, and their rusting cameras would remain to show they ever existed here. Their hands waved the flies away from their flushed faces, and their breathing was rapid and light.

Some of the tourists accepted Billy's offer and crammed themselves into the back of his vehicle and under the dinghy which, roped to a high rack level with the top of the cab, provided some shifting shade. Billy drove as carefully as he could, suddenly mindful of the frailty of the pale people behind him. The hot metal stung their thin skin, their soft flesh bruised, their eyes wept with the wind and dust. It seemed their brittle bones would break, their very skeletons fall apart within them as the Toyota lurched along.

Usually Billy and Milton distributed their catch as they came back among the houses. As they drove back through the camp Milton would tell Billy where to stop, and to whom they should give fish. It made them feel strong and generous. 'Proper hunters, eh?' one or the other of them would say.

They did the same today, otherwise the fish would be wasted. But they did it hurriedly, because of their cargo of frail humanity, but also because that cargo revived itself. They remembered they were paying passengers, and they transformed themselves from cargo to consumers. They cooed at the babies, wrinkled their noses at the smells, stared into the grimy gloom within doorways and shook their heads at the rubbish and the signs of neglect. Their cameras whirred clicked flashed in accompaniment. Such black skins, such bright sun; this would mean problems with film exposure for sure. The people receiving fish kept their heads bowed, and showed no pleasure in the gifts. They mumbled and turned away. The tourists wanted to be friendly, and shouted at them, apparently hoping that they could communicate with the aliens by doing so.

So everyone was pleased when they saw Jasmine. A white girl. A young white girl. Oh, all alone here. How does she do it? And Milton, awkward and grinning, gave a large fish to Jasmine. She was just outside her place. But he saw her standing, blank faced, with the heavy fish in her arms and changed his mind.

'I'll fillet it, clean it, bring it back to you.' The passengers, standing on the tray, looking down on Milton and Jasmine, nodded approvingly among themselves. Milton leapt back into the cab and, even from the driver's side, Billy felt himself wrapped in the curves of Jasmine's smile and cleavage as she leaned in the passenger window. She gave Milton a quick kiss on the cheek. 'For the audience,' she winked.

The tourists disembarked, slowly and stiffly, at the community office. They felt better now, having reasserted themselves. 'What an experience.'

Gerrard organised vehicles to ferry the others in and tried to arrange to get the bus fixed, somehow. He opened the artefacts store and invited the tourists to look through what was there. 'Feel free to have a look around,' he said, and some of the tourists continued to circle within the small store. The rest of them moved to just outside the doorway, and stood there, turning their heads from side to side, squinting and grinning. Then they headed for the community store which stood on the fringe of the housing and by one of the school's gates. One person detoured toward the stone buildings and green lawns of the mission grounds, and a couple walked over to the school and peered in the windows of a classroom, before Alex, putting in some more weekend work, and always guarding his territory, came out to investigate them.

The corroboree that night, the first held for tourists at the camp rather than one of the beaches, was not a success. Too many of the men were late getting back from helping Raphael with the bus, and his bad mood had tainted them all. Samson didn't turn up. It was a half-hearted affair, which didn't start until after dark, and even then the fires did not glow, but weakly flickered and sputtered because they were lit too late and no one cared to stoke them. The performance finished early. Many reasons.

Gerrard said afterward that he wasn't going to pay them, but he did when Samson started talking about the people getting together and sacking him. He was not a project officer's arsehole. They didn't want the bloody tourists here anyway.

Perhaps the tourists enjoyed the argument more than the dance.

Milton came over to visit Billy later in the evening. Billy had kept out of the way, not wanting to be asked to transport tourists back out to their catamaran. He was filleting fish, and putting them into small freezer bags when Milton arrived.

They filleted and packed the remaining fish together. It was a plan they had worked out this morning. Like most people in the camp Milton didn't have a refrigerator, let alone a freezer. Now he could come over during the week and get tucker for just him and his family. They kept the packs stacked separately.

When they had finished they sat under the air-conditioner in the lounge room and drank tea. Milton looked around the room and admired the house again. 'Maybe I'll get one like this next time, one of these new ones,' he said.

Billy looked at him across his cup. 'Who? How do you decide who gets the new ones?' he asked.

Milton shrugged. 'It just happens. We all talk about it. Chairman, them on the council, their mob first.'

He picked up an old newspaper from under the chair and found the motoring section of the classified advertisements. 'I want a Toyota like your one, strong one. My father can have my little old one then.' He pointed at the small photographs. Billy read out the advertisements and prices, and they speculated on whether it was best to go all the way to Perth or Darwin and drive one back. Billy calculated how much Milton would need to save from each pay, and for how long. The result was depressing, so they ignored it.

'I could leave it here, with you, in your yard then, maybe, when I wasn't using it? Hey, I can leave my car here now, when I want to?'

'Sure Milton, but why would you want to do that?'

'All right for you, you haven't got everyone, like family, cousin-brothers, everybody, using your stuff all the time. I need a box with a lock to keep everything in.

'Then I could maybe get rich, go on holidays like these tourists that come here, if I wanted to. But I wouldn't expect the people, where I went, to put on shows for me like in a zoo or something. And I wouldn't complain to their boss and say I won't pay, for seein' nothin' but a lot of old men and kids kickin' dust and drunk men yelling.'

But many times the tourists come to the camp here, to look at the real Aborigine people. Them tourists from the *Kimberley Cruiser* boat, but them terrorists (tourists, yes?) always here in the dry time with their shiny four-wheel drives.

That *Kimberley Cruiser* is one big boat. Carpet all through it, little swimming pool on it, little pub there. Everybody has their own room, for himself and his wife or husband. Them people proper old but, most of them. Moses been on that boat. He went with Gerrard one time to have a look. He told us about it. Gerrard took a trip from here to Wyndham, or Darwin. He told us how food is cooked for you and is like on videos. He had a good time, and it cost him nothing. It was free for him. This last year that boat started coming in here for us to dance for them, because Karnama has the best dancers. Or pretty close to best anyway.

Most times we all go out to the beach and dance at about sunset. Fire dance. We have a fish, get oysters, maybe camp out. But sometimes now we get Gerrard's bus and we bring them in here, if they come early in the day.

They drive in and their heads all turn around and around and they wave back like they are toys. They get off the bus slowly, because they all so old. They look mostly the same. White, big hats, clothes so clean. Pink spots, little pink bits around their nails and eyes. And they all smell sweet like soap, and powder. People here thought they came in to see the river, and they didn't know why they just stayed around our store, and kept taking photographs. One man might take a photo of his old wife holding up one of our kids. Or a photo of her standing in the shop with all us mob, buying things. They think we monkeys maybe. Or sitting on the ground outside, in the shade, with us. We laughed when their clothes got dirty but.

Some of the people here say we should stop letting tourists in. They just treat us as we in a zoo, or something. Even government ones, not all of them. Talk to us like they can't talk proper English.

Those boat people, we can laugh at them, even though we get sick of their cameras. We can get away from them. But the tourists that drive in, ha! You go to a beach and you can't be alone with your own. We tell you, it's not so good if there's strangers on the beach with you. One mob stole an outboard from a big boat the government gave us. That was the only outboard we had then. They take all our oysters. Sometimes they make more rubbish than us, and some of our mob bad enough, for sure. They shit everywhere. You go to some of the beaches and there be toilet paper everywhere through the bush behind the beach.

People everywhere in dry time. If you stay at the office, the basketball court you can see them coming in. School holidays time especially. One, two, three, more. Dust with them, but sun still shining off them. Stuff packed everywhere; on top, on trailers, crammed against windows. And they look look look. Stop outside the shop, come in and stand around with us.

We can make money from them. Gerrard says that, lots of people say that to us. What for? What we want their money for? What can they give us for what we have? More grog? More card games? We must be mad bastards. That's what some other people think. Father Pujol's time, no tourists here.

Not even museum people come in then. Plenty now. And too many people want to go with them, show them things. Drive around in a big four-wheel drive, just like tourists themselves. They say they will help us to look after our sites, and guard the old things. But, how come?

In the old days we did look after our sacred sites ourselves, without letting white people, white men, women, take care of them. We know what to do. These others shouldn't interfere with our sacred things. Kiddies of ours, young men even, they not allowed to go near our sacred sites, trees even, that was anywhere in the bush. We didn't let them know because they wasn't men. They had to be initiated before they could go to these things and they sacred to us. They are very sacred things. We didn't say nothing to nobody, we just look after these things ourselves. That's why we don't like white women or white men coming to ask different things about our things, or saying we should do this, and why don't we . . . That's our sacred things. What they want them for, too. It's not right for so many people to show them things. And what are we? They studying us too? Like animals? Or maybe they want to steal our secrets, and when even the black man has lost his special things and his magic, then—hey, here it is!—the whitefellas have it and they use it on us.

Maybe we will have to change. Maybe make more things sacred, not just places, and keep them just for us. But then, we already sell some things to tourists.

Maybe we make a little building like a church, ourselves.

You know, you can't act the fool with our Law. It'll kill you. True. Like when a young man, uninitiated man, eats food that he shouldn't. Maybe he eats bush turkey. Well, you see. He get feathers and bones growing out of his knees. I hear one man got cancer from showing and working on sacred sites that were too powerful for him. That might happen you know.

But it is maybe true we have had tourists for a long time. Old Dr Oliver, he been coming up here every year since he was a young fella. He stays with Fatima, in her hut, on the little verandah there. He brings up a big Toyota and takes her and some of the other old people out to show him things. He takes photos and videos of old camps, and ovens. Indonesian ones. So those Indonesians, they tourists too, long time ago. White people also. But they stay.

There's another story, very good story, about early days and tourists, about this place. It was somewhere about Long Reef, somewhere about there. This bloke, Indonesian bloke, came in with a lugger, and he saw this girl. Young girl, and pretty. He made love with her, and he tell her, 'Come on, we can go on this lugger. We'll take you.'

But the girl wanted her husband too. Silly girl, she did jump on the lugger, with her husband. Her husband Walanguh, or the one who father for Walanguh, I forget. Walanguh told this story.

They sailing sailing sailing. This white bloke told him, told the husband, this Aborigine man, 'Climb up there and take rope to tie it with.' The Aborigine man climbed up to the top of the sails on the rope.

And this man cut that rope! This white bloke cut that rope. And he fell, that Walanguh one, he fell into the sea. They left him, swimming, swimming right out there in the ocean.

But this Aborigine man, he's a magic man and he was swimming across and he sing for that whale. He sing song for that whale, and that whale was way out swimming in deepest ocean. The whale went in close to the man, and the man get on top of his back next to his head.

He sat there above the water, in the sun and the spray, and he patted the whale, and he told him, 'We go for that lugger and we smash that lugger!'

The whale swam fast with that Walanguh man up on its back. They went straight for that lugger, and smashed it. Smashed it to pieces!

The man got his Aborigine girl, put her on the whale, and away they went to their home, to their island. When they got to that special island the whale came into the shallow water. They gave it fish, all kinds of fish. They patted him, and they let it go.

And this is a true story this one, this is a true story again. This mob here can tell you. Same words again.

And where is that island? You thinking that, eh? You want to know? But it might not be there, where it was, that land. Maybe just bones, nothing.

Listen, we tell no lies to you. Not ever. But we could help you there, maybe.

PART EIGHT

Encounters with the Law

Rea, detail 1 of 6 from *Definitions of Difference,* 1994, installation, 100 x 60 cm. Courtesy of Boomalli Aboriginal Artists Cooperative, Sydney, New South Wales, and the artist.

John Pat

JACK DAVIS

John Pat was a 16-year-old Aboriginal boy
who died of head injuries alleged to have been
caused in a disturbance between police and
Aborigines in Roebourne, Western Australia, in
1983. Four police were charged with manslaughter
over the incident. They were acquitted.

Write of life
the pious said
forget the past
the past is dead.
But all I
see in front of me
is a concrete floor
a cell door
and John Pat.

Agh! tear out the page
forget his age
thin skull they cried
that's why he died!
But I can't forget
the silhouette
of a concrete floor
a cell door
and John Pat.

The end product
of Guddia law
is a viaduct
for fang and claw,
and a place to dwell
like Roebourne's hell
of a concrete floor

a cell door
and John Pat.

He's there—where?
there in their minds now
deep within,
there to prance
a sidelong glance
a silly grin
to remind them all
of a Guddia wall
a concrete floor
a cell door
and John Pat.

Escape!

GRAEME DIXON

Spiteful rifle spits
slices through still night
Fragile life flickers
dying beneath searchlight
Faceless, uniformed figure
caresses hot, faithful toy
Warm blood gushes
shattered skull, tender boy.

Institutionalised keepers
blood lusted by the kill
gaze upon the carcass
Overwhelming power thrills!
Nobody mentions
victims a hungry thief
fallen from life's tree
like browned autumn leaf.

World eternally spinning
nothing breaks this move
Deafening silence returning
prison's eerie gloom
Bloody razor-wire glistens
beneath silvery moon
Night, quietly mourning
life escaped too soon.

Excerpt from *When the Pelican Laughed*

Alice Nannup with Lauren Marsh and Stephen Kinnane

Radio Theatre: Geraldton, 1950

I used to take my kids every Saturday afternoon to the matinee in town. We'd all go in, sit down and try to enjoy ourselves, but there were a few white kids in town who were really terrible. They'd turn around and poke their tongues out, or sling off at us with 'Nigger, Nigger, pull the trigger—BANG BANG you're dead.'

On this particular day a Tom Mix picture was on. Tom Mix was a cowboy, and he'd be going 'bang, bang' too, you see, so those kids would just turn it on to us.

There was one boy, and he was the main one. On this day he had chewing gum and he went and stuck it on my son's seat while he was out of the room. I didn't see him do it, of course, and I was that cross because these were brand new melange pants. They were the only pair in Wright's and because they were a bit damaged, shop soiled it was, they let me have them cheap.

The kid that did it thought it was a great joke. I said to my daughter, 'I've had enough of this Pearl. You tell me when the picture is nearly over.'

'Why, what are you going to do?' she asked.

'I'll show you what I'm going to do. You just tell me.'

'Well, it's just about finished now, Mum.'

Right, I thought, and I got up with my baby and I walked outside.

Out in the foyer, near the place where you buy the tickets, there was a rail running right to the other end of the room. There was a break in the rail where the audience goes in, so I went and stood there with my little bloke on my hip.

Before long they all started coming out, but I was blocking the way see, so some of the little kids started slipping under the rail. I was holding on to one baby, and I had another one of my kids at my feet clutching my dress, when I put up my hand. 'Just a minute, I've got something to say—and I want you all to listen.'

Everyone just stood there and looked at me, and there were quite a few of them too; the foyer was full.

'Look,' I said, 'I've been coming here every Saturday afternoon, bringing my children to enjoy the matinee, just like you people, and what do we get? Nigger, nigger, boong, boong, pull the trigger, this, that, and the other. Well I've had it. I want you people to try and understand how that feels. Why don't you bring your children up, don't drag them up—it's a disgrace!'

Well, they were all standing there, not saying anything. They were shocked, I suppose, that the likes of me could get up there and dress them down.

'You know,' I said, 'it's not fair. We're all the same, we're all human beings; we walk, we talk, we eat the same kind of food, we are all just made the same, Colour is skin deep and I think we should all be treated as human beings.'

Pearl was standing next to me and I said to them, 'I'll send my daughter next door to the tearooms to get two saucers. Then whoever of you is willing to come up here can be blindfolded. I'll take blood from me and from you, swirl it around in the saucers . . . then you come and tell me which is your blood.'

While I was saying all this two policemen came in, broke past and went and stood in front of me. I saw them there but I kept on telling them. I said, 'When we come into this theatre we don't throw off at you people, yet we're called everything. I'll tell you another thing too, there were three of your goody-goody boys across the road the other day and an old lady came out of the butcher's shop. She had two bags of groceries and every time she went to step off the kerb a car would come, and she'd have to step back. Well, those goody-goodies would laugh their heads off. That's shame,' I told them. 'But my son was with me, this "boong kid," and he walked across the road and carried that old lady's parcels home for her. That's what a "boong boy" does. And why? Because I brought him up to respect other people, not like you people. You're dragging your children up.'

They were all quiet, all just looking at me. The police were looking too and I tried not to look at them. But you should have seen these police, grinning from ear to ear, and one of those policeman didn't like Aborigines much either.

Then I said, 'I'll be back next week, don't worry about that. And I want to be treated as such, no names called, because we want to enjoy the matinee as well, Furthermore, before I go, if any of you can defend yourselves, come out here and tell me if I'm wrong. You come out here and tell me.'

But they didn't tell me, they just stood there.

'Right,' I said, 'you haven't got anything to say. You can go.' And I just stepped aside.

One Hot Night

ARCHIE WELLER

The train smashes away the hot, still, trembling body of the night and leaves it crumpled upon the hard rocks beside the sleepers. Black and bloody and flecked with light from the dying sun and the prosperous shops or the comfortable middle-class houses or the rushing vehicles on the highway or the arrogant street lights that guard the highway. The train charges noisily onwards, high up on its embankment. It will never reach the stars, but it is too proud for the common, crowded highways. It floats on a lonely uniform course between reality and dreams.

The train rattles and rocks in rhythm to its music. Inside its throbbing belly the black boy who huddles in the very corner is rocked too.

When he got on at Guildford, the three sailors with their painted giggling girl and the old, faded, white couple in their faded best eyed him furtively and coldly.

Just a skinny, scrawny part-Aboriginal boy, with a ragged mop of tangled blue-black hair on top of his hatchet face and a black beard and moustache surrounding it and his thin lips. He holds up his head in pride. His royal black eyes flick scornfully around the carriage for a brief second before he drifts up to the other end and throws himself into the corner to stare out of the window, ignoring the world.

He had a fight with his woman and punched her to the ground. She stared up at him reproachfully with her large sad eyes. Faces going red and orange, then black again in the flickering firelight. People stood silent. Blood ran out of his woman's mouth.

'Don't go to town, Elgin. Ya know the munadj's on the lookout for ya. Specially that big Fathers. Ya wanna go back to jail or what? Ya don't even think of me, unna? I may as well be dead, as much as you care, any rate.'

'Block up, Maydene. I'll do what I wanna do, see? I'm me own boss now.'

'I was better off when you was inside!' the girl cried and he backhanded her across the face and kicked her in the stomach so she gave a queer half-cry.

He knelt down beside her in remorse, and stroked her long black hair back from her bruised face before leaving abruptly. He went away from the communal campfire that held the ever-present circle of shadowy forms close to its warmth or comfort.

People get on the train. People get off. All white. They stare at the dark, sullen youth gazing out the window.

The sailors' girl leaves. Her high-heeled shoes clicketty-clack off the platform, then she is swallowed up by the lips of the stealthy night. The Nyoongah's eyes devour her plump white body then, from the corner of his eyes, he spots the three sailors glaring at him. He smiles at them, an evil smile. Spits out the window.

The Indian ticket collector bustles along the corridor. He stares through the youth with arrogant eyes, as if no one is there. He takes the youth's money, though.

Perth station.

Full of noise and colour and dancing lights. Shouting people and shunting trains.

Early yet.

He hunches into his clothes and shuffles outside. He rolls a smoke while the cars roar and rumble around him and people pass him by So alone in the crowded city.

Over on the other side of the river, the flats stand high and alert, like a tribe of advancing warriors. Lights flicker from balconies and rest on the serene back of the river. Soft music from record players, radios or guitars drifts around the dark shore like a lazily swooping seagull.

Tonight is a night for romance.

Little Caesar Jackell struts importantly down the cool white footpaths. He flits in and out of the shadows like a busy black hummingbird searching for honey.

He disappears.

Silent as a thought, he creeps between the trees and bushes of the garden. Only the whites of his eyes are seen in this world that he knows all too well, if only through the stories of his brothers and cousins.

No one is home.

No dogs.

Big house means big money.

He slinks around to the back and tries a window. Locked. He notices a small louvred window high up on the wall, big enough for him to crawl through.

Quickly and quietly, he drags a box over to the window. He pecks out the glass louvres one by one with agile fingers, like a black crow ripping out the eye of affluence, as it squats, powerless, in its green garden. Then he scurries through the hole he has made, to feed off the living juicy insides.

First he pulls out a packet of smokes from his coat pocket and lights one up to calm his nerves. This is only the second house he has ever broken into, and the first time he has done it alone.

Wait till his eyes become accustomed to the dark, then slip quietly through the house.

He comes to the bedroom. A photograph of an earnest young man glares out at the cheeky thief from among various bottles of perfume on the dressing table.

It can do nothing to him.

He flattens down his bushy hair with a brush and pulls faces in the mirror. Then he sets to work.

He finds a small locked metal cashbox with a lucky-sounding jangle inside it, various rings and necklaces in another box and a watch that takes his fancy. In the kitchen, he takes two bottles of beer and a flagon of riesling from the fridge. In another room, he finds more cigarettes, three cigars, and a $10 note. He shoves the biggest cigar into his mouth and grins into another mirror.

On top of a cupboard. his searching fingers feel a hard, cold object.

It is a rifle. A telescopic .303. He searches the drawers of the cupboard until he finds four packets of bullets. This truly is a prize.

He shoves all his loot into a bag he finds, and lowers it out the window. Then the .303, then himself.

Same stars, same people, same lights.

He goes.

Keeps to the back ways as much as he can. No one sees him—or would care if they did.

He reaches the riverside and lights up another cigar. He decides to dump the bag and .303 and come back for them later.

'Takes me, unna?' he brags to the waves that gently slap-lap-lap against the shore. 'Pooooh! Ya one solid man, Caesar Jackell.'

Takes one of the bottles of beer from the bag and wrenches off the top with his white teeth. He pours his cold, golden triumph down his throat. Starlight and city light glint off the bottle. No one is at his celebration party. Only the waves, and the floating rubbish and a few drifting ghostly gulls.

Across the water, the city beckons with crooked fingers and winks from tempting eyes. The buildings dance the dance of the night people, the street people, the nobody people.

His people.

Caesar finishes off the bottle and tries to open the cashbox.

He curses and swears and rips his knuckle open before he smashes the lock with a rock.

Open it eagerly.

Shells.

'Shit'

Hurl the useless box away, spewing beautifully patterned shells into the air.

He still has the $10.

Drinks the other bottle of beer. Slowly. He relishes the bitterness, and remembers he has robbed a whole house—a big, rich house—all on his own. Last time he was scared as he squatted under a tree chain-smoking, with his eyes darting about nervously, keeping watch for the others. Now he has proven he is as good as they. No, better, because he has a .303 and bullets.

He is drunk now.

Pats the barrel then aims it at the curious gulls.

'Bang, bang,' he mutters softly and smiles.

He hides the gun and bag, then stumbles away.

He staggers across the bridge and along the freeway, a small insignificant, drunken moth going to boast and be a big spender for at least one night in his miserable life.

The people pour onto the footpath in a noisy flow. They whirl and eddy, and cling to the sides of cars or heroes in bobbing groups. Inside is a comforting blast of music and synthetic gunfire as the youths become pretend cowboys or soldiers or gangsters or racing-car drivers; all fantasies that are so real for them. Then they squeeze out the door, to become black boys gazed upon in contempt or fear or black girls sitting on the seats, giggling and shouting, eyed over by the white man.

Big Murry James leans into the darkest doorway across the street from Crystal Palace, watching all the Kings and Queens and Princes and Princesses amble in and out.

He is the Court Jester.

He was fostered by a white family and lived with them for fourteen years. Last month, the murmurings of his people stirred in his heart and he wandered home again to Lockridge camp.

Very black, with large round eyes—and a deep voice. A small squashed nose and a low forehead. He hardly ever talks, for it takes a long time for him to work things out. He leaves the thinking to his cleverer cousins and friends while he just gets on with living.

Despite his huge size, he is gentle and kind.

Puff on a cigarette, and dream about the girl he would like to take to bed. The other boys shout and yell their love across the rooftops and drag names from dirty lip to dirty lip, sweetened by knowledgeable laughter. Then they will swoop in and rip a girl off the footpath like an owl pouncing on a squeaking, cowering mouse.

Not Murry. His woman is like a drink kept secure in a bottle so no one but he can partake of her. Her name slides down his throat and warms him whenever he thinks of her.

He sees her now, lost in a crowd of grinning girls gathered around two blonde-haired brothers who came out of Riverbank last week.

Saunter across.

'G'day. Lynette.'

'Look 'oo's 'ere' What ya doin'?' she shrieks.

Small and young with a beautiful body, a permanent grin and sparkling dark eyes that have not yet been dulled by brutal sex. She is only fourteen and still a virgin. He is sixteen and shy and not yet used to this dark world that laps around the marble pedestal he has stood upon for so long.

'Nuthin'. Wanna Coke?'

'Get away!' she cries, grinning at him. Then her grin fades to a half-smile. as she looks deeper into him.

'Orright then, if ya like,' she replies.

She understands. She always did from the first, when she caught him staring at her silently across the campfire the first week he drifted in.

He is tall and strong and handsome—in an ugly sort of way. He is quiet and gentle and kind. When he does make love to her, he will not be cruel.

They walk down the street to a coffee lounge.

'Lets go to Beaufort Park, Murry.'

'No. Ole Billy 'Owes died other day. The place is packed with 'Oweses now.'

'Elgin Broppo oughta look out, then. 'Im an' Mantan 'Owes 'ad one big fight, unna?'

'Yeah.'

'Ya got any boya, Murry?'

'Yeah.'

He is proud of the job he has at the panel beater's. He grins down at Lynette then away again at the staring, glaring lights all around him. They rip into his love like fruit fly boring into a delicate, delicious fruit. Get away from the harsh forest of lights. Go to the sea of darkness and shadows and softness and bushes down at Supreme Court Gardens.

'Stick around me, Lynette, an' we'll 'ave a good time.'

'Orright.'

They grin in unison and she moves a little closer to him.

Elgin Broppo slinks into a darkened, rutted lane way near the Beaufort Hotel and peers around the corner at the crowded park. Obscure figures flutter from one circle to another. Furtive mumblings and occasional yells of recognition. The Howeses drink to the death of old Billy.

An ebony trio is squeezed from the park and ambles across the street towards Elgin. He tenses, ready to run, then notices his cousin Jimmy Olsen.

Grins and soft punches as the cousins meet.

'Hey, Elgin, brother. Doan' 'ang round 'ere, budda. Manny 'Owes is drunk as all buggeries.'

'Shootin' off 'ow ya fought 'im dirty, like.'

'Go an' get 'im, Elgin.'

'Doan' talk silly, Larry. Mantan 'ud kill 'im with 'is own mob,' Jimmy growls.

Elgin's sombre eyes gaze thoughtfully over the park. He lifts his lips a little in a suggestion of a smile.

'Another night, yeah.'

'Let's buy a drink. you fellahs.'

'Oo's got the boya?'

'Jimmy busted into a shop, unna? Ya still got monies?'

They troop over to the bottle shop leering out at the dark parked cars.

The proprietor eyes them in an unfriendly way because last night there had been a big brawl in the front bar where the Aborigines drank. But money's money, so he sells them a flagon of Brandevino and half a carton of cans.

Fade away behind the toilets, in the grubby, scuffed sea of dirt. Broken bottles blink their last as they drown in the sea.

The youths drown, too.

Caesar Jackell stumbles into the light-blasted circle outside Crystal Palace. His stage light. His big performance.

'Hey, Donny, I got a gun, ya know.'

'Yeah, an' I got a million dollars.'

'No. True's God. I got a real gun. Bushted thish 'ouse. Easy as pissin', it wash.'

'Look 'ere! Caesar drunk, or what?' a girl shouts happily.

'Yeah, 'e's drunk. Finished.'

'Caesar drunk!'

They gather around him, gabbling and grinning. All blurs and noise. Caesar clutches hold of Donny's sleeve.

'I got a fuckin' gun—and bullets.'

'I'll give ya gun right up ya bony 'ole d'rectly, if ya don't bugger off.'

'I got ten dollars, too, if ya wanna know. I'm fuckin' rich, me.'

They gather closer. Caesar smiles around the group, then swaggers into the poolroom. He nearly trips over his feet and is saved from the disgrace of falling on his face by two girls grabbing him. Everyone howls louder than ever at the joke.

Caesar dances over to the counter. Everyone of importance gathers around, and he is a hero to the drifting night people.

Slaps the $10 note on the counter.

'Fill 'er up, buddy,' he grins.

'Gimme a lend of a dollar, Caesar.'

'Caesar, give me a few bob, please. Go on Caesar, baby.'

'I'm ya people, Caesar.'

Five dollars go.

'I'm keepin' the rest,' he says.

Staggers over to a pinball machine, which blinks at him with the knowledge of an old friend. The people disperse and only two bony, scraggly-haired girls hang around him in the hope of more handouts. He becomes lost in the world of bright lights and bouncing balls and flashing numbers. The only world he wants to know.

Murry and Lynette huddle on the corner with all the white people. They sip their Coke silently.

'Let's go down to Supreme Court Gardens, Lynette.'

She is thoughtful for a moment. Looks up at simple Murry's kind face.

'Yeah, orright.'

They cross over, rubbing against each other in the crowd.

Up the street, with busy people and screeching buses and windows full of white man things.

The gates: and beyond the gates is sweet obscurity that swallows them up.

The Gardens are quiet and cool. The young couple go down past the Court House and through the trees onto the lawn.

No one is there.

They lie under a spreading tree and let the silence and peace blanket them. They finish off their Coke, talking in whispers.

Murry forms the words in his mind and repeats them over and over before rising up above her. She stares up and the whites of her eyes glint in the city light.

'Lynette . . . Lynette, ya wanna be my woman?'

'Get away, ya silly bugger.'

'No. Ya know I'm mardong for ya, unna? I just gotta tell ya, that's all.'

She grins uneasily, yet knows that she *does* love him.

Soon, one day, a boy will grab her and suck what he wants from her, then toss her away. She would rather it was this boy than any other.

Murry's large clumsy hands encircle her and she gives an involuntary yelp before his face buries into her own and his lips devour her untainted ones. She struggles for a moment before relaxing. She is fearful of the unknown, yet happy in the comfort that will be her new life.

He peels her jeans down while his heavy fingers fumble around her body. Warm brown skin touches warm brown skin, and a unison of young, gentle, love is born.

The buildings, like stern priests, gaze down. The moon runs in naked freedom across her field, while the stars, clustered like daisies, wait to be put in a chain around her head.

The night—the hot, dusty night—presses down upon the city. Its misshapen head peers over the mountains of tall buildings while its grotesque fingers feel along the streets.

People go home.

Aboriginal children linger in large pulsating groups, sucking as much fun from the night as they can.

Elgin wanders up from Beaufort Park with his cousin Jimmy Olsen. Both are half-drunk and happy.

Caesar Jackell slumps in a dingy doorway, feeling sick. Drags listlessly on a cigarette.

Money all gone. Friends all gone. He is just like everyone else now. Waiting for the police to come and send him on his way.

'Give us a cigarette,' Elgin mutters and sits beside his little cousin. He grins up at slim, watchful Jimmy.

'What ya reckon, J.O.? Our main man is pissed as a parrot, yeah.'

Ruffles the boy's wiry hair. Caesar turns bleary, dull eyes on Elgin, his hero.

He remembers, and clutches at the straw that is going to save him from drowning.

'I got a gun, Elgin,' he mumbles as he extracts the crumpled cigarettes.

Elgin and Jimmy grin as each takes a cigarette.

'Yeah, I got a gun too. Right 'ere, unna. Big shotgun.' Elgin grins and jabs a finger at his groin.

The older boys laugh.

Caesar sits dazed.

'No, I *'ave* got a gun, ya know. An' jewels, I even got a watch.'

No one listens to him. Jimmy Olsen squints down the street.

''Ere come them 'Owes, budda. Time we was movin'.'

Half-drunk Elgin stares away, with his quiet eyes in some far-off thought of his own.

'You c'n go, Jimmy. I'll wait 'ere. Go later, yeah.'

'Doan' you get in no fight, Elgin, that's all I ask or else ya 'istory. None of our people around tonight, ya know, 'cept Murry—an' 'e's gone somewhere—an' this silly little prick.'

'Yeah. Well, see ya, J.O. See ya t'morrow, then.'

'Yeah.'

Jimmy disappears.

Just Caesar and Elgin and the city left.

'Ya gunna fight Mantan again, Elgin?'

'Naw. Fightin's stupid. Where's fightin' get ya? In jail, that's where, brother.'

'If ya get me gun, ya can shoot bloody ole Mantan full of 'oles.'

'So ya truly 'ave got a gun.'

'Course. An' jewels an' a necklace an' everything.'

They puff away on another cigarette.

Some Howeses wander by and look the two over with hard Oriental eyes.

'Goin' to be a smash, directly, Caesar. Let's get goin' and find Murry.'

Elgin, the boss, climbs off the seat. Everything is going hazy. but he still walks with a sort of pride. His grubby little page boy swaggers behind him.

Big cousin Elgin who held up a bank and has stolen a dozen cars and beat up two munadj. Big Caesar who broke into a house.

Black boys who idle along. Shy of the bright white lights that expose them for what they really are.

They go up Murray Street.

Past the fire station where the firemen whistle and shout and jeer.

They sit down on the low wall outside the nurses' quarters where girls in short, tight uniforms glide between the iron gates, comfortable in the knowledge of their whiteness and virginity.

No one notices the two Nyoongahs in the shadows under the huge Moreton Bay fig tree that erupts from the footpath in a green volcano. It leads a doomed life, one day to be chopped down by the hands that nurtured it. Just like the people it shelters now.

'Hey boy, 'ow'd you like 'er?' Caesar grins and spits as a pretty, buxom, young nurse walks past.

'Roasted, with two eggs.' Elgin grins.

Eyes follow her as they would a dream.

'Yeah, just like I was thinkin'.'

Elgin glances at his little cousin and bursts into laughter.

'Listen to 'im talk. Ya couldn't 'ave a moony to save yaself. Don't try foolin' me. I'm almost ya brother, yeah.'

'I done all right with Jenny Doolan.'

'Garn. Y'never touched 'er, even. I was there.'

'Any rate,' Caesar sulks, 'I thought we was lookin' for Murry. What we doin' up 'ere?'

'Walkin',' Elgin grunts.

Staggers to his feet. 'Let's get goin'.'

'What we goin' up 'ere for? I wanna get me gun before some jerk finds it, ya know.'

'I'm goin' to say a prayer to turn me white.' Elgin smiles, and his eyes take in the cathedral that looms down upon them, its spire silhouetted against the sky. The Virgin Mary looks out over the city that surrounds it like broken eggshells.

'What ya reckon we steal the cashbox, Elgin?'

'Don't talk silly. 'Ow'd ya know God won't blast ya to bits, eh?'

Caesar laughs loud and young, while Elgin gives a mocking smile.

They leave the cathedral with its awesome shadows and tranquillity up on the hill.

Past the now-silent school. In the daytime (with all its blue heat and flies and dust) green-clad schoolgirls shout in play and hide their self-conscious womanhood behind starched uniforms.

Past the mint, looking like a caged animal behind the iron bars and twisted barbed netting. A snarling white man's animal.

The two descendants of the kings of the old civilisation glance from hooded eyes as a police car swishes past.

Elgin digs his hands deeper in his pockets, and his sharp eyes flick over to the taxi parked beside a block of flats that rear up into the sky. It taunts him with its sleek whiteness. The sleek white owner is upstairs in the flats, fondling his white girlfriend between white sheets.

'Ya can't even pinch a car, Elgin.' Caesar sneers, still sullen from Elgin's gibes about his sexual prowess.

Elgin's eyes flash.

'Couldn't I, ya little jerk? Just you keep watch, budda, an' I'll show ya 'ow one Nyoongah can steal a car.'

The wiry youth crouches beside the taxi and his teeth pull back in a grin. His thin fingers find a crack where the window is wound down and he heaves with all his might. Puts in his hand and unlocks the door.

Caesar stands, tense and afraid, under a tree.

A utility glides past.

Elgin leaps onto the other side of the taxi, while Caesar melts into the tree. Door open. Silver paper on the fuses.

Two shadows pushing a taxi down the hill. The gentle crunch of tyres on cement. A sudden kick, and the engine bursts into life. Doors slam and Elgin lets out a howl of laughter as he screeches around the corner.

Caesar clutches the door in fright.

Elgin Mortimer Broppo lets all his drunken frustration bubble out in one long whoop of joy.

'*Now* we'll get ya bloody gun an' shoot bloody ole Mantan so full of 'oles 'e'll look like a piece of lace, yeah,' Elgin cries.

Caesar lights a nervous cigarette.

'Not so fast, couz. I wanna live, ya know.'

A faint, persistent thought hammers at Elgin's mind.

Back to jail; back to jail
E. M. Broppo back to jail

The wheel between his thin agile hands whisks the thought away. It bobs with the coloured lights here, then is gone.

Down in the cool peace of the gardens, Murry lies beside Lynette. She smiles serenely at him and he rubs a calloused hand through her hair.

She has become a woman tonight. In the way she dreamed about, down at the dusty camp, when she was small, and read, over and over again, the tattered book on 'Sleeping Beauty.'

Caressed and kissed and loved on this hot night. And her man is still here beside her, tracing patterns in her hair.

'We'd better go soon, Murry. The 'Owes'll be everywhere.

'They won't bother us,' the giant rumbles.

The girl realises he is still white, in many ways as well as in his manner of making love. She sits up and takes out cigarettes for them both.

'They will if they know ya one of Elgin's people.'

They finish their cigarettes. The incense-like blue smoke drifts around them and the tree squats above them like a buddha. They kiss again, never wanting to leave.

But there are Lynette's father and three brothers to think about—and her uncles and cousins. Just as everything is going well, Murry doesn't want to start a feud of his own.

'Better go.'

They amble up into the lighted city that is becoming dark and empty now. The buses are all gone.

The Howeses are all there. Too many glowering, hunched Howeses stalking the streets for gentle Murry and feminine Lynette to fight.

They slink back the way they came and down towards the river.

'We'll get a taxi, if there's any goin'. I got the money,' Murry murmurs.

Elgin and Caesar, on their way to get the .303, find them.

The squeal of brakes rips out the guts of the night. The taxi reverses back to gaping Murry and surprised Lynette.

'Shut ya mouth an' open the door, Murry,' rasps little Caesar, eyeing Lynette. He feels more sure of himself now, and happy that—at last—he is going to get his rifle.

Elgin cocks his head over his slight shoulders. Bright eyes twinkle at Murry.

'Where ya been, Murry?'

'Where ya think, Elgin? Down Supreme Court Gardens, unna, Murry?' Caesar says before Murry can answer.

Ya *wanna* punch in the 'ead, Caesar Jackell, ya big prick?' Lynette snarls.

'Da's true,' returns Caesar, and nudges Elgin. Their teeth gleam as they shudder in silent laughter.

Lynette glowers.

'Ya steal this taxi, Elgin?' Murry mutters as he slides in.

'Nah! 'E bought it, unna?' Caesar cackles.

Elgin smiles a superior smile.

They drive over the bridge. Elgin idles along the riverside slowly.

'Where ya goin', Elgin?' Lynette asks from the back. She is the only girl there. She has heard about these sort of rides before. After all, the two in the front *are* Murry's cousins. Share and share alike is their code.

'Just gettin' some of Caesar's stuff.'

''Ere. Turn off,' Caesar orders. He is the boss again, just as he was up in front of Crystal's.

The taxi rocks and bumps down the gravel track until it reaches the water's edge.

Caesar leaps out and searches in the long grass until he finds the .303 and the bag. He holds them up and shouts a challenge to the soaring flats and the dancing moon and the cold, white, impassive stars.

The cab screeches back onto the main road, spitting dust and gravel in defiance.

Caesar produces the flagon of riesling. Drunk and happy again, he hands out pieces of jewellery to everyone. He keeps the .303 on his knee and the watch and two earrings in his pocket. He takes a long swig of the flagon, then hands it to Elgin.

'Ya smart little bugger. 'Oo'd of believed it, eh?' Elgin gives Caesar a proper grin. A man-to-man grin for the new hero of the clan.

Caesar aims his rifle at buildings and boats and the occasional bird, Murry and Lynette snuggle up close to one another and take the odd sip of wine from the offered flagon.

Elgin drives, drowning in bitter riesling and his own thoughts.

They will be looking for the cab by now. When they catch him, they will make sure he goes to jail for a long time, if Big Pig Fathers has anything to do with it.

He thinks about his woman, lying alone in their tent out at the camp. Her round, bright eyes and quiet voice, and the gentle smile that can calm his wildness.

A still part of town.

A tired sign above a building, flashes blue and red: LAWSON HOT L.

He swings the taxi into the gloom of the parking area.

Two o'clock in the morning. No one around.

The others stare at him in curiosity as he grins around the dark cab.

'We just goin' to break into 'ere an' get some beer. 'Ave one big party, when we get back to camp.'

'Yeah?' Murry, uneasily.

'Nothin' to it, Murry. Wait 'ere a bit, you mob. Be back d'rectly.'

Elgin slips out and scuttles over to the wall. A sharp crack as the window breaks. Protesting squeaks as it jerks open.

A low whistle.

Murry clambers out noisily, not used to this sort of thing. Caesar floats beside him, holding his .303. Lynette huddles in the cab, with just a cigarette and the riesling to keep her company, feeling terribly alone, without big Murry beside her.

Elgin's head peers out of the window like a fox glancing out of his lair. A sly, thin, black fox, about to grab the fluttering white chickens and make them squawk.

'Come 'ere, Murry. Caesar, keep watch.'

The two coloured boys stand inside the murky lounge, while their eyes become used to the gloom. Elgin leads the way as they sneak into the storeroom.

'We right now, baby,' Elgin whispers. 'Fuckin' Christmas, unna, out at camp, when we deliver this little lot.'

Murry is afraid. It is strange that he is here, in someone else's place, taking all this beer. The pictures on the wall scowl down at him. He passes out the carton to drunk Caesar, who staggers over to the cab.

Carton after carton of bottles and stubbies and cans.

Murry is a criminal now. If he gets caught, it's an end to all his dreams. And all he wanted to do was go home.

'Grab some gnummerai, Murry. Geeze, do ya 'ave to be told everything?' Elgin hisses as he dashes past with an armload of spirit bottles. Murry gets a small cardboard box and quickly fills it up with cigars and packets of cigarettes. His strong hands wrench open the till and he stuffs about $200 in notes into his pockets.

'Come on. Murry, ya ole woman!'

He rushes over to the window and leaps out.

They roll start the taxi. Head for home. Home amongst the gaunt trees, beside the wide river flat.

They weave through the streets, keeping clear of police vehicles and taxis. Out on Guildford Road, Elgin pushes his foot down hard and lets the power and freedom of his body and mind echo in the taxi engine.

Reedy voices crackle feebly over the two-way in a vain search for the cab. Black Elgin is supreme once more. For the second time in his life he has the radios of Perth spread like a spider's web to catch him as he buzzes along.

'What ya reckon they'll say out at camp when we roll up?' he grins.

''Appy birthday,' Caesar laughs.

A train roars past and Elgin tries to beat it.

The only car on the whole lonely road.

Caesar pretends to shoot the people in the train.

Lynette sniggers. 'Look 'ere at Clint Eastwood!'

Caesar turns and laughs with her. All he can do now is laugh. If he stops laughing, he will spew up. He sways and rolls and clutches his .303 even tighter. His smile is a fixed one.

Lynette is only happy-drunk. She leans against broad Murry and his big hand covers her child's breast. He broods about the crime he has committed, then thinks about the money that will buy his woman a lot of joy.

Elgin is remote from the others. Just him and his car and the road.

They are almost at Guildford when they zoom past a speed trap.

Caesar hears the eerie wailing and jerks around.

'Hey couz, bloody munadj 'ave got us!'

Fear settles like a mist over the remnants of the tribe.

"Old tight. When I tell ya to run, ya bloody run—understand?' Elgin says, through clenched teeth.

More cars join in the chase: two blue vans and a CIB car. They bay and howl like hounds after the fox.

'I'll stop 'em!' screams Caesar, and loads the magazine of his .303.

Six bullets.

He leans out the window of the swaying cab so the wind whips his hair back and shrieks through the curls.

He fires the rifle and the bullet whines away. Fires again and again.

On his last shot, the bullet smashes through the windscreen of the foremost van so it slows to an abrupt halt. The RTA car also stops, but the others come relentlessly onwards.

The CIB car comes up alongside them. They think they are Starsky and Hutch, in their olive-green Kingswood. Elgin sees the fat, pale face of Detective-Sergeant Fathers peering in at them.

Slides over to the other side of the road in an attempt to block off the CIB car.

It only comes up on the other side of the road, so Elgin rams the taxi into it.

Twice he smashes the taxi against the car, desperately trying to escape. He has visions of smirking Fathers and his mates, like white toadstools growing on Elgin's black rotting body, down in the forest of Central police station.

The second time he rams the CIB car, Caesar Jackell's arm breaks with a snap like the click of his stolen rifle bolt.

He gives a cry of pain.

Just over the Swan River bridge, Elgin slams on the brakes. The taxi careers up onto the footpath.

'Run! Run!' he yells, and is out sprinting even before the car has stopped. Down over the bank and towards the river.

Caesar stumbles across the road, in the headlights of the pursuing CIB car. He scrabbles painfully down the opposite bank from Elgin, and staggers across the paddock, trailing his .303.

Dull Murry is stunned for three vital seconds and Lynette clings fearfully to him. When he explodes from the taxi, the area is surrounded by police.

He has more to lose than the other two boys. He has his pride at never having committed a crime and his good job and his girl whom he *does* love. He pushes Lynette down the bank after Elgin. Turns to face the approaching horde with the anger of a cornered wildcat.

He lifts one policeman off his feet with a powerhouse right and smashes huge Fathers in the mouth, rocking him.

Six police pounce on the giant Aboriginal and grapple him to his knees with punches and kicks. Hurl him into the van where he crouches in the corner with dead eyes.

'Who's your mates? Who was drivin'? What was the girl's name? How old was she, sonny? Do you know what carnal knowledge is all about? What's your name, arsehole? You 'ad the gun, eh, Jesse James? Well, who did, then? Where did you get all this beer and grog, matey? By Christ, you're in the shit now. Tell us who the others were, or we put everything on you. Hey, sarge, one went down along the river. Where'd that bloody girl go? I wouldn't mind arresting her, eh, Billy? . . . Hey, sarge, Central want you on the radio: Get every man you can down here, a mob of Abos have split everywhere . . . one of them is fucking dangerous . . . got a gun . . . took a shot at one of our cars . . . No, no one is hurt, only shaken . . . Listen, Jacky, yer better start talkin' soon, before I belt yer bloody ears off . . . How's Mal? Pretty crook, that boong's got a hard punch. Yaaah! They all think they're Baby Cassius.'

Words, words. Going round and round inside Murry's battered head. He drops his eyes and chews on his bottom lip while white faces gaze in at him as though he were a monkey in the zoo, not a human at all. Hard eyes, contemptuous eyes, wondering eyes: slit mouths and Hitler moustaches.

White faces, blue uniforms.

Being the only one caught is such a bitter feeling. The loneliness is more acute. He remembers Caesar joking and Elgin grinning, and Lynette smiling and pressing against him—so close—in a world so far away.

They take him to Midland lockup.

Caesar huddles, moaning, down beside the river. He stares at the blank brown water. His arm hurts now and tears run down his face. He sniffs noisily and wonders if he has killed anyone. The excitement of the chase wears off and he feels sicker then he has ever been. Leans over and vomits all over the ground. Fades among the trees as he hears the droning of a car bouncing over the paddock. Two yellow eyes stare out of the darkness and pick him up, cringing against the tree.

Car stops. Doors open. Feet crunch on the dead grass.
'Look out! He's the crazy bastard with the gun!'
'G'day, Caesar.'
Fathers and company.
'I never meant to kill no one.'
'No one's dead, Caesar. Now. suppose you give me that gun.'
'I busted me arm, ya know.'
The men close in around him.
'Well, we'd better get it looked at, then, hadn't we?'
He is escorted to the car.
The stars watch from above. His people.
They can't help him now.
No one can.
Inside the CIB car, on his way to Midland regional hospital, with the stale fingers of the evening's enjoyment ripping at his small body, he babbles out the truth of everything.

Just as the sun is crawling over the hills to begin a new day, Elgin creeps into the camp. He has run and slipped and swum his way along the river, then over the paddocks.

Safe back at home, in his tent.

His young woman stares at his silhouette in the tent opening with chiding eyes. He is angry, yet ashamed, of her disapprobation.

'Where ya bin, Elgin?' she whispers, tired of asking the same question. Tired of trying to settle her thin husband's turbulent soul.

'Nowhere.'

He throws himself down on the blanket and lights up a cigarette. He cannot meet her dark, all-knowing eyes.

Blood from a rip in his arm where he got caught on a barbed wire fence, trickles down the brown skin like a teardrop.

'Ya badly 'urt, 'oney?' she murmurs.

'No. Go back to sleep, Maydene.'

'It's almost mornin', an' ya been stealin' again, Elgin! 'Ow *can* I go to sleep, with yaself moonin' all over the countryside?' she cries. 'Ya only come out of jail last month, too. Ya *want* ole Fathers to flog ya again, or what?'

And Elgin was going to ride into camp on his white horse and unload all the beer. Everyone was going to gather around, and there would have been jokes and laughter and fun. His woman would have smiled at him and hugged him, and forgiven him—because he had brought some light into the dusty reserve.

He digs his hand into a pocket and pulls out one of Caesar's necklaces. His feral eyes meet her bruised ones.

'I got ya this, Maydene,' he mutters.

'Ooohh, Elgin! What ya tryin' to do to me, boy?' she weeps.

Elgin gets up abruptly, and moves outside. Muffled sobs pierce him like the first shafts of the orange-red sunlight from the new day.

Excerpt from *True Country*

KIM SCOTT

There were too many at the pub. All different peoples. Chinese ones, Aborigine, gardiya; old, young; men, women. There were singlets, jeans, long socks, white ankles under tanned legs, cracked bare feet. There was music. and roaring and shouting. Sometimes, in some places Franny stood, the music was so loud he listened to it with his chest. It was like he was hollow inside, and his chest vibrated like a drum. He smelled sweat, soap, perfume sharply sweet, stale beer, urine, tobacco and clove cigarettes. The interior bar was gloomy. There were strips and slices of light scattered around and over pool tables, and the old carpet was soggy and sprouting cigarette butts. Voices everywhere; taking off, screeching, snarling, flapping through the curling smoke and thin trunks of light like bats and birds. They alighted on shoulders and repeated repeated themselves, pecked and stabbed, or stroked with soft downy wings. Sometimes in a relative quiet, you could hear the click of ball and cue. Stabbing sounds of glass and stainless steel. But then the music would start again, a great blanket of it, angry and smothering.

Outside, in the yard where the band is playing, it is bright sun and people must squint. Their faces wrinkle up, their eyebrows come down. Sometimes, with beer in the belly, and a little craziness in the head, you might not know if it's noise hitting you or someone thumping bumping your back and chest. Out in the sun, the music noise is not like a great blanket, not even a bit soft. It is hard. The bass notes are maybe like bricks wrapped in hessian slamming into you. But it's all right. It's happy time. You shouting with the rest of them. Sing, dance, wriggle and stagger about. The white froth of the beer goes up into the hot and patient blue sky. The yellow liquid settles in scrawny guts and big hairy belly.

Franny is there. He too young, but he be there all right. Sitting hunched, then laughing and showing the cord of his throat as he lifts his head back. Others leave. Franny won't go with them.

Franny getting tired. Head on his arms on the table.

The day goes on. Much drinking. much noise. Some people get cranky and argue. Maybe if the people in this hot and sunny place stopped shouting touching dancing drinking for even just a little time then they feel unhappy, sad, angry. Hollow maybe. Maybe that helps explain why such bad things can sometimes happen.

This day goes on. The dark time comes. The sun falls below the noise and the floodlights of the concrete and fibro courtyard.

Franny lifts his head from the table when some people sit at it. He feels sick. His mouth is furry and his head aches. The faces of the people around him are those of strangers. They are caked with powder. Many are pale, stubbled, and streams of blood run through their eyes.

Out in the car park, in the comforting darkness again, Franny leans on a car. He vomits. With tears in his eyes he stumbles to the next car. Somehow, he opens the back door, and sways there, gripping the handle. The poor silly boy. He knows nothing, alone and sick.

It doesn't matter who the two men were that saw him. Their names don't matter. One was a bouncer, come up from Perth to work here. The other one worked on station, lived up this way long time. They been all day in a motel room, drinking and complaining and making themselves heavy, and only now come out.

Franny is about to fall onto the soft seat of the car.

Those two men stood at the edge of the car park and saw. They didn't shout. They ran over there, angry angry. Angry and wild. They pulled him out of the car, almost like he bounced up from the seat. Oh, he was black! Aborigine! They hit him, kicked him, punched him. He was like a bag, he didn't fight back. Groaned. Maybe they enjoyed feeling their fists and feet striking his flesh. They held him up to hit him. He slid to the ground; maybe yelled, sobbed, whimpered. Pick him up, hit him more. He fell again. Bang! Hit head on the bitumen. One of them killers hit him with a big brick. Oh, yes, they told us later. Oh, they jumped up and down on him. His heart went away.

One of them, proper thinking like, not like crazy, got his knife. They held his head back and sawed through his throat. Fish scales still on the knife. Cut his throat like he was bullock kangaroo turtle. Oh he was dead dead dead. Blood bits of meat on the ground. His heart floating around. Him, him no more.

How can this be? And those men? Well. They bayed at the moon maybe, savage dogs. Mad as mad. Very bad things. What did they do, those killers? They drink some more beer? Tell their mates they just stuck a boy, killed him? Wipe the blood and skin from that knife on the beer mat in the bar? Who can know the truth or their minds? They cannot be real people, these ones.

We thought, when we knew, that the law would get them. We stopped some of our people that wanted to kill them. We thought. you know, justice. White man's justice.

True. Silly buggers we be. We need a say. . . .

Yes, those murderers of Franny been clear off proper quick all right. They been run out of that court, into their cars, gone! Gone like a bullet. They frightened, see. Want to get back to Perth, Melbourne, and away. Away from us mob.

Oh, it be a long drive but. You drive all day all night day night day night, like that if you want to get there. No sleep, or only little bit. They not drive together. Not friends no more, you know.

One of them with his girlfriend. He make some stops on the way down, took it slowly slow.

Other one, him drive drive driving. One bit of road out there, long skinny lonely straight road out there in the dark time, something happened. Maybe he get out to check if he moving or not, because that road so long straight dark through the desert. Maybe a sharp shell from the ocean far away long ago come out of the ground and stab his tyre. Might be a kangaroo appear disappear in front of him and make him swerve, you know. And it could be that he see a fat belly black man flyin', swoop into the tunnel his headlights make.

Crash! He crash that car. Rolling and rolling over and over in his car, he so frightened even before that car start going arse over tit again and again and again.

He screaming out there in the cold cold dark time, no one to hear him, them black things in the sky between the sparkling stars looking down on him not caring. Him screaming, car upside down, wheels spinning motor hissing steaming. Blood all over him, arms and legs bent all wrong anykind, chest smashed, and heart still parked but going fast fast faster. Then stop. There. Dead dead proper dead bastard. Got him.

Other one? His mate? Death in our custody, eh? Can't make love, you know, can't make love with his girl no more. His dick shrivel up like a baby's, soft like a string. You put a special poison in his blood, make him go that way. Proper worried then. He have poison in his blood, have nightmares about us old people watching him. He see our eyes in dogs, in the kangaroos his car hits and hits. He see us watching him from the eagles high in the sky, from crows sitting on carcasses he passes. Even the seagulls back nearing Perth, they watch him with their all the time open eyes.

His girl goes. In his little place in Perth there he is like in a box. He start thinking about him being in a box, you know. Another box, small small one that fit him tight.

So we got him too. He makes a tube—he make it like a snake—that go from his exhaust pipe to the window of his car. He just sit in car then, start the motor, listen to radio.

Him dead. We got him. Just like old times. Still got power, see?

True. True story. Listen! We could do that. Could could could.

PART NINE

Hidden Histories

Brenda Croft, *Michael Watson in Redfern on the Long March of Freedom, Justice and Hope, Invasion Day, 26 January 1988*, Sydney, NSW, 1988, black and white gelatin silver photograph, 50.5 cm x 40.5 cm. Courtesy of the artist.

Leah King-Smith, Untitled (5/13), from the series *Patterns of Connection*, 1991, direct positive color photograph, 102.5 x 103 cm. Courtesy of the artist.

Artist Unknown

LISA BELLEAR

(For all indigenous/colonised artists inspired by a visit to the Art Gallery of New South Wales to look at Destiny Deacon's work)

Artist unknown
Location Liverpool River
The Rainbow Serpent
Narama and her sons 1948
Acc pl 1956

Artist unknown
Kimberley Area
Hammerhead Shark
And Black Fish 1948
Acc no p15 1956

Artist unknown
Location Oenpelli
Mimi Family 1948
Ochre on cardboard
Original collection presented by
The Commonwealth Government
Acc no pl 16 1956

Artist unknown
Location
Ochre on cardboard
Mimi man and woman 1948
Acc no14 1956

Artist unknown
Location Milinginbi
Hive of wild honey 1948
Ochre on cardboard
Acc p24 1956

Artist unknown
Location Oenpelli
Crocodile
Ochre on cardboard
Acc no p17 1956

Artist unknown
Location Oenpelli
Two fish 1948
Accp19 1956

Artist unknown
Divisions of fish
Acc no 22 1956

Artist unknown
Ochre on cardboard
Acquisition number
And purchase date
No name
No tribe
Or clan
Or Language group
No gender
No spirituality
The unknown artist
reads like a memorial

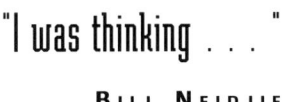

"I was thinking . . ."

BILL NEIDJIE

I was thinking . . .
no history written for us when white European start here.
Only few words written.
Should be more than that.

Should be written way Aborigine was live.
That floodplain . . .
my father, my mother, my grandfather
all used to hunt there,
use ironwood spear.
No clothes then.

When I was growing up
good mob of people all around then.
Now people bit wicked.
My time never do little bit wrong . . .
Otherwise get spear straight away.
Now . . . little bit cheeky mob.
Old time they would all be dead now.
Old people were hard . . .
I frightened when young.
Only few people now,
but it easy for this mob.

Anyway, got to be made that book.
There's still time.
No man can growl at me for telling this story
because it will be too late . . .
I'll be dead.

The Past

OODGEROO OF THE NOONUCCAL TRIBE

Let no one say the past is dead.
The past is all about us and within.
Haunted by tribal memories, I know
This little now, this accidental present
Is not the all of me, whose long making
Is so much of the past.

Tonight here in suburbia as I sit

In easy chair before electric heater,
Warmed by the red glow, I fall into dream:
I am away
At the camp fire in the bush, among
My own people, sitting on the ground.
No walls about me,
The stars over me,
The tall surrounding trees that stir in the wind
Making their own music,
Soft cries of the night coming to us, there
Where we are one with all old Nature's lives
Known and unknown.
In scenes where we belong but have now forsaken.
Deep chair and electric radiator
Are but since yesterday,
But a thousand thousand camp fires in the forest
Are in my blood.
Let none tell me the past is wholly gone.
Now is so small a part of time, so small a part
Of all the race years that have moulded me.

Holocaust Island

GRAEME DIXON

Nestled in the Indian Ocean
Like a jewel in her crown
The worshippers of Babel come
To relax and turn to brown
To recuperate from woe and toil
and leave their problems far behind
To practice ancient rituals
The habits of their kind

But what they refuse to realise
Is that in this little Isle
are skeletons in their cupboards

of deeds most foul and vile
Far beneath this Island's surface
In many an unmarked place
lie the remnants of forgotten ones
Kia, members of my race.

Are There Abo Schools?

LIONEL FOGARTY

At the abo school what are our children taught?
Are they told of our sisters being raped now
Are they told of our Mothers crying sorrowfully
Will they be told that all whites are not the enemy
Are they told of capitalism—the enemy
Australian Aboriginals—will they know their culture?
Are they told violence is ahead
Are they told that revolution
is the only solution
Are they told that Jacky Jackys and Marys are going to be killed
Tell the abo child the true history
But 'member white man keeps inventions to destroy
And never let them step in abo's ways
If so we know who they can turn to
The abo education
Are there
Revolutionists
Educationists.

A Letter to the Shade of Charles Darwin

JACK DAVIS

We sincerely wish to thank you
for the assistance you have unwittingly given us
in the occupation of this continent
It is better far better that we
that we the intelligent and superior ones
were able to enlighten and lighten the burden of those poor
miserable halfstarved
bottlenosed caricatures
of humanity who aimlessly wandered this land
for centuries before our arrival
It was better far better that we
that we led them out of barbarism
into the era of Christendom by baptising
bibling blanketing and clothing them
As a small token of gratitude
for we are grateful in being able to assist you
and your colleagues we are forwarding to you
The heads of Pomawoy and Yagan
which I believe are two of the purest specimens
of skulls of brute man
ever to leave our shores
Caucasian man has much to thank you for
in propounding the laws of selectivity
In relation to Homo Erectus
in Australia and beyond

Yours faithfully
Sylvester Squatter

    p.s. My friends and I
        will send you further specimens
        when they come to hand
        S.S.

Historical Journals

LISA BELLEAR

(for Tony Birch)

Historical journals offer frameworks
to
      rationalise
      demystify
and
      historisise
constructs of deception
Reference points
are
      neutral
      safe
settler • explorer • coloniser • drovers • dyke

Reach for truth

Sue and Du: The Spirit of One Tribe Is All

LIONEL FOGARTY

The Wakka Wakka are there
walking, talking singing
in the land.
The Gabi Gabi are there, walking
talking, singing in the land.
The Gurang Gurang are there walking,
talking, singing in the land.
The Dungidau are there walking,
talking, singing in the land.
The Booyooburra are there walking,

talking, singing in the land.
They are all full blooded past and
futures. They are looking at us
doing what's wrong—yes they are
listening to us, saying silly things
Do you remember dat story
No it was never told. Yes
but can you sit in the bush and
think of the chants peace they had.
Can you sit and easy your spirit
to feel their presence
can your mind picture what
they looked painted up like.
Yea Murri it's hard when few
are here, but some have
spoken long time ago, some are
here today willing to tell us.
Have you ever heard of Fred Embrey?
Well his stories are recorded in
book, may be taped. And have you
heard Willie Mackenzie—he gave
knowledge to migglou of lot of
tribes many old are still here
walking, talking, singing. Where
are they dat come from the land?
You Murri of today have it here
speaking, telling and reliving.
Wakka, Kabi are still there
they are all there in the wind,
rain, sun, bush morning and night;
you will feel proud to be Aboriginal
if you give all your tribes
the POWER TO LIVE.

Excerpt from *My Place*

SALLY MORGAN

My name is Daisy Corunna. I'm Arthur's sister. My Aboriginal name is Talahue. I can't tell you when I was born, but I feel old. My mother had me on Corunna Downs Station, just out of Marble Bar. She said I was born under a big, old gum tree and the midwife was called Diana. Course, that must have been her whitefella name. All the natives had whitefella and tribal names. I don't know what her tribal name was. When I was comin' into the world, a big mob of kids stood round waitin' for to get a look at me. I bet they got a fright.

I was happy up North. I had my mother and there was Old Fanny, my grandmother. Gladdie 'minds me of Old Fanny, she's got the same crooked smile. They both got round faces like the moon, too. I 'member Old Fanny always wore a handkerchief on her head with little knots tied all the way around. Sometimes, my granddaughter Helen 'minds me of her, too. They both short and giggly with skinny legs. Aah, she was good for a laugh, Old Fanny.

She loved panning for tin. All the old people panned for tin. You could see it lyin' in the dirt, heavy and dark, like black marbles. Old Fanny said I had good eyes, sometimes she took me with her for luck. We traded the tin for sugar or flour. They never gave us money.

Old Fanny went pink-eye[1] to Hillside one day. I never saw her again. They tell me she died on Hillside, maybe she knew she was going to die. She was a good old grandmother.

On the station, I went under the name Daisy Brockman. It wasn't till I was older that I took the name Corunna. Now, some people say my father wasn't Howden Drake-Brockman, they say he was this man from Malta. What can I say? I never heard 'bout this man from Malta before. I think that's a big joke.

Aah, you see, that's the trouble with us blackfellas, we don't know who

---

1. *pink-eye*—term used by Aboriginal people of north-west Australia, similar to the more widely known term *walkabout*. A period of wandering as a nomad, often as undertaken by Aborigines who feel the need to leave the place where they are in contact with white society, and return for spiritual replenishment to their traditional way of life. Can also simply mean a holiday, usually without leave.

we belong to, no one'll own up. I got to be careful what I say. You can't put no lies in a book.

Course, I had another father, he wasn't my real father like, but he looked after us just the same. Chinaman was his name. He was very tall and strong. The people respected him. They were scared of him. He was Arthur's Aboriginal father, too. He was a powerful man.

My poor mother lost a lot of babies. I had two sisters that lived, Lily and Rosie. They were, what do they call it? Full blood, yes. I was the light one of the family, the little one with blonde hair. Of course, there was Arthur, but they took him away when I was just a baby.

I 'member Old Pompee, he was the old boy that looked after the vegetable garden, he told me my mother cried and cried when they took Arthur. She kept callin' to him like. Callin' to him to come back. The people thought Arthur was gettin' educated so he could run the station some day. They thought it'd be good to have a blackfella runnin' the station. They was all wrong. My poor old mother never saw him again.

Rosie and I was close. Lily was older than me. I spent a lot of time with Rosie. I was very sad when she died. She was only young. My mother nursed her, did everything for her, but we lost her. Good old Rosie, you know I been thinkin' 'bout her lately. She was what you call a good sport.

I'll tell you a story about our white man's names. My mother was in Hedland with the three of us when an English nursing sister saw her near the well. She said, 'Have you got names for your three little girls?'.

Mum said, 'No'.

She said, 'Well, I'll give you names, real beautiful ones. We'll call this one Lily, this one Rosie and this little one Daisy'. I was the short one of the family. We didn't mind being called that, we thought we were pretty flowers.

I haven't told you about my brother Albert, yet. He was light, too. He used to tease me. He'd chase me, then he'd hide behind a big bush and jump out and pretend he was the devil-devil. Oooh, he was naughty to me. They took Albert when they took Arthur, but Albert got sick and came back to the station. He was a good worker. He liked playing with me. He called me his little sister.

They was a good mob on Corunna. A real good mob. I been thinkin' 'bout all of them lately. There was Peter Linck, the well-sinker. I think he was German, he lived at the outcamp. He had Rosie, not my sister Rosie, another one. Then there was Fred Stream, by jingoes, there was a few kids that belonged to him. He had Sarah, her children were really fair, white blackfellas, really.

Aah, that colour business is a funny thing. Our colour goes away. You mix us with the white man, and pretty soon, you got no blackfellas left. Some of these whitefellas you see walkin' around, they really black underneath. You see, you never can tell. I'm old now, and look at me, look at the skin on my arms and legs, just look! It's goin' white. I used to be a lot darker than I am now. I don't know what's happened. Maybe it's the white blood takin' over, or the medicine they gave me in hospital, I don't know.

The big house on Corunna was built by the natives. They all worked together, building this and building that. If it wasn't for the natives, nothing would get done. They made the station, Drake-Brockmans didn't do it on their own.

At the back of the homestead was a big, deep hole with whitewash in it. It was thick and greasy, you could cut it with a knife. Us kids used to mix the whitewash with water and make it like a paint. Then we'd put it all over us and play corroborees. Every Saturday afternoon, we played corroboree. We mixed the red sand with water and painted that on, too. By the time we finished, you didn't know what colour we were.

I 'member the kitchen on Corunna. There was a tiny little window where the blackfellas had to line up for tucker. My mother never liked doin' that. We got a bit of tea, flour and meat, that was all. They always rang a bell when they was ready for us to come. Why do white people like ringin' bells so much?

Every morning, they woke us up with a bell. It was only 'bout five o'clock, could have been earlier. We all slept down in the camp, a good way from the main house. Every morning, someone would light a lamp, walk down into the gully and ring a bell. When I was very little, I used to get frightened. I thought it was the devil-devil come to get me.

There was a tennis court on Corunna. Can you 'magine that? I think they thought they were royalty, puttin' in a tennis court. That's an Englishman's game. They painted it with whitewash, but it didn't stay white for long, I can tell you. I had a go at hitting the ball, once. I gave up after that, it was a silly game.

I saw plenty of willy-willies up there and cyclones, too. By jingoes, a cyclone is a terrible thing! When one was coming, my mother hid me. I wasn't allowed to move. She was worried I might get killed. Get taken away by the wind. I was only small. I 'member one time we hid in the kitchen, when my mother wasn't looking, I sneaked up to the window and peeked out. You should have seen it! There was men's hats, spinifex, empty tanks, everything blowin' everywhere. It's a funny thing, but those old tanks always ended up settlin' on the tennis court.

There was a food store on Corunna. It had tin walls, tin roof and a tiny window near the top covered with flywire. You wouldn't believe the food they had in there, sacks of apricots, potatoes, tobacco, everything. It makes my mouth water just thinkin' about it. When it was siesta time, the other kids used to lift me up and poke me through the window. I'd drop down inside as quiet as a mouse when the cat's after him. Then I'd pick up food and throw it out the window. If they heard someone coming, they'd cough, then run away. I'd hide behind the sacks of potatoes and wait for them to come back for me. I had a good feed on those days.

The people were really hungry sometimes, poor things. They didn't get enough, you see. And they worked hard. You had to work hard, if you didn't do it, then they call the police in to make you work hard. When things was like that, one of the men would put me through the window again. I suppose I should feel bad about stealin' that food. Hunger is a terrible thing.

Aah, you see, the native is different to the white man. He wouldn't let a dog go without his tea.

Of course, the men all wanted their tobacco as well. The white man called it Nigger Twist. It was a twist like a licorice, only thicker. It's terrible, when you think about it, callin' something like that Nigger Twist. I mean, we all called it that because we thought that was its name.

Sometimes, we'd pinch the eggs the chooks lay in the hay shed. Aah, that old hay shed, it's kept a lot of secrets. Now there was plenty of stockmen up North, then, and they all wanted girls. We'd be hearin' all this noise in the hay shed, the hay'd be goin' up and down, the hens'd be cluckin', the roosters crowin'. Then, by and by, out would come a stockman and one of the girls. They'd be all covered in hay. We just bin lookin' for eggs', they'd say.

There was a government ration we used to get now and then. It was a blanket, we all called it a flag blanket, it had the crown of Queen Victoria on it. Can you imagine that? We used to laugh about that. You see, we was wrappin' ourselves in royalty.

Then there was a mirror and a comb, a cake of soap and a couple of big spotted handkerchiefs. Sometimes, the men were lucky and got a shirt, the women never got anything.

I 'member my mother showin' me a picture of a white woman, she was all fancied up in a long, white dress. 'Ooh, Daisy', she said, 'if only I could have a dress like that'. All the native women wanted to look like the white women, with fancy hairdos and fancy dresses.

Later, my mother learnt how to sew, she was very clever. She could draw anything, she loved drawing. She drew pictures in the sand for me all the time. Beautiful pictures. Maybe that's where you get it from, Sally.

We were cunning when we were kids. There was a big water trough on Corunna, it was used for the animals, even the camels had a drink from it. Mrs Stone always warned us not to muck around in the trough. We'd wait till she was sleeping, then we'd sneak down to the garden and dive in the trough. It was slimy and there was a lot of goona in the water, but we didn't care. I 'member holding my breath and swimming under the water. I looked up and I could see the faces of all the animals lookin' down at me as if to say, 'What are you doin' in our water, child?'.

They had a good cook on Corunna for a while, Mrs Quigley. She was a white woman, a good woman. I think Nell and Mrs Stone, the housekeeper, were a bit jealous of her. Nell was Howden's first white wife. They were real fuddy-duddies and didn't like her talkin' to anyone.

The cook had a little girl called Queenie and it was my job to look out for her. We were 'bout the same age, ooh, we had good times! We'd laugh and giggle at anythin'. We were giggling gerties, that's what Queenie's mother used to call us.

I taught Queenie all about the bush. We'd go out after a big rain. Sometimes, the rain was so heavy up North, it hurt when it hit you. That's the kind of rain you get in the wet. One day, the place would be desert, the next day, green everywhere. Green and gold, beautiful, really. I'd take Queenie out into the bush and we'd watch a little seed grow. 'Look now', I'd say to Queenie, 'it's getting bigger'. By the time we finished lookin', that seed'd be half an inch long.

In the evenings, I liked to sit and watch the kangaroos and other animals come down and drink at the trough. The crows and the birds would have a drink, too, and do a bit of goona. I just liked to sit and watch them all. Course, you know, Corunna has blue hills all round it. They always looked soft that time of night. Sometimes. my mother would sit and watch, too. We knew how to count our blessings, then.

I was a hard worker on Corunna. I been a hard worker all my life. When I was little, I picked the grubs off the caulies and cabbages at the back of the garden. I got a boiled sweet for that. Now the blackfellas weren't allowed to pick any vegetables from the garden. You got a whipping if you were caught. Old Pompee, he used to sneak us tomatoes. And so he should have, he was eatin' them himself.

We all loved the orphaned lambs. We were their mother and their father. We fed them with a bottle with a turkey feather stuck in it. There was one lamb I fed, dear little thing she was, she was blind. She kept bumpin' into the fence and the other lambs. Poor thing. I was so upset I told cook about it and she told me this story.

'You know, Daisy, when I was a young child in Sydney, I had very bad eyesight. One day, an old lady came to visit us and she asked my mother if she could have a go at curing me. Mother said yes. They sat down and put a single grain of sugar in each eye. Ooh, it hurt! I cried and cried, but pretty soon, I could see. I'll give you some sugar, you try that with your lamb'.

I did what she said, and pretty soon, that lamb's eyes were watering all over the place. Next thing I knew, it was runnin' around like all the other lambs, not bumpin' into anything. She was a wise woman, that cook.

Aah, we played silly games when we were kids. I always played with Rosie and Topsy. That Topsy, she was one of a kind, I tell you. One day, Mrs Stone gave her a cake of soap and told her to take a bath. You know what she did? She threw the soap back and said, 'I'm not takin' no bath!'. Can you 'magine cheekin' a white woman like that? Aah, she was great fun, old Topsy.

There was a creek that cut across Corunna in the wet. We loved swimming in it and catching fish. They were like sardines, we threw them on the hot ashes and then gobbled them up. They were nice, but you had to be careful of the bones.

All sorts of wild fruit grew along the creek. There was a prickly tree with fruit like an orange, but with lots of big seeds in it. You could suck the seeds. Then there was another one shaped like a banana, that was full of seeds, too. You ate the flesh and spat out the seeds. There wasn't much food in that one, just juice. There was another prickly tree that had yellow flowers like a wattle, wild beans grew off that tree. When they swelled up, we picked them and threw them in the ashes. They were good.

The best one of all was like a gooseberry bush. Aah, if you could find a patch of that, no one saw you, you just stayed there and ate. You could smell those ones a good way away, they smell like a ripe rockmelon. We'd sniff and say, 'Aah, something ripe in there, somewhere'. We'd lift up all the bushes looking for them, they were only tiny. When we found them, we'd say, Hmmmn, mingimullas, good old mingimullas'. I never tasted fruit like those mingimullas. They had soft green leaves like a flannel, ooh, they were good to eat.

There was another tree we used to get gum from to chew. It grew on little white sticks. We'd collect it and keep it in a tin. It went hard, like boiled lollies. You know, jubes always 'mind me of that gum. Perhaps that's why I like jubes.

Rosie and I were naughty. We'd pinch wild ducks' eggs and break up their nests. And we'd dig holes to get lizards' eggs. We could tell where the lizards had covered up their eggs. We'd dig them all out, get the eggs and bust them. Those poor creatures. They never harmed us and there we were, breakin' up their eggs. We're all God's creatures, after all.

Rosie and I used to catch birds, too. We'd get a bit of wire netting and make a cage, then we'd take it down the creek and throw wheat around. We kept the cage a little bit lifted up and we tied a long bit of string to the wood underneath.

You should have seen all the cockies, they loved wheat. When there was a big mob of them, we'd pull the string, down would come the cage and we would have them trapped. Trouble was, we couldn't do anything with them, they kept biting us. In the end, we let them go. We did silly things in those days.

When I got older, my jobs on Corunna changed. They started me working at the main house, sweeping the verandahs, emptying the toilets, scrubbing the tables and pots and pans and the floor. In those days, you scrubbed everything. In the mornings, I had to clean the hurricane lamps, then help in the kitchen.

There were always poisonous snakes hiding in the dark corners of the kitchen. You couldn't see them, but you could hear them. Sssss, ssssss, ssssss, they went. Just like that. We cornered them and killed them with sticks. There were a lot of snakes on Corunna.

Once I was working up the main house, I wasn't allowed down in the camp. If I had've known that, I'd have stayed where I was. I couldn't sleep with my mother now and I wasn't allowed to play with all my old friends.

That was the worst thing about working at the main house, not seeing my mother every day. I knew she missed me. She would walk up from the camp and call, 'Daisy, Daisy', just like that. I couldn't talk to her, I had too much work to do. It was hard for me, then. I had to sneak away just to see my own family and friends. They were camp natives, I was a house native.

Now, I had to sleep on the homestead verandah. Some nights, it was real cold, one blanket was too thin. On nights like that, the natives used to bring wool from the shearing shed and lay that beneath them.

I didn't mind sleeping on the verandah in summer because I slept near the old cooler. It was as big as a fireplace, they kept butter and milk in it. I'd wait till everyone was asleep, then I'd sneak into the cooler and pinch some butter. I loved it, but I was never allowed to have any.

Seems like I was always getting into trouble over food. I'm like a lamb that's never been fed. I 'member once, Nell asked me to take an apple pie to the house further out on the station. Nell's real name was Eleanor, but everyone called her Nell. Anyway, I kept walkin' and walkin' and smellin' that pie. Ooh, it smelled good. I couldn't stand it any longer, I hid in a gully and dug out a bit of pie with my fingers. It was beautiful. I squashed the pie together and tried to make out like it was all there. Hmmmnnn, that was good tucker, I said to myself as I walked on.

When I gave the pie to Mrs Stone, I had to give her a note that Nell had sent as well. If I had have known what was in that note, I'd have thrown it away. It said, if any part of this pie is missing, send the note back and I will punish her.

Mrs Stone looked at the note, then she looked at the pie, then she said, 'Give this note back when you go'. I did. And, sure enough, I got whipped with the bullocks cane again.

Nell was a cruel woman, she had a hard heart. When she wasn't whippin' us girls with the bullocks cane for not workin' hard enough, she was hittin' us over the head. She didn't like natives. If one of us was in her way and we didn't move real quick, she'd give us a real hard thump over the head, just like that. Ooh, it hurt! White people are great ones for thumpin' you on the head, aren't they? We was only kids.

Aah, but they were good old days, then. I never seen days like that ever again. When they took me from the station, I never seen days like that ever again.

They told my mother I was goin' to get educated. They told all the people I was goin' to school. I thought it'd be good, goin' to school. I thought I'd be somebody real important. My mother wanted me to learn to read and write like white people. Then she wanted me to come back and teach her. There was a lot of the older people interested in learnin' how to read and write, then.

Why did they tell my mother that lie? Why do white people tell so many lies? I got nothin' out of their promises. My mother wouldn't have let me go just to work. God will make them pay for their lies. He's got people like that under the whip. They should have told my mother the truth. She thought I was coming back.

When I left, I was cryin', all the people were cryin', my mother was cryin' and beatin' her head. Lily was cryin'. I called, 'Mum, Mum, Mum!'. She said, 'Don't forget me, Talahue!'.

They all thought I was coming back. I thought I'd only be gone a little while. I could hear their wailing for miles and miles. 'Talahue! Talahue!' They were singin' out my name, over and over. I couldn't stop cryin'. I kept callin', 'Mum! Mum!'

I must have been 'bout fourteen or fifteen when they took me from Corunna. First day in Perth, I had to tidy the garden, pick up leaves and sweep the verandahs. Later on, I used an old scythe to cut the grass. All the time, I kept wonderin' when they were goin' to send me to school. I saw some white kids goin' to school, but not me. I never asked them why they didn't send me, I was too 'shamed.

Funny how I was the only half-caste they took with them from Corunna. Drake-Brockmans left the others and took me. Maybe Howden took me 'cause I was his daughter. I don't know. I kept thinkin' of my poor old mother and how she thought I was gettin' educated. I wanted to tell her what had happened. I wanted to tell her all I was doin' was workin'. I wasn't gettin' no education. How could I tell her, I couldn't write. And I had no one to write for me.

It wasn't the first time I'd been in Perth. I'd been there before with the first wife, Nell. Now I was with the second wife, Alice. Nell had died. When I'd been there before, I'd had to look after Jack and Betty, they were the children. I was only a kid myself. I was 'bout ten and Jack was 'bout six, I can't remember how old Betty was. We was all kids, but I had to do the work.

Aah, she was a hard woman. She was hard on her own kids, too. She bossed Howden around. He didn't step out of line with Nell around. She was a suspicious type of woman. I don't think many people liked her. When I was in Perth with her, she didn't even give me a place to sleep. I had to find my own place. There was a big, empty trunk on the verandah of the house we were stayin' in, I climbed in there at night. At least, it kept me out of the wind.

You see, I went to Perth with Nell, and I came back. My mother would be thinkin' I'd come back this time, too. She'd be thinkin' it was like before, but it wasn't. They just wanted me to work.

We moved into Ivanhoe, a big house on the banks of the Swan River in Claremont. I was lookin' after children again, there was Jack and Betty, Judy, June and Dick. I was supposed to be their nanny. You know, like they have in England. I had to play with them, dress them, feed them and put them to bed at night. I had other chores to do as well. I never blamed the children, it wasn't their fault I had to work so hard. I felt sorry for them.

At night, I used to lie in bed and think 'bout my people. I could see their campfire and their faces. I could see my mother's face and Lily's. I really missed them. I cried myself to sleep every night. Sometimes, in my dreams, I'd hear them wailing, 'Talahue! Talahue!', and I'd wake up, calling 'Mum! Mum!' You see, I needed my people, they made me feel important. I belonged to them. I thought 'bout the animals, too. The kangaroos and birds. And, of course, there was Lily. I wondered if she had a new boyfriend. I missed her, I missed all of them.

Alice kept tellin' me, 'We're family now, Daisy'.

Thing is, they wasn't my family. Oh, I knew the children loved me, but they wasn't my family. They were white, they'd grow up and go to school one day. I was black, I was a servant. How can they be your family?

The only friend I had then was Queenie's mother, Mrs Quigley. She was housekeeping for the Cruikshanks in Claremont. I used to sneak over and visit her whenever I could. She understood the North, she knew how hard it was for me. She never said much, but I knew she understood. I never stayed with her long, I was worried they'd notice I was missing. And, of course, you had times in those days when you had to be in. The blackfella couldn't live his own life, then.

Aah, Queenie's mother was a kind woman. She told a real good story. Sometimes, she'd tell me something funny to cheer me up.

I did all the work at Ivanhoe. The cleaning, the washing, the ironing. There wasn't nothing I didn't do. From when I got up in the morning till when I went to sleep at night, I worked. That's all I did really, work and sleep.

By jingoes, washing was hard work in those days. The old laundry was about twenty yards from the house and the troughs were always filled with dirty washing. They'd throw everything down from the balcony onto the grass, I'd collect it up, take it to the laundry and wash it. Sometimes, I thought I'd never finish stokin' up that copper, washin' this and washin' that. Course, ever thing was starched in those days. Sheets, pillowcases, serviettes, tablecloths, they was all starched. I even had to iron the sheets. Isn't that silly, you only goin' to lay on them.

The house had to be spotless. I scrubbed, dusted and polished. There was the floors, the staircase, the ballroom. It all had to be done.

Soon, I was the cook, too. Mind you, I was a good cook. I didn't cook no rubbish. Aah, white people, they got some funny tastes. Fussy, fussy, aaah, they fussy. I 'member I had to serve the toast on a silver tray. I had to crush the edges of each triangle with a knife. Course, you never left the crusts on sandwiches, that was bad manners. Funny, isn't it? I mean, it's all bread, after all.

I had my dinner in the kitchen. I never ate with the family. When they rang the bell, I knew they wanted me. After dinner, I'd clear up, wash up, dry up and put it all away. Then, next morning, it'd start all over again. You see, it's no use them sayin' I was one of the family, 'cause I wasn't. I was their servant.

I 'member they used to have real fancy morning and afternoon teas. I never liked Perth much, then. I was too scared. I was shy, too. I couldn't talk to strangers. People looked at you funny 'cause you were black. I kept my eyes down. Maybe some of those white people thought the cat got my tongue. I don't know. I'm not sayin' they was all bad. Some of them was nice. You get nice people anywhere. Trouble is, you get the other ones as well. 'Cause you're black, they treat you like dirt. You see, in those days, we was owned, like a cow or a horse. I even heard some people say we not the same as whites. That's not true, we all God's children.

Course, when the white people wanted something, they didn't pretend you wasn't there, they 'spected you to come runnin' quick smart. That's all I did sometimes, run in and out. Someone was always ringin' that damn bell.

I'm 'shamed of myself, now. I feel 'shamed for some of the things I done. I wanted to be white, you see. I'd lie in bed at night and think if God could make me white, it'd be the best thing. Then I could get on in the world, make somethin' of myself. Fancy, me thinkin' that. What was wrong with my own people?

In those days, it was considered a privilege for a white man to want you, but if you had children, you weren't allowed to keep them. You was only allowed to keep the black ones. They took the white ones off you 'cause you weren't considered fit to raise a child with white blood.

I tell you, it made a wedge between the people. Some of the black men felt real low, and some of the native girls with a bit of white in them wouldn't look at a black man. There I was, stuck in the middle. Too black for the whites and too white for the blacks.

I 'member when more native girls came into Perth as servants, they all looked to Nellie and me. Nellie worked for the Courthope family, they were good to her. The other native girls thought we were better than them because we had some white in us.

It was a big thing if you could get a white man to marry you. A lot of native people who were light passed themselves off as white, then. You couldn't blame them, it was very hard to live as a native. One of my friends married a Slav. I think that's how you call it. He was a foreigner, anyway. She came to say goodbye to me and Nellie. We was all cryin'. She'd promised her husband never to talk or mix with any natives again. We didn't blame her, we understood. He wouldn't have married her, otherwise.

Nellie was from Lyndon Station, she was the daughter of the station manager, Mr Hack, but he never owned her. The Courthope family got her from Mogumber to be a servant in their house. Nellie was lucky, because she got treated kindly. She worked very hard like me, but they was good to her. She had a lovely room.

Aah, she was a laugh, that Nellie. She always wanted to be white. All those baths in that hydrogen peroxide and dyin' her hair red. Sometimes, she'd forget to take those baths and then she'd go black again.

You know, I been thinkin' a lot 'bout this. People mustn't say the blackfella has never done anythin' good for this country. I knew this black woman, Tillie, she was a servant and she joined the Salvation Army. She led a real good life, helpin' her own people when she could. She made me feel bad for not goin' to church on Sunday night when she could take me. I didn't like church. People there didn't understand what it was like for the natives.

I 'member the minister at Christ Church started up a sewing circle for all the native servants. We had to go down there and he'd give us a talk, then we'd sew. One time, he went on and on, tellin' us how we must save ourselves for marriage. It was very embarrassing, we couldn't look at him. Most of us had already been taken by white men. We felt really 'shamed.

One day. we were sittin' in the garden sewing when boys from Christ

Church Grammar School came past. They laughed at us and called us awful names. Then, they threw pebbles at us. I never went back there, I was too 'shamed to say why.

Now Sal, this is just between you and me. I don't want Amber hearin' this, she's too young. You watch out for her after I'm gone. She's goin' to be very beautiful. All the men'll want her. Some men can't be trusted. They just mongrels. They get you down on the floor and they won't let you get up. Don't ever let a man do that to you. You watch out for Amber. You don't want her bein' treated like a black woman.

We had no protection when we was in service. I know a lot of native servants had kids to white men because they was forced. Makes you want to cry to think how black women have been treated in this country. It's a terrible thing. They'll pay one day for what they've done.

Aah, white people make you laugh the way they beat the native to teach him not to steal. What about their own kids? I seen white kids do worse than that and no one touches them. They say, he's sowin' his oats or that kid got the devil in him, but they not belted. Poor old blackfella do the same thing, they say you niggers don't know right from wrong and they whip you! I tell you, this is a white man's world.

The only one I had in Perth was Arthur. Now if I had've been livin' with my big brother Arthur, he'd have protected me. He was a strong man. I 'member I was standin' in the kitchen cooking when I heard this knock. I turned around and there's this big native lookin' through the flywire.

'Is that you, Daisy?' he said.

'Who are you?' I asked.

'Aah, you not Daisy', he said. 'She had real fair hair. Come on Mrs, you tell me where Daisy is'.

'What you want her for?' I wasn't gunna let him in the door.

'That's for me to know and you to find out', he said. Aah, I thought, he's got tickets on himself.

'You listen here', I growled at him. 'We don't like strange blackfellas hangin' round here. You better get goin' before the mistress comes home. She'll take a stick to you'. I was tryin' to frighten him, he was a big man.

'Don't you go gettin' uppity with me, Mrs', he said. 'Thinkin' you're better just 'cause you work for white people. I got every right to be lookin' for my little sister Daisy. I want her to know she's got a brother who's gettin' on in the world'.

I couldn't believe it. Can you 'magine that? This big, ugly blackfella was my brother.

'You Arthur?'

'Now how did you come by my name, Mrs?'

'You cheeky devil', I said. 'I'm your sister Daisy'. He just stood there. 'Well, come in', I said. I didn't want him out there clutterin' up the verandah.

'What did you dye your hair for?' he asked. 'You was the only one of us with blonde hair'.

'Don't be stupid. This is the colour of my hair!'

Cheeky devil, he pulled my hair. Maybe he 'spected the colour to come off. Maybe he thought I put boot polish on my hair, I don't know. 'By gee, you a devil!' I told him. I should have known he was my brother, I was fightin' with him, wasn't I?

It wasn't so bad after that. Arthur would come and take me out. Sometimes, he even took me in a car. Can you 'magine that? All us natives drivin' round Perth in a real car? Aah, he thought he was somebody, that Arthur. All the girls wanted him, then. He was the only blackfella they knew with a bit of money in his pocket. He was nice to them all, wasn't he cunning?

We always went to see the horses. We loved horses. One time, he took me to the Show. By gee, he was tough. He'd take on anyone. I said to him, 'Don't you get into no fights when you're out with me. It's not proper. I'll give you what for if you get silly.' You see, he loved showin' off, lived for it.

If he wouldn't settle down, I'd say, 'You just a silly old blackfella'. He'd settle down quick smart after that. He didn't want any of those girls thinkin' he was old.

One day, he said to me, 'Daisy, don't talk to me like that when we out. I'm your brother, you got to show me some respect'. Hmmph, the way he carried on you'd think he was a white man.

When he didn't come, I missed him. We always had a good laugh together. Sometimes, he was too busy puttin' crops in to bother with me. He was a hard worker, he did it all on his own.

When he couldn't come to see me, he'd write. I felt real important, gettin' a letter with my name on it. Trouble was, I couldn't read. I couldn't have nothin' private 'cause I always had to get someone to read it for me.

Aah, he was a clever man. We had fights all the time. but I was proud of that man.

I hadn't seen Arthur for a long time when I had Gladdie.

Before I had Gladdie, I was carryin' another child, but I wasn't allowed to keep it. That was the way of it, then. They took our children one way or another. I never told anyone I was carryin' Gladdie.

Now how this all came about, that's my business, I'll only tell a little. Everyone knew who the father was, but they all pretended they didn't know. Aah, they knew, they knew. You didn't talk 'bout things, then. You hid the truth.

Alice bought me a cane pram to wheel Gladdie in. She gave Gladdie a doll. I kept Gladdie with me in my room.

Howden died not long after she was born. When I came home from hospital, he said, 'Bring her here, let me hold her'. He wanted to nurse Gladdie before he died.

After he died, I never had time for anything. I had Gladdie and the other children to look after. There were times when Gladdie ate so much she 'minded me of the little baby pigs runnin' round the station.

It was hard for me with her. Sometimes, she'd be cryin', cryin', and I couldn't go to her. I had too much work to do.

When Arthur saw her, he thought she was beautiful. I think he was jealous, he wanted her to belong to him.

Strange, isn't it, at one time, I was goin' to live with Arthur. It was before I had Gladdie, they said they didn't want me any more. Then, they changed their minds. Arthur told me he had a real nice whitefella for me to marry. After Gladdie was born, Arthur wanted us both to go with him. I wasn't allowed to go anywhere. I had to have permission and they wouldn't let me go. I knew Arthur would be good to Gladdie, she had him by the heart-strings. When it came to little ones, that Arthur was tender-hearted.

When Gladdie was 'bout three years old, they took her from me. I'd been 'spectin' it. Alice told me Gladdie needed an education, so they put her in Parkerville Children's Home. What could I do? I was too frightened to say anythin'. I wanted to keep her with me, she was all I had, but they didn't want her there. Alice said she cost too much to feed, said I was ungrateful. She was wantin' me to give up my own flesh and blood and still be grateful. Aren't black people allowed to have feelin's?

I cried and cried when Alice took her away. Gladdie was too young to understand, she thought she was comin' back. She thought it was a picnic she was goin' on. I ran down to the wild bamboo near the river and I hid and cried and cried and cried. How can a mother lose a child like that? How could she do that to me? I thought of my poor old mother then, they took her Arthur from her, and then they took me. She was broken-hearted. God bless her.

When Gladdie was in Parkerville, I tried to get up there as often as I could, but it was a long way and I had no money. When I did get paid, Alice was always takin' money out that she said I owed her. It was a hard life. I always got Gladdie something nice to eat when I went up. She loved food, I think she gets that from me.

Parkerville wasn't a bad place, there was plenty of kids for her to play with and there was bush everywhere. I knew she'd love the bush. I used to take her for a bit of a walk, show her the birds and animals like. She was always real glad to see me. I knew she didn't want to stay there, but what could I do? It wasn't like I had a place of my own. It wasn't like I had any say over my own life.

It was during the thirties that they told Gladdie I might die. My cousin Helen Bunda was real sick. They asked me to give blood for her. I said yes. She belonged to me, I had to give blood, but I was real scared.

You never know what doctors are goin' to do to you. The silly buggers, they lost the first lot of blood they took, so they took some more. I was so weak I couldn't lift my head. I was that weak. I think I turned white with all the blood they took from me.

Helen died and I heard the doctors say, 'Doesn't matter, she was only a native'. Then, they looked at me and the nurse said, 'I think this one's going, too'. You see, they treat you just like an animal. Alice came and got me, she was very cross. She took me back to Ivanhoe and nursed me. She was a good bush nurse.

They brought Gladdie down from Parkerville to say goodbye to me. She looked real frightened when she saw me. I tricked all of them, I didn't die, after all. Pretty soon, I was up and doin' all the work again. That's the last time I give blood.

Helen had been a good old cousin. She was mean, though. She'd walk five miles to save a ha'penny. She was good with her hands. No one could sew the way she could. She'd had a hard life, work, work, work. They'd sent her to Moore River. I don't know if you ever heard of it, terrible place. She had three kids there and was made to leave them there and go back to service. I think all those kids died. It was a terrible place. No one wanted to go to Moore River, no fear. Poor old Bunda. I knew how she felt, it was the same with all of us.

When she died, I thought her things would come to me. I was her family. Turned out I got nothin', not a penny. The white family that she was workin' for got it all. They said she made a will leavin' it to them. Bunda didn't know nothin' 'bout will-makin'. I don't think she could even write much. That family even come and asked me to give back the brooch she'd given me. The cheek of it. Bunda belonged to me, she'd given it me before she died and they come and asked for it back. 'That brooch doesn't belong to you now, Daisy', they said, 'it's ours now, you got to hand it over'. I felt very bitter 'bout that. Right inside my heart, I felt bitter.

Arthur finally got married in the thirties and I lost track of him. The Depression was on and I knew he'd be havin' trouble makin' ends meet. It was just as well Gladdie and I hadn't gone with him. We'd be only two more mouths to feed. He worked real hard, did anythin' to put food on the table. I think he lost his farm in the Depression. Those white people at Mucka, they were always after his farm. Funny, isn't it, the white man's had land rights for years, and we not allowed to have any. Aah, this is a funny world.

Couple of times. Arthur saw Gladdie at Parkerville. He had a real soft spot for her. Then he got too busy with his own family to see her. I think she missed him. She loved visitors.

The thirties was hard for everyone. You never threw anythin' away, there was always someone who could use it. It broke my heart to see men standin' round for food. Not just black men, white ones, too. If I knew someone who was hungry, I'd give them food. I gave away some of my clothes and shoes, whatever I could find. You can't be rotten to people when they in trouble, that's not the blackfella's way.

When Gladdie was 'bout fourteen, she left Parkerville. She'd been with me for holidays at Ivanhoe, and when I took her back, she didn't want to stay. You see, she found out she was havin' this new House Mother and she was a cruel woman. Gladdie was real frightened. I said to them, 'Can she come with me, she's almost grown up, now'.

They asked Gladdie if she wanted to leave Parkerville and she said, 'Too right!'. She didn't want to be stayin' with a cruel woman.

I took her back to Ivanhoe with me. I thought she could stay in my room, but, after two days, Alice said, 'Look Daisy, you can't keep her here. You'll have to find somewhere else for her to go'. I was real upset 'bout that.

They'd told me to leave before, reckoned they couldn't afford me. I had to go and work for Mrs Morgan. Then, a few years later, Alice begged me to come back. She said it was for good. That Ivanhoe was my home. I thought it would be Gladdie's, too. Aah, you see, promises, promises. The promises of a wealthy family are worth nothin'.

I found a family to take Gladdie in. They was religious people and they often took girls in. I knew they'd be good to her. She was real upset, she couldn't understand why they didn't want her at Ivanhoe.

One day, the Hewitts, that was their name, they said they couldn't trust Gladdie no more. 'She's been goin' to the pictures', they said, 'Pictures are a sin'. They said they didn't want her bein' a bad influence on the other kids. They packed her bags and said I had to take her.

I was livin' in my own place by then. Alice had kicked me out again. Aah, I was silly to believe her. She owed me back wages, got me to work for nothing, then kicked me out. I was just used up. I been workin' for that family all those years, right since I was a little child. and that's how I get treated. I left a good job to go back to Ivanhoe. I was silly. I should have known. When they didn't want Gladdie stayin' there, I should have known.

I reckon they wasted their money, it was all that high livin'. Everyone thought they was real important. Hmmph, I never seen any of their money. Howden, he promised Arthur and me money. He said he'd leave us some. Haa, that's how you get treated by rich people, real rotten. I think they get greedy, they live for the money. All Alice ever gave me was a couple of odds and ends and an old broom. After all those years, that was all I got. I hear now when you leave a job, you get a gold watch. That's better than a broom.

I 'member there was this beautiful picture of Fremantle that Alice had. She was sendin' a lot of stuff to auction houses, then. You see, they was goin' to live in Sydney. I asked if I could have that picture, but they said it was goin' to auction. There was some other pictures I asked for, but they made a big bonfire and burnt them. God will make them pay, they was religious pictures.

I thought, well, I got wages now, I'll buy my own things. Some people you're better off without.

My new job was a cook in a restaurant. All the soldiers and sailors loved to come in, because we served good tucker and I gave them plenty. I never cook rubbish. By gee, they could eat. They all wanted second helpings. I felt sorry for them. Some of them were only kids. Goin' to war like that, it's not right.

I shared a house with a good woman. She liked Gladdie, she was good to her. Gladdie and I was livin' together for the first time. She was makin' new friends and so was I. Pretty soon, I was goin' to the trots and other places. I really loved the horses. I'm like Arthur, I got a tender spot for all God's creatures.

Gladdie left school and Alice got her a job as a florist. They didn't want to take her, because she was a native. They were pleased they took her in the end, because everyone loved Gladdie.

Now you'd be thinkin' that, after all those years apart, we'd get on real good. Well, we didn't. Gladdie liked to do things her way and I liked to do things my way. We was fightin' and fightin'. By jingoes, we had some rows

Gladdie was silly in those days, always wantin' to know her future. She didn't know what she was meddlin' with. You leave the spirits alone. You mess with them, you get burnt. She had her palm read, her tea leaves read, I don't know what she didn't get read. I never went with her to any of these fortune tellers. They give you a funny feeling inside. Blackfellas know all 'bout spirits. We brought up with them. That's where the white man's stupid. He only believes what he can see. He needs to get educated. He's only livin' half a life.

Gladdie didn't like some of my friends and I didn't like some of hers. Now maybe she was right 'bout some of my friends and maybe she wasn't, but I think it's true that you don't get many real true friends in this life. There's not many that'll stand by you in trouble. They the rare ones. Gladdie was always tellin' me I was too suspicious. She said I didn't trust her. Maybe I didn't. Maybe it was the men I didn't trust. Gladdie was innocent. She knew nothin' 'bout life. She didn't know what could happen.

One day, she just went off and got married. She was only twenty-one. I s'pose she didn't tell me because she knew I didn't like Bill. He was a drinker. I never liked men who were drinkers. What was she goin' and gettin' married for, anyway? She should have been home, lookin' after her mother.

Well, there's no use cryin' over spilt milk. What's done is done. They got a State Housing place in Mulberry Farm, that's near Beaconsfield. It wasn't a bad little place. I used to visit them, take them a bit of meat. There were some poor families there. Sometimes, I gave them meat, too. I don't 'member anyone sayin' thank you. Still, you can't let people go hungry.

Pretty soon, I was havin' grandchildren. You was the first, Sally, but you was so sick. Jilly wasn't like you, she was real healthy and she wasn't naughty. We never had to play with Jilly in the middle of the night.

I felt real sorry for Gladdie. She didn't realise how bad Bill was when she married him. He kept disappearing. She was worried sick. She never knew where he was. It was the grog, you see. The grog got the better of him. I'm not sayin' he was a bad man. He had a hard time during the war.

When Gladdie was carrying Billy, she got polio. There wasn't one family in Mulberry Farm that wasn't touched with polio. It was a terrible thing. I was worried you kids might get sick, too. That's when I moved in. Gladdie couldn't walk, she was stuck in bed. There was no one to look after you and Jilly. Bill didn't like me there. He was jealous. He wanted Gladdie to himself. What could she do? She needed someone to mind the kids. He was no good around the house.

Now, I tell you something, Sal, this is a sacred thing, so I better speak quiet. I helped your mother with that polio. You see, our family's always had powers that way. I don't want to say no more. Some things I'm tellin' you 'cause I won't be here much longer. That's something you should know.

Gladdie and Bill was offered a house in Manning. It was made from bricks and bigger than the one we was livin' in. Billy was a baby then, and Gladdie was over the polio. I liked the new place. There was bush everywhere. You couldn't see nothin' but bush, and it was near the river. Aah, the birds and the wildlife, it was wonderful. Trouble was, it stank at night. We was near the swamp. That night air was bad for you, Sally. It made you sick. You should have been up North, you're no good in the cold.

Now, this is something I've told no one. You mightn't believe me. 'Member when we first moved there? Couple of nights, you came out on the back verandah and found Gladdie and me sittin' there, 'member we made you go away? You was always in the wrong place at the wrong time. Well, we was listenin' to music. It was the blackfellas playin' their didgeridoos and singin' and laughin' down in the swamp. Your mother could hear it. I said to her one night, 'I'm goin down there and tell those natives off. Who do they think they are, wakin' all the white people up'. That's when Gladdie told me. She said, 'Don't go down there, Mum, there's no one there, only bush'. You see, we was hearin' the people from long ago. Our people who used to live here before the white man came.

Funny, they stopped playin' after your father died. I think now they was protectin' us. Fancy, eh? Those dear old people. You see, the blackfella knows all 'bout spirits.

It was hard for us with Bill. He couldn't get away from the grog. We had no money. Grog's a curse. I'm glad you didn't marry a drinkin' man. I 'member when Bill used to see all those little red devils sittin' on the end of his bed. He kept beggin' me to take them away. I don't think he should have been takin' that medicine and drinkin' too. It made him worse. Aah, doctors don't know nothin'. They kept sendin' him home. He needed help. Gladdie and I couldn't help him.

There was rows all the time with Bill. You know all 'bout that, so I'll say no more. Just between you and me, Bill's parents didn't like natives. They said things 'bout Gladdie behind her back. They said she wasn't good enough for Bill. They blamed her for his troubles. It wasn't her fault, she was doin' the best she could.

'Member we used to keep you kids out the way? We didn't want to upset him. Any little thing upset him. We was frightened of what he might do.

I never told anyone this, but you was close to your father, you knew what he was like. I never even told your mother. I just kept it to myself. When Gladdie wasn't around, Bill used to call me a bloody nigger. I know he had a bad time in the war, but he shouldn't have called me that. No one should call anyone a bloody nigger. I kept quiet 'bout that 'cause I didn't want to cause trouble, but it hurt me real bad to hear him say that.

I was glad when he got real sick. It meant he couldn't touch Gladdie no more.

We was lucky we had those old people protectin' us. Bill could have killed us all.

One time, he asked me to hide the axe. It was the voices he used to hear. They kept tellin' him to kill us all, even you little ones. Bill said to me, 'Dais, hide the axe tonight. They want me to kill you all again and I'm afraid I'll do it'.

He wasn't a bad man, he was just very sick. Sometimes, he'd put himself in hospital. Sometimes, he'd keep himself awake all night, just pacing up and down, up and down. He really had to fight hard not to kill us. You see, there was a part of him that was real good.

When he died, I'd been expectin' it. I had that feelin' inside he might be goin' soon. I think Gladdie knew, too. We didn't talk 'bout it. You didn't talk 'bout things like that.

Course, you know little David found the body. Poor little bloke, he was only 'bout two, then. He thought Bill was asleep, he kept tryin' to wake him up.

David and you are a lot alike, Sal. He wasn't naughty like you, mind, but you both got a feel for the spiritual side of things. I 'member you played on your own a lot. Course, you wasn't on your own, was you? The angels was with you. Your mother was like that, and me, too, I s'pose. You see, you never know what's gunna get passed down. Our people was strong in the spirit.

I think Bill knew he was goin' to die. He made his peace. He knew where he was goin'. 'Member he played footy with Billy and David? Aah, it was a sad time. If it hadn't been for the grog and the war, he'd have been a different man. A good man.

Bill's parents were mongrels after he died. They didn't help Gladdie. They wasn't interested in you kids. We had no money, nothin' left to sell. We didn't know what we was goin' to do, we was desperate. Gladdie wrote to the Drake-Brockmans in Sydney to see if they could give us a loan. They said they was broke, too.

Lois was good to your mother, then. She gave us some money. Frank Potter was good to us. Turned out his heart was as big as his belly.

We was worried 'bout you kids, then. We thought the government might come and get you. They didn't like people like us rearin' kids with white blood in them. Seems like no one took account of the black blood. You belonged to us, Bill's family didn't want you. You kids loved the bush, you got things passed down to you from Gladdie and me. Things that you only got 'cause we was black.

I tried to stay out the way after Bill died. Gladdie could pass for anythin'. You only had to look at me to see I was a native. We had to be careful. 'Tell them they're Indian', I told her. 'You don't want them havin' a bad time'.

Your mother got work, and pretty soon, we had food on the table, good food. Bill drank money and we ate it.

There was men interested in Gladdie, she was a beautiful woman. She didn't want no one. All she wanted was you kids. Good men are rare in this world.

Well, Sal, that's all I'm gunna tell ya. My brain's no good, it's gone rotten. I don't want to talk no more. I got my secrets, I'll take them to the grave. Some things, I can't talk 'bout. Not even to you, my granddaughter. They for me to know. They not for you or your mother to know.

I'm glad I won't be here in body when you finish that book. I'm glad I'm goin'. You a stirrer, you gunna have a lot of talkin' to do. I can't stick up for myself, you see. It's better you do it. Look out for your mother, she's like me.

Aah, you've always been naughty. I'm not frightened for you any more, Sal, you'll be protected. I think maybe this is a good thing you're doin'. I didn't want you to do it, mind. But I think, now, maybe it's a good thing. Could be it's time to tell. Time to tell what it's been like in this country.

I want you grandchildren to make something of yourselves. You all got brains. One of you could be like Mr Hawke, Prime Minister, one day. I hope you'll never be 'shamed of me. When you see them old fellas sittin' in the dirt, remember that was me, once.

Aah, I'm tired of this world, now. I want to get on to the next one. I'm afraid I'll go before I'm ready, can you understand that? God's got a spot up there for me, I dunno what it's like, but it's a spot. Probably a bit of bush, eh? What do you think? Old Arthur'll be waitin' for me. We can have a good old fight. I bet he's causin' trouble up there.

I feel real tired, now, Sal, the fight's gone out o' me. I got no strength left.

Now you asked me 'bout the future. That's a hard question. I got no education, how can I answer a question like that? You think I'm a fortune teller, eh?

But I'll tell you what I'm wonderin'. I'm wonderin' if they'll give the blackfellas land. If it's one thing I've learnt in this world it's this, you can't trust the government. They'll give the blackfellas the dirt and the mining companies'll get the gold. That's the way of it.

I don't like this word Land Rights, people are gettin' upset 'bout it. I dunno what this word means. I've heard it on the news.

You know what I think? The government and the white man must own up to their mistakes. There's been a lot of coverin' up. Maybe they want us all to die off so no one'll talk. No use you goin' on at me, Sal, you can't blame us old ones for not wantin' to talk. We too scared.

Well, I'm hopin' things will change one day. At least, we not owned any more. I was owned by the Drake-Brockmans and the government and anyone who wanted to pay five shillings a year to Mr Neville to have me. Not much, is it? I know it's hard for you, Sal, hard for you to understand.

You different to me. I been scared all my life, too scared to speak out. Maybe if you'd have had my life, you'd be scared, too.

Aah, I can't really say what will happen. I s'pose it don't concern me no more.

As for my people, some of them are naughty, they drink too much. Grog's a curse, I've seen what it can do. They got to give it up. They got to show the white man what they made of.

Do you think we'll get some respect? I like to think the black man will get treated same as the white man one day. Be good, wouldn't it? By gee, it'd be good.

Glossary

abo derogatory term for Aborigines

Aboriginal English an Aboriginal dialect of English

Aboriginal Inland Mission mission established in Central Australia in 1900s

Aboriginal Legal Service government-funded agency

Aboriginal Protection Board government bureaucrats charged with negotiating Aboriginal affairs

Act, the Aboriginal Protection Act

Arthur Phillip governor of first colony in Australia

baalay lookout, warning

Banjil eagle? (a Tasmanian Aboriginal term)

barcoo rot streptococcal skin infection (from Barcoo River, Queensland)

barjun poison (Wakka Wakka and Pitjara language)

Barkly Barkly Tableland

barramundi fish, tropical perch

barrister lawyer who can present cases at the Bar

Bassetts family surname

bedourie oven, cast-iron covered pot

billy can cylindrical metal container with close-fitting lid for boiling water or making tea

black trackers Aboriginal people skilled in tracking, learned from hunting, often hired by police

blokes men

bob a shilling (now ten-cent coin)
bog wet ground
bombing at Darwin Japanese Naval Air Attacks in 1942
bonnet hood of car
bookah nasal congestion (Wakka Wakka and Pitjara language)
boong Aboriginal person (derogatory)
boot trunk of a car
bora ground ceremonial site
bora ring circular indentation in ground surface at ceremonial site
boughshed shade shelter
boya money (Nyoongah term from Western Australia)
brolga Australian crane (large bird)
budgie cage bird cage for a budgerigar (small parrot)
buggy two-wheeled horse-drawn carriage
bull oak casuarina (native Australian) tree
bullock steer or cattle
bullock's cane cattle stick
bush trackless countryside, general term for outback Australia
bush tucker wild food
by jingoes exclamation for "truthfully"
calico cotton cloth
cane pram perambulator, baby buggy
Captain Cook English navigator who "discovered" the east coast of Australia for Britain in 1770
captains white men whom Aboriginal women exploit for an evening's entertainment
catamaran twin-hulled boat
caulies cauliflower
ceremonies ceremonial dances with song, sometimes sacred, single-sex
CES Commonwealth Employment Service
Charlie Perkins outspoken Aboriginal politician
cheeky disrespectful or unlawful
choo exclamation of disbelief, shame (also spelled "tju")
chooks hens
cleanskins unbranded cattle
cockatoo Australian parrot
cockies cockatoos or parrots
corgi small, short-legged Welsh dog
corroborees ceremonial dances with song and rhythmic music
Croeses King of Lydia, Asia Minor, c. 550 B.C., renowned for his wealth
Cross, the Kings Cross, Sydney, suburb with nightclubs

cuppa cup of tea
damper bread cooked in coals
daruk prison
department government department
department, the Department of Aboriginal Affairs, previously called the Department of Native Affairs
Didgeridoo musical wind instrument made of a hollowed tree bough
dingo native wild dog
dole unemployment welfare payment
dray low cart without sides pulled behind horse
Dreaming Aboriginal belief system incorporating creation law sites passed on through story, song, place, and dance
Dreamtime *see* Dreaming
drover trail hand
droving trail driving
duff rustle
emu large flightless bird similar to but smaller than ostrich
farex brand name of baby cereal
flagons half-gallon bottles, usually of wine
footy football (soccer) final series
footy goals football scores
Fred Embrey grew up at the Cherbourg Aboriginal Mission in southeast Queensland; passed on stories of traditional Aboriginal life, law, and custom to white anthropologists in the 1930s and 1940s.
furphy water-tank cart or a rumor
galah pink and grey parrot
gaol jail
gardiya white people
Gerties *see* "giggling gerties"
giggling gerties expression for tittering girls
gins Aboriginal women, used in the past as a derogatory term
gnummerai cigarette, originally native narcotic plant (Nyoongah term from Western Australia)
goal aim, target, or score
goanna large lizard
good go cynical attempt
gooly-up wild or angry (Wakka Wakka and Pitjara language)
goom alcohol
goona excrement
graziers ranch owners

grog alcohol

grubs insect larvae

gubba white bosses, from the word *governor*

guddia Kimberley term for white men

Guilin city in People's Republic of China

guinea one pound one shilling, now A$2.10

gullies ravines

gum eucalyptus tree

gum nut seed pod of eucalyptus tree

gunduburrie baby or small child (Wakka Wakka and Pitjara language)

gunin gunin poor thing (Wakka Wakka and Pitjara language)

gunna going to

gydgea tree acacia tree

ha'penny half-penny, small copper coin

hessian burlap

hobble chains chains attached to horses or camels to stop them from straying

hoied thrown away

Holden ute small General Motors pick-up truck

homestead ranch house

ILO International Labor Organization

jackaroo trainee ranch manager

jirruping happy, keen on, likes, wants

johnny cakes flat bread cooked over coals

JP Justice of the Peace, a civil official

jubes jelly candy

kadaitja man Aboriginal law enforcer

kadaitja shoes made of human hair string and emu feathers to disguise footprints

Keeper of the Rock holder of custodial rites over sacred site

Kiwi whitened shoes; Kiwi brand shoe whitener

koondang ashamed, shy

Koori common self-description of SE Australian Aboriginal people

land rights Aboriginal peoples' claims for return of land

Lands Council Aboriginal Political Organization

lavvy lavatory or toilet

leaving year final year at high school

Long Bay jail in Sydney

Lord Carnarvon English aristocrat

lugger small, usually two-masted sailing ship used for pearl or trepang fishing

Maori Polynesian New Zealanders

mardong sexual attraction (Western Australian term)

marsupials mammals that have a pouch for their young, e.g., kangaroo, wombat, koala

metho methyl alcohol

micky young wild bull

middies ten-ounce glasses of beer

migaloos white people (Wakka Wakka and Pitjara language)

migglou *see* migaloos

mimi spirit figures on rock art in Arnhem Land

mingimullas gooseberry-like native fruit

mob group (usually of people)

Molotov cocktail bottle-and-rag petrol bomb (after Molotov, Stalin's Foreign Minister)

moon-bird small desert bird

moony sexual intercourse

Mr Hawke former prime minister of Australia, Robert J. Hawke

mucking around playing around

mulga desert acacia tree

munadj police (Nyoongah term from Western Australia)

muntha bread (Wakka Wakka and Pitjara language)

munyoos lice

Murri or Murries Aboriginal person from northeast Australian state of Queensland

napaljarri kinship category, also known as a "skin" group

napkins diapers

niggi niggi making love (Wakka Wakka and Pitjara language)

"not the full quid" mildly retarded

oleander evergreen shrub

outcamp campsite away from main living place

paddock enclosed field

pandanus thorny, spiral palm

pictures cinemas

played the wag playing hooky from school

poddy-dodging cocky calf-stealing small farmer

pom British migrant

Pomawoy alternative spelling of Pemulwuy, a resistance warrior near Sydney, c.1800

privet bushy, evergreen shrub

quid one pound currency (A$2)

race meeting horse race

Rainbow Serpent Creation ancestor from the Dreaming who lives on in the landscape, common to many Aboriginal language groups

rollies hand-rolled cigarettes

roo kangaroo

Royal Commission government inquiry

sandy blight trachoma (eye disease)

scruff to wrestle a calf to the ground

seersucker crinkled, usually striped cotton

singlets cotton-knit, sleeveless undershirts

spinifex sharp, desert grass

squatter rich and influential rural landowner

station ranch

Stradbroke island where poet Oodgeroo lived

straight proper relationship according to kinship rules

St Vinnies Saint Vincent de Paul, charity providers

sulky two-wheeled, one horse carriage

sumpin' something

swag rolled bundle, including bedding and personal belongings

TAFE Department of Technical and Further Education Community Colleges

thimbun female (Wakka Wakka and Pitjara language)

tip garbage dump

toff rich, well-dressed person

totems animal or plant with which one has a spiritual relationship

tranny transistor radio receiver

treacle refined molasses

tucker food

Uluru impressive sandstone monolith in Central Australia, also called Ayers Rock

unna isn't that right?, do you think so too?, etc.

ute pickup truck

Veterans Affairs government department

waadow what about that?

Waddy wooden club

Wadjala(s) white people

wag a truant, also a humorous person

wattle acacia tree

Wee-uns little spirit people

Willie McKenzie (tribal name Gaiarbau) Queensland Aboriginal elder and storyteller; main informant to Dr. L. P. Winterbotham of Aboriginal life and custom in and around the Kabi and Waka territory of southeastern Queensland in the 1950s.

willy-willy small, mostly dust tornado

winyarn sorrowful, pitiful, sad sight

wopping huge

wudjella women white women
Yagan resistance warrior in Western Australia
yarned told stories
yarraman horse (Wakka Wakka and Pitjara language)
yoke shoulder harness
yumba fringe camp

Bibliography of Works by the Authors

BELLEAR, LISA (NOONUCCAL).
Dreaming in Urban Areas. St. Lucia, Qld.: University of Queensland Press, 1996.

BRUSNAHAN, MARGARET.
Raukkan and Other Poems. Broome, WA: Magabala Books, 1992.

BURKE, JOHN MUK MUK.
Bridge of Triangles. St. Lucia, Qld.: University of Queensland Press, 1994.

DAVIS, JACK.
The Dreamers. Paddington, NSW: Currency Press, 1996.
Black Life: Poems. St. Lucia, Qld.: University of Queensland Press, 1992.
A Boy's Life [memoir]. Broome, WA: Magabala Books, 1991.
Burungin (Smell the Wind) [play]. Sydney: Currency Press, 1989.
The First-Born and Other Poems. Sydney: Angus and Robertson, 1970.
Honey Spot [play]. Sydney: Currency Press, 1987.
Kullark and the Dreamers [plays]. Sydney: Currency Press, 1982.
Our Town [play]. Paddington, NSW: Currency Press, 1992.
John Pat and Other Poems. Ferntree Gully, Vic.: Dent, 1988.
Jagardoo: Poems from Aboriginal Australia. Sydney: Methuen, 1977.
No Sugar [play]. Sydney: Currency Press, 1986.

Ed., with Stephen Muecke, Mudrooroo Narogin, and Adam Shoemaker. *Paperbark: A Collection of Black Australian Writings*. St. Lucia, Qld.: University of Queensland Press, 1990.

DIXON, GRAEME.

Holocaust Island. St. Lucia, Qld.: University of Queensland Press, 1990.

FOGARTY, LIONEL G.

Kargun. North Brisbane: Cheryl Buchanan, 1980.
Kudjella. Spring Hill, Qld.: Cheryl Buchanan, 1983
Ngutji. Spring Hill, Qld.: Cheryl Buchanan, 1981.
Jagera. Coominga, Qld.: Cheryl Buchanan, 1990.
New and Selected Poems: Munaldjali, Mutuerjaraera. Introduced by Mudrooroo Narogin. South Melbourne, Vic.: Hyland House, 1995.
Yoogum Yoogum. Ringwood, Vic: Penguin, 1982.

GILBERT, KEVIN.

Aboriginal Sovereignty: Justice, the Law and Land. Canberra: Burrambinga Books, 1993.
Because a White Man Will Never Do It. Sydney: Angus and Robertson, 1973.
The Blackside: People are Legends and Other Poems. South Yarra, Vic.: Hyland House, 1990.
Black from the Edge. South Melbourne: Hyland House, 1994.
The Cherry Pickers: The First Written Aboriginal Play [play]. Canberra: Burrambinga Books, 1988. (First pub. in 1970.)
End of Dream-Time. Sydney: Island Press, 1971.
Me and Mary Kangaroo. Ringwood, Vic.: Viking, 1994.
People are Legends: Aboriginal Poems. St. Lucia, Qld: University of Queensland Press, 1978.
Ed. *Inside Black Australia: An Anthology of Aboriginal Poetry*. Ringwood, Vic.: Penguin, 1988.
Ed. *Living Black: Blacks Talk to Kevin Gilbert*. London: Allen Lane and Ringwood, Vic.: Penguin, 1977.

LANGFORD GINIBI, RUBY.

Don't Take Your Love to Town. Ringwood, Vic.: Penguin, 1988.
My Bundjalung People. St. Lucia, Qld.: University of Queensland Press, 1994.
Real Deadly. Pymble, NSW: Collins/Angus & Robertson, 1992.

HUGGINS, RITA AND JACKIE HUGGINS.
Auntie Rita. Canberra: Aboriginal Studies Press, 1994.

MILLER, OLGA.
Fraser Island Legends. Brisbane: Jacaranda Press, 1993.

MORGAN, SALLY.
My Place. Fremantle, WA: Fremantle Arts Centre Press, 1987.
Wanamurraganya: The Story of Jack McPhee. Fremantle, WA: Fremantle Arts Centre Press, 1989.

NANNUP, ALICE WITH LAUREN MARSH AND STEPHEN KINNANE.
When the Pelican Laughed. Fremantle, WA: Fremantle Arts Centre Press, 1992.

NEIDJIE, BILL.
Kakadu Man—Bill Neidjie. Edited by Stephen Davis and Allan Fox. Queanbeyan, NSW: Mybrood, 1985.
Story About Feeling. Edited by Keith Taylor. Broome, WA: Magabala Books, 1989.

OODGEROO OF THE NOONUCCAL TRIBE (FORMERLY KNOWN AS KATH WALKER).
The Dawn is at Hand. Brisbane: Jacaranda Press, 1966.
Father Sky and Mother Earth. Brisbane: Jacaranda Press, 1981.
My People: Oodgeroo. 3rd ed. Milton, Qld.: Jacaranda Press, 1990 [1970].
Stradbroke Dreamtime. Pymble, NSW: Angus and Robertson, 1993.
We Are Going: Poems. Brisbane: Jacaranda Press, 1964.
Ed. *Australian Legends and Landscapes.* Illustrated by Reg Morrison. Milson's Point, NSW: Random Century, 1990.

SCOTT, KIM.
True Country. Fremantle, WA: Fremantle Arts Centre Press, 1993.

WARD, GLENYSE.
Unna You Fullas. Broome, WA: Magabala Books, 1991.
Wandering Girl. Broome, WA: Magabala Books, 1987.

WELLER, ARCHIE.

Blackfellas. A screenplay adapted from Weller's novel *The Day of the Dog* by James Ricketson and Archie Weller. Screen adaptation directed by James Ricketson, 1993.
The Day of the Dog. North Sydney: Allen and Unwin, 1981.
Going Home: Stories. North Sydney: Allen and Unwin, 1986.
Ed., with Colleen Glass. *Us Fellas: An Anthology of Aboriginal Writing.* Perth: Artlook Books, 1987.

WHARTON, HERB.

Ed. *Cattle Camp: Murri Drovers and Their Stories.* St. Lucia, Qld.: University of Queensland Press, 1994.
Unbranded. St. Lucia, Qld.: University of Queensland Press, 1992.
Where Ya' Been, Mate? St. Lucia, Qld.: University of Queensland Press, 1996.

Select Bibliography of Books on Indigenous Australian History, Art, and Literature

Ashcroft, Bill, Gareth Griffiths, and Helen Tiffin, eds. *The Empire Writes Back. Theory and Practice in Post-colonial Literatures.* New York: Routledge, 1989.

Attwood, Bain. *The Making of the Aborigines.* Sydney: Allen & Unwin, 1989.

———, ed. *In the Age of Mabo: History, Aborigines and Australia.* Sydney: Allen & Unwin, 1996.

———, and John Arnold, eds. *Power, Knowledge and Aborigines.* Melbourne: La Trobe University Press in association with the National Centre for Australian Studies, Monash University, 1992.

Beckett, Jeremy R., ed. *Past and Present: The Construction of Aboriginality.* Canberra: Aboriginal Studies Press, 1988.

Bell, Diane. *Daughters of the Dreaming.* 2nd ed. Sydney: Allen & Unwin, 1993.

Berndt, R. M., and C. H. Berndt, with J. E. Stanton. *Aboriginal Australian Art: A Visual Perspective.* Sydney: Methuen Australia, 1982.

Bieir, Ulli. *Dreamtime Machinetime: The Art of Trevor Nickolls.* Sydney: Robert Brown and Associates in association with Aboriginal Artist's Agency Ltd., 1985.

Brantlinger, Richard. *Rule of Darkness: British Imperialism, 1830–1914.* Ithaca, NY: Cornell University Press, 1988

Brewster, Anne. *Literary Formations: Postcolonialism, Nationalism, Globalism.* Melbourne: Melbourne University Press, 1995.

———. *Reading Aboriginal Women's Autobiography.* Sydney: Sydney University Press, 1996.

Carter, Paul. *The Road to Botany Bay: An Essay in Spatial History.* London: Faber and Faber, 1987.

———. *Living in a New Country: History, Travelling and Language.* London: Faber and Faber, 1992

———. *The Lie of the Land.* London: Faber and Faber, 1996.

Caruana, Wally. *Aboriginal Art.* London and New York: World of Art Series, Thames and Hudson, 1993.

Chryssides, Helen. *Local Heroes* [interviews with Aboriginal writers]. North Blackburn, Vic.: Collins Dove, 1993.

Darian-Smith, Kate, Roslyn Poignant, and Kay Schaffer. *Captured Lives: Australian Captivity Narratives.* London: SRMCAS, Institute of Commonwealth Studies, University of London, 1993.

Flood, Josephine. *Archaeology of the Dreamtime.* Rev. ed. Sydney: Collins, 1989.

Goldie, Terry. *Fear and Temptation: The Image of the Indigene in Canadian, Australian, and New Zealand Literatures.* Kingston, Ontario: McGill-Queen's University Press, 1989.

Hodge, Bob, and Vijay Mishra. *Dark Side of the Dream: Australian Literature and the Postcolonial Mind.* Sydney: Allen and Unwin, 1990.

Horton, David, gen. ed. *The Encyclopaedia of Aboriginal Australia.* 2 vols. Canberra: Aboriginal Studies Press, 1994.

Isaacs, Jennifer. *Australia's Living Heritage: Arts of the Dreaming.* Sydney Lansdowne Press, 1984.

———. *Aboriginality: Contemporary Aboriginal Paintings and Prints.* St. Lucia, Qld.: University of Queensland Press, 1989.

———, and Rosemary Crumline. *Aboriginality: Aboriginal Art and Spirituality.* St., Lucia, Qld: University of Queensland Press, 1989.

Jennings, Karen. *Sites of Difference: Cinematic Representations of Aboriginality.* Melbourne: Australian Film Institute, 1993.

Jordan, Glenn, and Chris Weedon. "Racism, Culture and Subjectivity; Australian Aboriginal Writing." In *Cultural Politics: Class, Gender, Race and the Postmodern World.* Cambridge, MA, and Oxford: Blackwell, 1995. Pp. 489–539.

Langton, Marcia. *"Well I heard it on the radio and I saw it on the television . . . "* North Sydney: Australian Film Commission, 1993.

Loos, Noel. *Invasion and Resistance.* Canberra: Australia National University Press, 1982.

McGrath, Ann, ed. *Contested Ground: Australian Aborigines under the British Crown.* Sydney: Allen and Unwin, 1995.

Meucke, Stephen. *Textual Spaces: Aboriginality and Cultural Studies.* Sydney: University of New South Wales Press, 199S

Michaels, Eric. *Bad Aboriginal Art: Tradition, Media and Technological Horizons.* Sydney: Allen and Unwin, 1994.

Morgan, Sally. *The Art of Sally Morgan.* Ringwood, Vic.: Penguin, 1996.

Mudrooroo, Narogin. *Writing from the Fringe: A Study of Modern Australian Literature.* Melbourne: Hyland House, 1990.

———. *Us Mob. History, Culture, Struggle: An Introduction to Indigenous Australia.* Sydney: Angus and Robertson, 1995.

Nelson, Emmanuel S. *Connections: Essays on Black Literature.* Canberra: Aboriginal Studies Press, 1988.

Parbury, N. *Survival: A History of Aboriginal Life in New South Wales.* Sydney: Ministry of Aboriginal Affairs, 1988.

Pettman, Jan Jindy. *Living in the Margins: Racism, Sexism and Feminism in Australia.* Sydney: Allen and Unwin, 1992.

Reynolds, Henry. *Frontier: Aborigines, Settlers and Land.* Sydney: Allen and Unwin, 1987.

———. *The Law of the Land.* Ringwood, Vic.: Penguin, 1987.

———. *Dispossession: Black Australians and White Invaders.* Sydney: Allen and Unwin, 1989.

———. *The Other Side of the Frontier: Aboriginal Resistance to the European Invasion of Australia.* Rev. ed. Ringwood, Vic.: Penguin, 1990.

Rowse, Tim. *After Mabo: Interpreting Indigenous Traditions.* Carlton, Vic.: Melbourne University Press, 1993.

Rutherford, Anna, ed. *Aboriginal Culture Today.* Sydney and Mundelstrup, Denmark: Dangaroo Press, 1988.

Ryan, Lyndall. *The Aboriginal Tasmanians.* 2nd ed. Sydney: Allen and Unwin, 1996.

Schaffer, Kay. *In the Wake of First Contact: The Eliza Fraser Stories.* Cambridge: Cambridge University Press, 1995.

Shoemaker, Adam. *Black Words. White Page: Aboriginal Literature 1977–88.* St. Lucia, Qld.: University of Queensland Press, 1989.

Smith, Heide. *The Life and Art of Australia's Tiwi People.* Sydney: Angus and Robertson, 1990.

Summers, Anne. *Damned Whores and God's Police.* 2nd ed. Ringwood, Vic.: Penguin, 1994.

Sutton, Peter, ed. *Dreamings: The Art of Aboriginal Australia.* New York: Viking Press, 1988.

Thomas, Nicholas. *Colonialism's Culture: Anthropology, Travel and Government.* Melbourne: University of Melbourne Press, 1994

Thompson, Liz, ed. *Aboriginal Voices: Contemporary Aboriginal Artists, Writers and Performers.* Sydney: Simon & Schuster, 1990.

Van Toom, Penny, and David English, eds. *Speaking Positions: Aboriginality, Gender and Ethnicity in Australian Cultural Studies.* Melbourne: Victoria University of Technology, 1995.

Webb, Hugh. "Aboriginal Writing: Twisting the Colonial Supernarrative." In *Sourcebook of Postcolonial English Literatures and Cultural Theory,* edited by R. Mohanram and G. Rajan. Westport, CT: Greenwood Publishing, 1996.

Yunupingu, Mandawuy, et al. *Voices From the Land.* 1993 Boyer Lecturers. Sydney: Australian Broadcasting Corporation, 1993.

About the Contributors

EILEEN BELIA

Unlike many other Aboriginal people, Eileen was able to remain close by her traditional tribal country as she grew up in Northern Queensland. She was taken from the station camp as a young girl and made to work in the homestead, unlike many other members of her family who were forcibly removed to Queensland's infamous Palm Island, where they lost touch with their country and traditions. Eileen now lives in a small outback town in Western Queensland, providing a focus for many of her kinsfolk who want to maintain their heritage.

LISA BELLEAR

Lisa Bellear was born in Melbourne in 1961 and was the first female Koori graduate to hold a Bachelor of Social Work (1986) and then a Master of Arts (Women's Studies, 1996) from the University of Melbourne. Passionate about social justice, she is an executive member of the Black Women's Action in Education Foundation and has taught and lectured at universities in Australia, the United States, and Thailand. Presently working on a higher degree in creative writing at the University of Queensland, she has been a volunteer broadcaster on community radio in Victoria for eleven years and a writer in residence at the Australian Catholic University in Ballarat, Victoria.

Margaret Brusnahan

Margaret Brusnahan was born in Kapunda, South Australia, one of nine children. Her mother, Iris Rankine, was from the Ngarrindgeri people of Raukkan (Point McLeay) on Lake Alexandrina, and her father, Arthur Woods, was white and of Irish descent. She and her brothers and sisters were all taken from home at an early age and lived in various orphanages, government institutions, and white foster homes, not seeing each other for several years at a time. She believes that her writing has helped her deal with being of one culture yet reared in another, an Aboriginal woman raised in a white community. "My poetry has not been designed for any political purposes, rather it is life experiences, and all the encounters, written for the enjoyment of those who would like to read it. I hope that all Aboriginal people, no matter where, can relate to my poems and identify not only with the sad occasions but the happy times as well."

John Muk Muk Burke

John Muk Muk Burke is descended from the Wiradjuri people and was born in Narrandera, New South Wales, in 1946. He left school at fifteen, working in Australia and New Zealand in jobs ranging from the post office to scrub clearing and factory work before returning to study in 1967 to qualify as a teacher. He has taught in New Zealand, Darwin, and outback Northern Territory, and has been a specialist art teacher and music adviser for the Northern Territory Department of Education. He has also worked and traveled in Europe, most recently giving a series of lectures on Australian indigenous literature in Germany. He is now assistant dean in the faculty of Aboriginal and Torres Strait Islander Studies at Northern Territory University, where he teaches Aboriginal Studies. He has a twenty-year-old son and is currently working on a second novel.

Jack Davis

Jack Davis, born in Perth in 1917, has been writing since he was fourteen years old. The fourth child in a family of eleven, he spent his childhood in the mill town of Yarloop, Western Australia. He worked for several years as a stockman and boundary rider in the north before returning to Perth and settling into full-time writing and a long life of service to the Aboriginal cause. His poetry and plays have been published and performed widely inside and outside of Australia. His play *No Sugar* received standing ovations at festivals in Vancouver and Edinburgh in 1986.

One of Australia's foremost indigenous writers, Davis has received numerous distinctions, including the British Empire Medal, the Order of Australia, a four-year Australian Creative Fellowship, honorary doctorates from the universities of Murdoch and Western Australia, and the Bicentennial BHP Award for the Pursuit of Excellence in literature and the arts. An elder of the Manguri Management Committee, he served for several years as Managing Director of the Aboriginal Advancement Council and as

Editor of Aboriginal Publications. Today he continues his active support for Australia's indigenous writers.

Graeme Dixon

Graeme Dixon, a South Western Nyoongah, was born in Perth in 1955. Between the ages of ten and fourteen, until being expelled from high school, he lived in a Salvation Army Boys Home. He spent much of the next two years in reformatories, and at the age of sixteen was incarcerated in Fremantle Prison. With a record of violence and escaping legal custody he was considered a security risk and was kept in maximum security until the age of twenty-four. He began writing poetry during this time, his major themes becoming injustice, the death in prison of friends, and the brutality to Aboriginal people of the prison environment. After being released he became actively involved in Aboriginal Rights issues. He returned to school to gain tertiary entrance and subsequently began a Bachelor of Arts degree at the University of Western Australia. He now studies music at the Abmusic center on the Clontarf Aboriginal Campus in Perth.

Lionel Fogarty

Lionel Fogarty was born on the land of the Wakka Wakka tribe at Barambah, Queensland, which is now known as the Cherbourg Aboriginal Reserve. This was one of the "punishment reserves" where individuals and their families who spoke out against the white authorities were sent from all over Queensland. As a result, the land of the Wakka Wakka became a place of many people from many different tribes.

Lionel left the Reserve at the age of sixteen with little formal education and worked as a ring-barker, a railway worker, and cleaner. He became deeply involved with the Aboriginal struggle for land rights and justice, and has traveled widely throughout Australia, the United States, and Europe reading his poetry and acting as an ambassador for his Murri culture and the Aboriginal cause.

Kevin Gilbert

Kevin Gilbert was born to the Wiradjuri nation on the banks of the Kalara (Lachlan) River in 1933. Orphaned at the age of seven, his life became split between living in city orphanages, fruit picking with his elder sisters' families, and living with his mother's people who had remained independent from the missions by living in "humpies" (shacks) on their sacred land.

He worked his way up to station manager of a property in central New South Wales, but was jailed after unintentionally killing his wife. While in jail he came to see that conditions for prisoners were often better than those in which his own people lived. On being released from jail he joined the struggle for Aboriginal rights and, in

1972, initiated the idea of the Aboriginal tent embassy in Canberra, which was established for a time on the lawns of Parliament House. One of the first Aboriginal printmakers and a distinguished writer, he died in early 1993 at the age of fifty-nine.

Ruby Langford

Ruby Langford, who is now known as Ruby Langford Ginibi, was born at the Box Ridge Mission, Coraki, on the north coast of New South Wales in 1934. She was raised in Bonalbo in northeastern New South Wales, moving to Sydney at the age of fifteen, after her second year of high school, to train as a clothing machinist. She raised her family of nine children, the first born when she was seventeen, mostly by herself, living in the Koori areas of Sydney and working in clothing factories. At other times she lived for long periods camped in tin huts in the bush around Coonabarabran, working at lopping and ring-barking, burning off, pegging kangaroo skins, and fencing. She is now the grandmother of twenty children.

Rita Huggins and Jackie Huggins

Rita and Jackie Huggins were the first Aboriginal authors to collaborate on a mother-daughter piece of work. Both are well known and respected in their fields: Rita for her graciousness and enormous capacity to love and share with all people, to tell stories so proudly and vehemently to all who care to listen and read; Jackie as a historian who used the primary source of oral history and academic history as a backdrop to *Auntie Rita*. Sadly, Rita passed away on 27 August 1997. Jackie is presently the deputy director of the Aboriginal and Torres Strait Islander unit at the University of Queensland.

Olga Miller

Olga Miller was born in 1920 and is a direct descendant and elder of the Butchulla people of Fraser Island, three hundred kilometers north of Brisbane. She is recognized by her people as an Aboriginal historian and has an extensive knowledge of the Wide Bay/Fraser Island district of Queensland. She has been teaching and writing about Aboriginal culture for over thirty years, and has become known to her people as "Caboonya" (Keeper of Records), a title given to her by her grandfather and passed down from generation to generation.

Sally Morgan

Sally Morgan was born in Perth, Western Australia, in 1951. She completed a Bachelor of Arts degree at the University of Western Australia in 1974 and has postgraduate diplomas from the Western Australian Institute of Technology (now Curtin University of Technology) in both counselling psychology and computing and library studies. She is married with three children. As well as writing, Sally Morgan has established an international reputation as an artist, printmaker, and designer. Her works are held in all major art galleries in Australia, including the Australian National Gallery, Canberra, and in numerous private collections.

Jennie Hargraves Nampijinpa

Jennie Hargraves Nampijinpa lives in the Warlpiri community of Hooker Creek, Northern Territory. About her experience as an Aborigine and as a writer in contemporary Australia working not only in English but in the language of her people, she says that she is very much aware of the traps and tribulations of media technology, but that she nevertheless loves the interest and excitement of languages.

Alice Nannup

Alice Nannup was born on Pilbara station in Western Australia in 1911, of an Aboriginal mother and white father. She was taken from her community at the age of twelve and sent south, where she was trained in domestic service. After her marriage in 1932, Alice raised ten children. Now known as "Nan," she lives in Geraldton, Western Australia, and enjoys contact with her large family.

Pansy Rose Napaljarri

Pansy Rose Napaljarri works at the Lajamanu School, Hooker Creek, in the Northern Territory, where she translates English curriculum materials into her native language, Warlpiri.

Rhonda Samuel Napurrurla

Rhonda Samuel Napurrurla works at the Lajamanu School in Hooker Creek, Northern Territory, where she translates English into Warlpiri and collects legends from the Old People, which she enters into a computer to make books for the children of her community.

Bill Neidjie

Bill Neidjie, an elder of the Buniti clan of the Gagudju people, was born on the East Alligator River in Arnhem Land in the Northern Territory in 1913. His father, Nadampala, was of the Buniti clan, and his mother, Lucy Wirlmaka, was from the Ulbuk clan. He was raised in the East Alligator River area until his early teens, and then in the Cape Don area, where he lived with his mother's family. As a young man he worked briefly as a buffalo hunter and then at an isolated timber mill in Mount Norris Bay, in time becoming a hand on a lugger carrying timber to Darwin. He worked on the luggers carrying cargo and passengers along Australia's northern coastline for several years. He later returned to live permanently at the East Alligator area.

In 1979 he was a claimant in the Alligator River Stage 2 Land Claim, which resulted in the Buniti people's being awarded title to their traditional land. This land (Kakadu National Park) was subsequently leased to the National Park Service. Neidjie is a park ranger at Kakadu.

Oodgeroo of the Noonuccal tribe

Oodgeroo was born in 1920 and spent her early childhood on Stradbroke Island, off the coast of Queensland near Brisbane. She left school to become a domestic, and when the Second World War broke out she served as a telephonist in the Australian Auxiliary Service, training later as a stenographer. Her first book of poems, *We Are Going*, was the first published by an Aboriginal poet, and her work has subsequently brought national and international focus to bear on Aboriginal oppression, human rights, and equality. She held the position of Queensland Secretary of the Federal Council of the Aboriginal Advancement League and served on a number of other organizations, and for many years fought for an "Aboriginal Charter of Rights," which seeks to alter the conditions under which Aboriginal people live. In 1988 Kath Walker changed her name to Oodgeroo of the tribe of Noonuccal in order to discard the namesake traces of the European colonial past. Oodgeroo is a traditional name of the Noonuccal people for the paperbark tree. Oodgeroo is of the Noonuccal tribe; her totem is the carpet snake, Kabool; her tribal land is Minjerribah, which the European invaders renamed Stradbroke Island (in the Whitsunday Islands of the Queensland coast).

Kim Scott

Kim Scott was born in 1957 in Perth, Australia, and grew up on Western Australia's south coast. He began writing for publication when he became a teacher of English. His first novel, *True Country*, was published in 1993 and shortlisted for the Western Australian Premiers Prize. Scott has had poetry and short stories published in a number of anthologies. He has been a guest writer and read his work on tour and at literary festivals throughout Australia. He is descended from people who have always lived on the south coast of Western Australia, and regards himself as extremely fortunate to be living in times when he is free to attempt to articulate the significance of that fact. In recent years he has worked mainly as a teacher and in 1996 was coordinator of the Aboriginal Bridging Course at Curtin University of Technology in Perth.

Glenyse Ward

Glenyse Ward was born in Perth, Western Australia, in 1949 and was taken from her parents at the age of one when her mother took her to a doctor when she was ill. At the age of three she was taken from the St. John of Gods orphanage in Perth to St. Francis Xavier Native Mission at Wandering Brook, eighty miles southeast of Perth, where she was brought up. Not doing well at school, she was made a working girl in the mission, assisting the nuns with domestic duties until she was old enough, at fifteen, to take on domestic duties outside the mission. She later worked as a domestic and as a nursing assistant in hospitals in rural Western Australia and Perth, and then worked within the Community Health Service. Married in 1975, she now has two children and lives and writes in Broom, Western Australia.

Archie Weller

Archie Weller was born in Perth, Western Australia, in 1957, and was raised in Cranbrook, about twenty miles south of Perth in the bush country near the Stirling Ranges, and later as a teenager in the depressed suburb of East Perth. Weller's paternal great-grandmother was from the South Australian Port Augusta tribe of Ellis, though little is known about her background. His mother is of Scottish ancestry. After Weller graduated from high school he spent a year at the Western Australian Institute of Technology (now Curtin University) before leaving to begin work on his first novel, *The Day of the Dog*, which was filmed as *Blackfellas*. He has lived and worked in various parts of Australia, from the wharf at Broome in Western Australia to the Australian National University in Canberra, where he was writer-in-residence. He has attended by invitation writers festivals in England, Glasgow, Johannesburg, and Germany.

Errol West

Errol West was born in Launceston, Tasmania, in 1947, and is a descendant of the Emeratta tribe of Northern Tasmania. He received only five years of formal education in schools on islands and the mainland of Tasmania, following his parents as they followed the cycles of seasonal work open to Aboriginal people in the late forties and early fifties. With the support and encouragement of his family, he reentered education and qualified as a teacher. West is presently chairman, and was the inaugural deputy chairman, of the National Aboriginal Education Committee, the Commonwealth Government's principal policy adviser on issues regarding Aboriginal and Torres Strait Islander education.

Herb Wharton

Herb Wharton was born and raised in Cunnamulla in the Yumba Aboriginal fringe dwellers' camp in southwest Queensland. His maternal grandmother was from the Kooma tribe, and his grandfathers were English and Irish. He went droving after leaving school at twelve and later broke in horses, becoming a successful rodeo rider and horse trainer, and more recently a life member of the Stockman's Hall of Fame. He is a former director of Queensland's South-West Aboriginal Housing Co-op and a trustee of the Eulo Aboriginal Reserve. He has participated extensively in writers' festivals, tours, residencies, and workshops throughout Australia and has been employed as a writer in communities in Victoria and the Northern Territory. He has lectured and read in such places as Hong Kong, Paris, Amsterdam, Berlin, and Munich, and his poetry, short stories, book reviews, and essays appear in journals published in Australia and abroad.

About the Editors

Jennifer Sabbioni is senior lecturer in Aboriginal Studies and head of research in Aboriginal Studies at Edith Cowan University's Kurongkuri Katitjin School of Australian Indigenous Studies. She has taught in Tasmania and has given presentations throughout Australia to both Aboriginal and non-Aboriginal audiences. A Nyungar woman actively involved in her community, she has been involved in cross-cultural training to demystify stereotypes of Aboriginal peoples.

Kay Schaffer is associate professor in the Department of Women's Studies at the University of Adelaide. She is the author of *In the Wake of First Contact: The Eliza Fraser Stories* (Cambridge, 1996) and *Women and the Bush* (Cambridge, 1988), as well as co-author of *Captured Lives: Australian Captivity Narratives* (with Kate Darian-Smith and Roslyn Poignant, 1993). She has authored numerous articles in literary, cultural studies, and feminist journals and has lectured extensively in women's studies and Australian studies programs in Europe and the United States.

Sidonie Smith is professor of English and Women's Studies at the University of Michigan, where she is also Director of Women's Studies. She is the author of *Where I'm Bound: Patterns of Slavery and Freedom in Black American Autobiography* (Greenwood, 1974); *A Poetics of Women's Autobiography: Marginality and the Fictions of Self-Representation* (Indiana, 1987); and *Subjectivity, Identity, and the Body: Women's Autobiographical Practices in the Twentieth Century* (Indiana, 1993); and co-author of *De/Colonizing the Subject: The Politics of Gender in Women's Autobiography* (with Julia Watson, Minnesota, 1992); *Getting a Life: Everyday Uses of Autobiography* (with Julia Watson, Minnesota, 1996); and *Writing New Identities: Gender, Nation, and Immigration in Contemporary Europe* (with Gisela Brinker-Gabler, Minnesota, 1997).